CN00959433

ETHNOCENTRISM

Ethnocentrism has made a huge conceptual contribution to the social sciences, but its popularity and usage have somewhat decreased over the last several decades. This book works to reinvigorate the study of ethnocentrism by reconceptualising ethnocentrism as a social, psychological and attitudinal construct.

Using a broad, multidisciplinary approach to ethnocentrism, the book integrates literature from disciplines such as psychology, political science, sociology, anthropology, biology, and marketing studies to create a novel reorganisation of the existing literature, its origins, and its outcomes. Empirical research throughout serves to comprehensively measure the six dimensions of ethnocentrism—devotion, group cohesion, preference, superiority, purity, and exploitativeness—and show how they factor into causes and consequences of ethnocentrism, including personality, values, morality, demographics, political ideology, social factors, prejudice, discrimination, and nationalism.

This book is fascinating reading for scholars, researchers, and students in psychology, sociology, and political science.

Boris Bizumic is a Senior Lecturer in psychology at the Research School of Psychology, the Australian National University. His research expertise is in social, personality, and political psychology. He has published widely in the areas of ethnocentrism, prejudice, personality, attitudes, cross-cultural research, and scale construction.

ETHNOCENTRISM

Integrated Perspectives

Boris Bizumic

Routledge
Taylor & Francis Group

LONDON AND NEW YORK

First published 2019
by Routledge
2 Park Square, Milton Park, Abingdon, Oxon OX14 4RN

and by Routledge
711 Third Avenue, New York, NY 10017

Routledge is an imprint of the Taylor & Francis Group, an informa business

© 2019 Boris Bizumic

The right of Boris Bizumic to be identified as author of this work has been asserted by him in accordance with sections 77 and 78 of the Copyright, Designs and Patents Act 1988.

All rights reserved. No part of this book may be reprinted or reproduced or utilised in any form or by any electronic, mechanical, or other means, now known or hereafter invented, including photocopying and recording, or in any information storage or retrieval system, without permission in writing from the publishers.

Trademark notice: Product or corporate names may be trademarks or registered trademarks, and are used only for identification and explanation without intent to infringe.

British Library Cataloguing-in-Publication Data
A catalogue record for this book is available from the British Library

Library of Congress Cataloging-in-Publication Data
A catalog record has been requested for this book

ISBN: 978-1-138-18772-6 (hbk)
ISBN: 978-1-138-18773-3 (pbk)
ISBN: 978-1-315-64297-0 (ebk)

Typeset in Bembo
by Out of House Publishing

 Printed in the United Kingdom
by Henry Ling Limited

For Bojana and Filip

CONTENTS

FIGURES

TABLES

ACKNOWLEDGEMENTS

I am grateful to John Duckitt, Daniel Bar-Tal, Sam McFarland, and Iain Walker, who all provided excellent comments on this book. I am also grateful to Ravi Iyer, who included a version of the Ethnocentrism Scale 1 on the website YourMorals. Org and collected data from over 4000 participants. Analyses based on that dataset are presented in this book. I also thank Elizabeth Huxley, who helped me collect and prepare data from several samples. I am grateful to three of my Honours students, Ayndri de Soysa, Ashley Dunne, and Philip Mullens, who collected data using a version of the Ethnocentrism Scale 1 for their Honours thesis and whose data I have reanalysed for this book. I would like to thank Bernd Heubeck for his help with German translations of Gumplowicz's writings on ethnocentrism. Several paragraphs that Bernd translated from German are quoted in the book. I am also indebted to Eleanor Reedy, Alex Howard, Julie Toich, and Kristina Siosyte at Routledge, and Céline Durassier at Out of House Publishing for all their help with this book. Roger Borthwick helped with copy-editing and proofreading, and I am grateful for his work. Several chapters include modified parts of two previous publications, and I am grateful to the publishers who hold copyright for letting me use the content from these publications.

INTRODUCTION

> The inhabitants of the Ladones believe, that their language is the only one in the world, and therefore that all the other nations of the earth are dumb.
>
> *Zimmermann, 1758/1797, p. 44*

> The Kubus of Sumatra believe illnesses arise from relations with people outside the tribal group. This group-egotism, which, among other things, causes so many tribes to denominate themselves 'Men,' as distinguished from the rest of the world, who do not measure up to that exalted title, is called ethnocentrism.
>
> *Keller, 1915, p. 58*

Ethnic group-egotism, or more widely known as ethnocentrism, is a phenomenon that does not exist only in tribes and non-industrial societies, but is found widely in ethnic groups across the world and time periods. Many people have observed ethnocentrism, and many more have exhibited it. For example, ethnocentrism can be seen in Aristotle's attribution of courage and lower intelligence to those living in the northern countries of Europe, intelligence but no courage to Asians, and both intelligence and courage to the Greeks (Gumplowicz, 1892). The Greeks, in fact, introduced the concept of barbarians to denote all people who speak languages other than Greek because the Greeks said that the other people speak unintelligibly, like birds, "bar-bar" (Jahoda & Krewer, 1997). The ancient Greek writer Aristophanes used the term "barbaroi" to describe birds because their chatter and chirping is inarticulate and impossible to understand (Evans, 1894). Later, many other ethnic groups would use the term barbarism to distinguish themselves, or the civilised, from others, or the barbarians. The term civilisation itself is ethnocentric as it distinguishes the civilised, who are superior, from everyone else.

Ethnocentrism can also be found among those usually seen as leaders of the Enlightenment and opponents of oppression. A distinguished Enlightenment thinker, the Scottish philosopher David Hume, wrote: "I am apt to suspect the Negroes, and in general all the other species of men ... to be naturally inferior to the whites. There never was a civilized nation of any other complection than white, nor even any individual eminent in action or speculation. No ingenious manufactures among them, no arts, no sciences" (Hume, 1742/1767, p. 234). The US Vice-President Henry Wallace reports how the British Prime Minister Winston Churchill, who fought against fascism and Nazi ethnocentrism, once told him: "why be apologetic about Anglo-Saxon superiority ... we were superior" (1973, p. 208). Even the Indian leader Mahatma Gandhi, a renowned advocate of freedom from oppression, was not free from ethnocentrism. His numerous ethnocentric remarks, such as, "Some Indians do have contacts with Kaffir women. I think such contacts are fraught with grave danger. Indians would do well to avoid them altogether" (Gandhi, 1999, p. 414), can be found on pages of his collected works, especially on those written during his life among the British and "Kaffirs" (an offensive term for Blacks) in South Africa. These are just several, out of thousands, recorded examples of ethnocentrism whereby one thinks that their ethnic group or culture is more important, better, and superior to others (e.g., see Gumplowicz, 1881, 1887, 1892, 1895; Keller, 1915; Sumner, 1906; Sumner, Keller, & Davie, 1928; Zimmermann, 1758/1797).

What is exactly ethnocentrism? Although there is no general agreement on what it is, I will argue and show that ethnocentrism is a social psychological construct that relates to people's belief that one's own ethnic group is in the centre of everything and is therefore extremely important. I will argue that ethnocentrism is an attitudinal construct centred on this belief, and that, as an attitude, it also has strong emotional and behavioural aspects. It is deeply rooted in the human mind and is almost universally found – though in different degrees – in all ethnic groups. Ethnocentrism is an attitude because it has cognitive (beliefs), affective (emotions), and behavioural (actions) aspects. Ethnocentrism has been with humans since prehistoric times and was already noticed by ancient thinkers, but the concept was introduced into the social sciences in the second half of the nineteenth century. Ever since that time, the concept has been widely used by social scientists and many other scholars.

Although ethnocentrism is a widely used social scientific concept, its popularity has somewhat decreased over the last several decades. This book, therefore, aims to reinvigorate this fundamental social scientific concept, to present a novel reorganisation of the existing literature, and to propose a broad approach to ethnocentrism. Its aim is broad because the phenomenon of ethnocentrism permeates the human mind deeply across all human societies and because the concept itself has captured the attention of numerous social scientists across disciplines.

There has been a large amount of research published on ethnocentrism, but the last three comprehensive books on ethnocentrism were published in the 1970s (Booth, 1979/2014; Brewer & Campbell, 1976; LeVine & Campbell, 1972). More recently, the political scientists Kinder and Kam (2009) wrote a book on the role of ethnocentrism in American public opinion. There are, however, many books on prejudice, diversity, group processes, and intergroup relations in psychology (e.g., R. Brown, 2010; Jackson, 2011; J. M. Jones, Dovidio, & Vietze, 2014; Lott, 2009), but these have not focused on ethnocentrism, although they covered relevant research. The concept of prejudice comes close to the concept of ethnocentrism, but I will show that ethnocentrism is distinct from prejudice. Nevertheless, ethnocentrism and prejudice often coexist within one person. Researchers have emphasised that ethnocentrism is the taproot (Altemeyer, 1996) or heart of prejudice (Sniderman & Piazza, 1993), but also that, in contrast to prejudice, the study of ethnocentrism has been neglected (Sniderman & Piazza, 1993).

If researchers wanted to learn about ethnocentrism, they would need to browse through many journal articles and chapters on ethnocentrism from many disciplines, they would need to consult books on prejudice, which often do not specifically address ethnocentrism, or they would need to read older – often out of print – books that discuss ethnocentrism (e.g., Adorno, Frenkel-Brunswik, Levinson, & Sanford, 1950; Brewer & Campbell, 1976; LeVine & Campbell, 1972). The readers may also become confused with this literature as it often treats the concepts of ethnocentrism, prejudice, racism, ingroup bias (or similar concepts such as intergroup or ingroup-outgroup bias), nationalism, xenophobia, and discrimination as interchangeable and equivalent. The present book differs because it explicitly focuses on ethnocentrism, clarifies the construct across disciplines, and presents an integrated approach. In this book I have several main aims.

The first aim of the book is to reinvigorate the concept of ethnocentrism. Ethnocentrism is a fundamental concept in psychology and the social sciences and has been used since at least the 1870s. Although it was popular in social psychology in the period from the 1950s until the 1980s, it was recently replaced by other concepts, such as prejudice, ingroup favouritism, ingroup bias, and discrimination, possibly because of the conceptual confusion in the field and because the concept has meant many things to different researchers and theorists. My and my colleagues' work (Bizumic, 2012, 2014; Bizumic & Duckitt, 2008, 2012; Bizumic, Duckitt, Popadic, Dru, & Krauss, 2009) has attempted to reinvigorate and clarify the concept. This book presents an overarching argument for why the concept is relevant to social psychologists and other disciplines. This aim is not unique to this book, and an independently conducted research programme was relatively recently presented in a book by Kinder and Kam (2009), who also argued that the concept of ethnocentrism needs to be reinvigorated.

In this book, I aim to present a multidisciplinary and historical perspective on the concept of ethnocentrism. The book primarily focuses on psychological work, but it also covers relevant work from: (a) sociology, focusing on historical perspectives and sociological explanations of ethnocentrism; (b) political science, focusing on political implications; and (c) biology, focusing on evolutionary theorising. The book also considers other contributions to ethnocentrism, such as those from anthropology, philosophy, and marketing studies.

Finally, in this book I aim to consolidate the current knowledge of ethnocentrism. This book integrates historical writings on ethnocentrism with modern research and shows how early theorists prefigured many modern ideas in the study of ethnocentrism. The book, therefore, integrates old writings with a variety of modern perspectives. The book outlines an integrative framework for ethnocentrism, which focuses on the role of diverse causes, such as fear, self-aggrandisement, social factors, biology, and evolution, and the role of diverse consequences, such as nationalism, prejudice, emotional reactions, discrimination, support for specific political issues, dehumanisation, ethnic wars, ethnic cleansing, and specific forms of ethnocentrism, such as consumer ethnocentrism. Finally, and in contrast to all influential publications on ethnocentrism (e.g., Adorno et al., 1950; Brewer & Campbell, 1976; Kinder & Kam, 2009; LeVine & Campbell, 1972; Tajfel, 1982), which incorrectly find the intellectual origin of the concept of ethnocentrism in the twentieth century, that is, in the book by Sumner (1906), the present book acknowledges and examines explicit discussions of ethnocentrism from the nineteenth century (Evans, 1894; Gumplowicz, 1879, 1881; McGee, 1898).

These aims are addressed in the seven chapters of the book. The first chapter discusses a history of the study of ethnocentrism across time periods and disciplines. It touches on many writings that were rarely linked to the study of ethnocentrism. The second chapter offers a reconceptualisation of ethnocentrism as a social psychological concept, or, more precisely, as an attitudinal construct, and shows how this reconceptualised ethnocentrism can be measured, using different versions of the Ethnocentrism Scale 1 and 2, across ethnic groups. The third, fourth, and fifth chapters discuss the origins of ethnocentrism, such as those pertaining to fear, self-aggrandisement, social factors, biology and evolution, as well as the consequences of ethnocentrism, such as nationalism, prejudice, and discrimination. The sixth chapter presents the results of empirical research, with thousands of participants, which investigated causes and consequences of ethnocentrism. It shows how ethnocentrism, including its six dimensions, relates to its causes, such as personality, values, demographics, political ideology, and social factors, as well as its consequences, such as prejudice, attitudes, emotional reactions, discrimination, and political attitudes. The chapter integrates the causes and consequences, and proposes that the need for ethnic strength and resilience is the overwhelming motivation that underlies ethnocentrism. The final, seventh chapter discusses how ethnocentrism, in addition to being an important focus of study in psychology, also affects the study of psychology itself.

Although this book is primarily written for psychologists, such as social, personality, political, and cross-cultural psychologists, other social scientists, such as anthropologists, sociologists, and political scientists, and potentially biologists, philosophers, and researchers interested in religious, marketing, business, and military studies should find it useful. Given that ethnocentrism is widely seen as a universal construct existing across cultures (D. E. Brown, 1991, 2000, 2004), the book reviews, discusses, and presents international perspectives on ethnocentrism. Accordingly, the book should be of interest to a diverse group of researchers from all over the world.

General public readership may also find the study of ethnocentrism interesting and useful because ethnocentrism is an aspect of our everyday life and deeply permeates our actions, such as our decisions regarding where to live, whom to marry, whom to have as friends, whom to vote for, and even whether in certain circumstances to die for our ethnic group. It is rare for humans to sacrifice themselves for certain attitudes, but for ethnocentrism, a complex attitude that is related to the belief that one's ethnic group is extremely important – much more than individual group members and other ethnic groups – countless people have died in the past, are dying now, and will die in the future.

1

THE HISTORY AND CONTEXT OF STUDY

The history of the study of ethnocentrism is somewhat ethnocentric, with almost all English-speaking researchers who have studied ethnocentrism attributing the origin of the concept to an English-speaker, US social scientist Sumner (1906). Nevertheless, Ludwig Gumplowicz, a Polish Jew who had an academic post in Austria-Hungary and who was one of the founders of sociology, had used the concept in publications written in German and Polish (e.g., Gumplowicz, 1879, 1884). Sumner, like many other US sociologists at that time, was influenced by Gumplowicz (Martindale, 1976), but failed to mention that Gumplowicz had also used the term. Accordingly, other social scientists, writing in English, did not read Gumplowicz's books and journal articles, but read Sumner's 1906 book and assumed that Sumner had invented the concept. Therefore, when one reads books, journal articles, and encyclopaedia articles on ethnocentrism, or when one does an internet search trying to learn about ethnocentrism, Sumner emerges at the person who invented the concept in his 1906 book.

Gumplowicz also proposed another related concept that, unfortunately, has never been adopted by the social scientists. The concept is acrochronism (Gumplowicz, 1895), and is similar to ethnocentrism in that it denotes a phenomenon whereby what is closely related to the self is seen as more important than what is distant. Here, however, the focus is on time, so that the present time is seen as more important, better, and superior to any past time. The past is seen as just the preparation for the superiority of the present time. Gumplowicz thought that acrochronism is also a fundamental bias and delusion as ethnocentrism is. Interestingly, Gumplowicz's writings on ethnocentrism have been ignored by modern theorists and researchers into ethnocentrism possibly because of these two biases (ethnocentrism and acrochronism): Gumplowicz did not write in English, and he is a nineteenth-century social scientist, and the social sciences tend to disregard the old in favour of the new (Andreski, 1972).

Writings on ethnocentrism before the development of the social sciences

Gumplowicz was not the first to notice ethnocentrism, and the phenomenon was recorded in ancient times and in all probability observed by many people in pre-historic times. Many writers across different ages recognised that people are eth-nocentric. This is, unfortunately, often overlooked in the modern literature on ethnocentrism, which assumes that we have only recently noticed and discovered ethnocentrism and that people were blind to ethnocentrism for a long time. Most often a review of the work on ethnocentrism starts with Sumner's 1906 book and then focuses on later contributions (e.g., Booth, 1979/2014; Brewer & Campbell, 1976; Kinder & Kam, 2009; LeVine & Campbell, 1972). For example, a recent book on ethnocentrism stated: "We are indebted to Sumner for noticing ethnocentrism in the first place, for naming it felicitously, for defining it sensibly" (Kinder & Kam, 2009, p. 29). In fact, there have been many who have noticed ethnocentrism in humans. I will not attempt to be exhaustive in my presentation, but I will present historical examples of scholars noticing and attempting to explain ethnocentrism. My aim is to correct the biases by showing that many have noticed ethnocentrism in human groups for a long time. I also include here certain writings by authors, such as Zimmermann (1758/1797), who have rarely, if ever, been connected to the study of ethnocentrism.

Early writings on ethnocentrism can be found in the works of several ancient Greek writers. For example, Aristotle in the eighth book in the *Nicomachean Ethics* wrote that animals, but especially humans, show affection and love for the members of the same race (Aristotle, trans. 1881). Aristotle used the term *tois homoethnesi*, which has been translated as the same race (Whiting, 2006), to indicate special affection among members of the same ethnos or clan. Jennifer Whiting (2006) claimed that Aristotle's point "is that human beings stand out among animals as especially *clannish*. We are the most *ethnocentric* – or, as Aristotle puts it, the most *homoethnic* – of animals. That is why we praise those who are (simply) *philanthropoi*: they have managed to overcome this common but regrettable tendency" (p. 291). Interestingly, observing the same bias, and many centuries later, Darwin (1875) wrote that social instincts, which include love and affection for one's community, exist in animals, including humans, but that they do not extend to the whole species.

Another ancient Greek, Herodotus (trans. 1947), wrote that preference for one's culture and its customs is universal among humans. Herodotus also wrote that this preference is not fully ameliorated, transcended, and corrected by having knowl-edge about other cultures. According to him, even upon examining and knowing other cultures, humans would select their own as the best:

> For if one were to offer men to choose out of all the customs in the world such as seemed to them the best, they would examine the whole number, and end by preferring their own; so convinced are they that their own usages far surpass those of all others.
>
> *Herodotus, trans. 1947, p. 160*

Here Herodotus put forward an idea that corresponds closely to the modern conceptualisation of ethnocentrism, which is the view that ethnocentrism is a universal phenomenon characteristic of all cultures (D. E. Brown, 1991, 2000, 2004). Herodotus also postulated that preference and superiority are two related aspects of this phenomenon.

Another ancient Greek historian, Diodorus Siculus (trans. 1725/1814), remarked that many ethnic groups believe that they are vastly superior to others. He also mentioned that many ethnic groups believed that all humans originated in their ethnic group and that their group alone is responsible for numerous discoveries from which all humans have benefited. For example, ancient Egyptians believed that gods and first humans were born in Egypt because the climate and nature were superior in Egypt to anywhere else: "The Egyptians report, that at the beginning of the world, the first men were created in Egypt, both by the reason of happy climate, and the nature of the river Nile" (Diodorus Siculus, 1725/1814, p. 18).

Ancient Chinese and Roman thinkers have also noticed ethnocentrism. For example, in the fifth century BC, an ancient Chinese philosopher, Mozi (also spelled Mo Tzu) asserted that because many people favour their own country over others, they dislike and want to harm people from other countries. The only way to ameliorate this unfortunate state of affairs, according to Mozi, is for people "to regard other people's countries as one's own" (Chan, 1963, p. 214). Writing negatively about the Jews, the ancient Roman Tacitus described them: "among themselves they are inflexibly honest and ever ready to shew compassion, though they regard the rest of mankind with all the hatred of enemies" (Tacitus, trans. 2003, p. 564). This association of strong ingroup positivity and strong outgroup negativity would later become the main conceptualisation and operationalisation of ethnocentrism (e.g., Adorno et al., 1950).

Ethnocentrism became salient during the time commonly known as the Age of Discovery, and authors such as Las Casas (1550/1974), Montaigne (1580/2003), and la Bruyère (1688/1885) recognised this phenomenon. The Age of Discovery was the time when people from Western countries began to "discover" the many "distant" lands – or what they called the "New World" – and in the process became acquainted with almost the entire spectrum of human diversity and with people who had strikingly different values, beliefs, morality, practices, and norms to those in the West. This was also the time of unbridled imperialism and colonialism, which resulted in the rampant exploitation of people in these "distant" lands. Ethnocentrism facilitated this exploitation as it helped the Western powers take advantage of the ethnic groups perceived to be too different and needing instruction and civilisation. The Western powers saw themselves as economically superior, being technologically more advanced, but also culturally and morally superior. They often relied on their own dominant religion, Christianity, to proclaim that they are superior to "savages and heathens" who worshipped "primitive" gods.

Although it is often perceived that people from Western countries were unified in their ethnocentric attitudes towards other human groups and approved of exploitation, there were alternative and deviating voices. One of the earliest recorded voices was that of Bartolomé de Las Casas, who lived in Spain during the fifteenth and sixteenth centuries. In his books, such as *In defense of the Indians* (Las Casas, trans. 1974), he argued forcefully against the Spanish exploitation of Indians in the Americas and confronted ethnocentric attitudes prevalent in his time. For example, while discussing the concept of barbarians and how the Spanish applied it to Indians, he maintained that the concept is relative as all groups with distinct languages perceive each other as barbarians. In another book, published only in the twentieth century, Las Casas maintained that "just as we consider the people of the Indians to be barbarians, they judge us the same way, since they do not understand us" (as quoted in Todorov, 2010, p. 20).

These same ideas are later revisited and further elaborated on by the French essayist Michele de Montaigne, when he wrote about indigenous peoples who lived on the coast of Brazil:

> I find (from what has been told me) that there is nothing savage or barbarous about those peoples, but that every man calls barbarous anything he is not accustomed to; it is indeed the case that we have no other criterion of truth or right-reason than the example and form of the opinions and customs of our own country. There we always find the perfect religion, the perfect polity, the most developed and perfect way of doing anything!
>
> *Montaigne, 1580/2003, p. 231*

Montaigne presented here a modern description of ethnocentrism, where people use the norms, practices, beliefs, morality, and values of their own ethnic group or culture to judge others, giving rise to the perception of superiority. Here, as in Las Casas's writings, we see the argument in favour of cultural relativism where there are no absolute criteria for judgement, and therefore no superior ethnic groups or cultures. Similar ideas are also expressed by another French author, Jean de la Bruyère (1688/1885):

> Our prepossession in favour of our native country and our national pride makes us forget that common sense is found in all climates, and correctness of thought wherever there are men. We should not like to be so treated by those we call barbarians; and if some barbarity still exists amongst us, it is in being amazed on hearing natives of other countries reason like ourselves.
>
> *p. 339*

The Italian philosopher Giambattista Vico (1744/1948), who lived in the seventeenth and eighteenth centuries, discussed national self-conceit in his influential book *New Science*. He referred to Diodorus Siculus's claim that all national groups believe themselves to be the oldest and that their history goes back to the beginning of time. He maintained that because people make judgements about things that are unknown and distant with the reference point of what is known and near to them, they tend to give a lot of importance to themselves – despite having objectively minor importance. Vico contended that, like nations, scholars are also self-conceited because they judge things that they do not know through the prism of what they do. Vico condemned scholars who attempt to interpret the world through the prism of the national self-conceit, and argued that their conclusions are most often biased and erroneous. This is in essence an argument that ethnocentrism leads to biased and poor science, and this argument would later be strongly endorsed by, for example, Gumplowicz, cultural relativists in anthropology, and contemporary cross-cultural psychologists.

Another elaborate discussion of ethnocentrism is in the Swiss author Johann Zimmermann's (1758/1797) book on national pride, which was widely read in the eighteenth century. The prominent political psychologist Harold Lasswell (1925), more than a century and a half later, discussed the importance of this "forgotten study" for the discipline of political psychology. Despite Lasswell's views, this book has almost never been mentioned explicitly in relation to the study of ethnocentrism and is largely forgotten now. Zimmermann conceptualised national pride as a sense of ethnic or cultural superiority, which is a central conceptualisation of ethnocentrism. Zimmermann wrote on national pride, but he made it clear that he used the term to describe a sense of real or imagined superiority among ethnic groups and cultures.

Although Sumner (see Sumner, 1906; Sumner et al., 1928) is usually praised for sampling diverse examples of ethnocentrism (Kinder & Kam, 2009; LeVine & Campbell, 1972), Zimmermann had already proposed numerous examples, many of which would be used later by both Gumplowicz and Sumner. For example, one such widely cited example is that of non-industrial societies often calling themselves the only and original humans: "Ask the Carribee Indians, who live at the mouth of the Oronoque, from what nation they derive their origin; they answer, 'why, we only are men.' In short, there is hardly any nation under the sun, in which instances of pride, vanity, and arrogance, do not occur" (Zimmermann, 1758/1797, p. 40). The other examples Zimmermann offered are about Egyptians, who believed that they had themselves already existed for 48,863 years before Alexander's age, and who believed that it was in Egypt where the first gods, then the first demigods, and then the first men lived. Similarly, he wrote about the Japanese, who believed that their real ancestors were gods; about Indians, who believed that the Indian culture had existed for millions of years; and about the Chinese, who believed that their empire was in the centre of the world, that it had begun even before the world was created, and that it occupied most of the world – with the rest of the world, as represented by Chinese maps, being small islands, which have peculiar and amusing names.

Zimmermann also attempted to describe and explain the phenomenon that would be later called ethnocentrism. For example, the following statement by Zimmermann (1758/1797) includes characteristics and explanations of ethnocentrism that would become prominent later: "Every nation contemplates itself through the medium of self-conceit, and draws conclusions to its own advantage, which individuals adopt to themselves with complacency, because they confound and interweave their private with their national character" (p. 1). Zimmermann assumed, similarly to modern social identity theorists, that a sense of group superiority is caused by perceiving oneself as being one with the group and by wanting to enhance one's own self-esteem (Tajfel & Turner, 1986; Turner, 1999). He also maintained that people tend to like other individuals whom they agree with because people want to be right and feel superior to others.

A contemporary of Zimmermann, the Scottish philosopher Adam Ferguson (1768) also recognised the phenomenon of ethnocentrism, and, like Vico before him, argued against ethnocentric biases, in particular against their influences on understanding humans and social life. He also claimed that when people judge others, they use their own group as a reference point. He maintained that national groups use different dimensions to assert their superiority. For example, he wrote in his book, titled *An Essay on the History of Civil Society*:

> No nation is so unfortunate as to think itself inferior to the rest of mankind: few are even willing to put up with the claim to equality. The greater part having chosen themselves, as at once, the judges and the models of what is excellent in their kind, are first in their own opinion, and give to others consideration or eminence, so far only as they approach to their own condition. One nation is vain of the personal character, or of the learning, of a few of its members; another, of its policy, its wealth, its tradesmen, its gardens, and its buildings; and they who have nothing to boast, are vain, because they are ignorant.
>
> *Ferguson, 1768, p. 312*

Ferguson also gave examples of different cultures being ethnocentric, such as Russians believing themselves to be superior to their western neighbours, whom Russians held in contempt and called *Nemci*, which can be translated as mute people. Ferguson's views have been directly linked to ethnocentrism (e.g., C. Smith, 2013), because he believed that people tend to use their own culture, and their own time period, as a standard while judging other cultures and other time periods, making them perceive other cultures as defective, wrong, and improper, or at least as less good than people's own culture. It should be noted that Ferguson also maintained that the positivity that members of a group have for each other goes hand in hand with negativity towards others, and that the two reciprocally influence each other. For example, he noted that "it is vain to expect that we can give to the multitude of a people a sense of union among themselves, without admitting hostility to those who oppose them" (Ferguson, 1768, p. 37).

Social scientific writings on ethnocentrism

A systematic social scientific study of ethnocentrism started in the nineteenth century with the development of the social sciences. Evidently, Vico and Ferguson could be seen as early social scientists, and they wrote on the phenomenon later to be labelled ethnocentrism. Nonetheless, the social sciences would experience more systematic and rapid developments in the second half of the nineteenth century, when disciplines such as sociology and psychology developed.

The increasing interest in ethnocentrism was in part influenced by the fact that many people, primarily those from a more educated background, had become increasingly acquainted with immense differences between cultures – stemming from growing anthropological work – and that many people began to question what is correct, good, and moral across societies. Additionally, with the development of Darwin's (1875) theory of evolution, many thinkers had begun to reject super-natural explanations, and attempted to find scientific explanations for the myriad phenomena, including social phenomena. Therefore, the view that had gained a lot of credence was that social phenomena, considered as just extensions of natural phenomena, are legitimate subjects for a scientific study. This view led to the rapid development of the social sciences. In fact, certain discussions of ethnocentrism can be found in Darwin's writings, such as his views about how intergroup competition and intragroup cooperation go hand in hand, and that animal species do not extend affection to their whole species, but just to those close to them (Darwin, 1875).

An early discussion of ethnocentrism can be found in the writings of one of the founders of sociology and an influential evolutionary theorist in his own right, the British sociologist Herbert Spencer. Spencer's (1874) chapter on patriotic biases in *The Study of Sociology* deals with the phenomenon that later social scientists would call ethnocentrism, a bias in favour of one's own ethnic group or culture. For example, Spencer (1874) asserted:

> Patriotism is nationally that which egoism is individually — has, in fact, the same root; and along with kindred benefits brings kindred evils. Estimation of one's society is a reflex of self-estimation; and assertion of one's society's claims is an indirect assertion of one's own claims as a part of it. The pride a citizen feels in a national achievement, is the pride in belonging to a nation capable of that achievement: the belonging to such a nation having the tacit implication that in himself there exists the superiority of nature displayed.
>
> *p. 205*

Spencer (1874) linked self-esteem and belonging to a nation to biases in favour of one's nation. Additionally, he explicitly linked individual egoism with group egoism. He also argued that although societies around the world reject excessive individual vanity, they celebrate excessive group vanity. Spencer claimed that the study of sociology is highly susceptible to this bias, which distorts objective views about other societies and precludes an objective study of social phenomena. Spencer gave the example of the French, who, according to him, thought that they were the only civilised nation in the world, that all other people should learn from the French, and that there was nothing that the French could learn from anyone else. Spencer opined that it could only benefit the French to learn from others because their patriotic bias produced dogmatic views and led them to incorrect conclusions.

It is ironic that Spencer (1892b) himself was a victim of ethnocentrism, writing against intermarriage between racial groups, claiming that his own study of this topic made him conclude that, as with interbreeding of animals, the consequences of interracial marriages are always negative.

Spencer (1892) also wrote about two moral codes that exist across societies: the code of amity, which is the moral code that enforces cooperation, reciprocity, affection, and altruism among people within one society; and the code of enmity, which is the moral code that enforces exploitation, aggression, hatred, and destruction, and which is followed in relations with outsiders. These two moral codes resemble Ferguson's (1768) previous arguments about the association of ingroup positivity and outgroup negativity, and anticipate later influential ideas about ethnocentrism being the association of ingroup positivity and outgroup hostility (Adorno et al., 1950; LeVine & Campbell, 1972). It is also relevant to mention that Spencer's writings about numerous social phenomena, including ethnocentrism, suggest that he saw them primarily stemming from individualistic and biological instincts. These could be contrasted with Ludwig Gumplowicz's views, which saw social phenomena to be entirely the products of groups (Gumplowicz, 1885/1963).

It was probably with Gumplowicz that the phenomenon of ethnocentrism already discussed in many writings got its name – or at the least, its first printed use. He mentioned ethnocentrism in at least eight publications, which include his conceptualisation of ethnocentrism and many examples of ethnocentrism (Gumplowicz, 1879, 1883, 1884, 1887, 1892, 1895, 1905, 1881). Given that his writings on ethnocentrism are generally ignored and do not seem to exist in the English language, I will present here translations of three passages where he discussed ethnocentrism. Interested readers are referred to the eight publications for more comprehensive discussions.

> Just as he regards himself as the centre of the earth (Anthropocentrism), as he regards the earth as the centre of the universe (Geocentrism), as every people and every nation regards itself as the most splendid (Ethnocentrism), so has the biblical saga, and similarly the sagas of other peoples invented the first couple created by God only for that reason to portray their own people always as the direct descendants of this first couple – as those whom God expressly called into life in this way as masters of the creation.
>
> *Gumplowicz, 1881, p. 71*

> But the reason why again and again one talks about a steadily progressive development of the whole of mankind as a unified whole, on the one hand lies in the unjustified transfer of the experience made in single social communities, especially in the single state in its existing phase of life, to the supposed course of development of the whole of mankind, on the other hand in a limited and self-complacent/smug view of the social world, that we would like to designate with one word as Ethnocentrism. According to this each people believe that they always occupy the highest position among the contemporary

people and nations, as well as with regard to all people of the historical past. If one now is caught up in the delusion that oneself is the highest and most accomplished work of the creation, and that all people and generations of the past were only bungling attempts of the Creator, until he succeeded with the masterwork of this people and this generation: then all past must indeed only appear as preparation for the present, and all the remaining people only as preliminary stages to the climax of the one people that Providence has been directly aiming for.

Gumplowicz, 1883, p. 352

(Before we can complete the argument), two ghosts prevent us from it. One is Ethnocentrism, that delusion of nations worth cursing, as if each of them forms the eminent "centre" or the "pinnacle" of humanity. Just as the Chinese consider themselves the "people of the middle", the Jews thought of themselves as the "chosen", the French strode "at the peak of civilisation", and Hegel assured the Germans (and they happily believed him) they were "the embodiment of the objective mind", which was meant to mean as much as "the God amongst the nations". Well, the modern sociology has shone into the face of the ghost of Ethnocentrism – and it [Ethnocentrism] begins to wane.

Gumplowicz, 1895, pp. 1–2

Gumplowicz therefore saw ethnocentrism as a delusion, whereby people believe that they are in the centre of everything, and superior to all other groups, and not only existing groups but all human groups that have ever existed. It is a phenomenon similar to both anthropocentrism, whereby humans believe that they are the most important and central species on earth, and geocentrism, whereby humans believe that the earth is central and the most important place in the universe. It is a delusion, but a powerful one, a delusion that can captivate numerous members of an ethnic group.

Living in the Austro-Hungarian Empire, Gumplowicz was exposed to a life of ethnic struggle and turmoil. During his life, many ethnic groups within the empire fought for independence. This, and the popularity of Spencer's and Darwin's writings, may have influenced his theory about the permanent racial struggle between the different racial groups – an idea that would later become prominent in the Nazi ideology. The term race in Gumplowicz's writings, however, is not a biological construct, but a cultural and social construct, and resembles the current usage of the term ethnic group. In fact, Gumplowicz "used the term 'race' where most would now use 'ethnicity'" (Scott, 2007, p. 59).

Gumplowicz's theory of group conflict, exploitation, and dominance is a theory that foreshadows later developments of realistic group conflict theory. According to his theory, ethnic groups want to exploit and dominate other groups, while wanting their own members to be obedient and devoted to the group. So, according to Gumplowicz, group cohesion and negative outgroup attitudes go hand in hand.

Gumplowicz (1881) also introduced the concept of syngenism, which can be seen as a strong sense of group consciousness. This concept incorporates the sentiments of group cohesion and devotion, which may in turn bring about exploitation and rejection of outgroups.

It should be noted that Gumplowicz was influenced by a fourteenth-century Arab scholar, Ibn Khaldun (1377/1958), and that Gumplowicz's concept of syngenism resembles Ibn Khaldun's concept *asabiyyah*, which is translated as a "group feeling". That concept had existed in the Arab language before Ibn Khaldun's writings, but became central in his theory of historical developments. It indicates a strong sense of group loyalty, cohesion, and devotion to one's own group. Ibn Khaldun argued that strong group feeling makes groups superior to other groups with weak group feeling. For example, a given number of individuals within a group rich in group feeling are always superior to the same number of individuals who belong to different groups and are without a unity of group feeling. Although Ibn Khaldun's writings are rarely related to ethnocentrism (but see Noor, 2003), they have had influence on later authors, such as Gumplowicz, and possibly through him on Sumner and others.

As mentioned before, in the nineteenth century, during the time of Spencer and Gumplowicz, sociology was being invented as a separate scientific discipline. In fact, Spencer and Gumplowicz belong to a group of early social scientists, together with Comte, Marx, Durkheim, and Weber, who can be seen as founders of sociology. Herbert Spencer and Gumplowicz were often placed together as social Darwinists, but, as mentioned above, Gumplowicz criticised Spencer's view that society can be reduced to a biological organism and his reductive individualism (Gumplowicz, 1885/1963). For Gumplowicz, the main unit of analysis for social phenomena is the group, and he argued that social phenomena are unique and cannot be reduced to biological and individual phenomena. He claimed that one cannot understand social groups and their relations based on "the properties of their constituent parts, i.e., … the properties of individuals" (Gumplowicz, 1885/1963, p. 98). Interestingly, this distinction between the view that social groups and their phenomena could be explained by either biology and individuals or by the whole groups or society is a distinction that would repeat itself over many years in psychology – as will be discussed later in the book.

Probably due to the influence of Gumplowicz's writings in the early social sciences, especially in the US, where his influence was as strong as the influence of Comte, Spencer, and Marx (Martindale, 1976), American scholars began to use the term ethnocentrism in the late nineteenth and early twentieth centuries. For example, the US historian and linguist Edward P. Evans (1891, 1894) used the term in two publications in the 1890s. Like Gumplowicz, he also linked ethnocentrism to anthropocentrism:

> We have happily rid ourselves somewhat of the ethnocentric prepossessions which led the Greeks, and still lead the Chinese, to regard all other peoples as outside barbarians; but our perceptions are still obscured by anthropocentric

prejudice which prevents us from fully appreciating the intelligence of the lower animals and recognizing any psychical analogy between these humble kinsmen and our exalted selves.

Evans, 1891, p. 179

Evans (1894) gave numerous explicit examples of ethnocentrism. For example, he saw ethnocentrism in the tendency of non-industrial societies to consider the physical environment of their tribe as the centre of the world. Additionally, he observed ethnocentrism among the English visiting Italy when they perceived Italians to behave in an un-English (meaning inappropriate, improper) way. He also maintained that even the countries that call themselves enlightened have not transcended ethnocentric ethics. Ethnocentric ethics, according to Evans, assumes that inflicting harm and being unfair to other people are unacceptable towards members of one's own ethnic group, but acceptable towards those who belong to another ethnic group.

Several publications by the US anthropologist William McGee (1898, 1899a, 1899b, 1900) also used and discussed the term ethnocentrism. McGee explicitly linked egocentrism with ethnocentrism, where egocentrism represents self-centred thinking and ethnocentrism represents tribal or ethnic group self-centred thinking. He noted that in tribes, "the egocentric and ethnocentric views are ever-present and always-dominant factors of both mentation and action" (McGee, 1900, p. 831). McGee also held the view that lack of knowledge and contact with others may lead people to believe that they, as individuals and groups, are in the centre of the world. His ethnographic analysis of Seri Indians described this tribe as exceptionally ethnocentric:

> [Seri Indians] typify primitive culture in their collective thinking, which is tribe-centered (or ethnocentric), i.e., they view extraneous things, especially those of animate nature, with reference to the tribe, like all those lowly folk who denote themselves by the most dignified terms in their vocabulary and designate aliens by opprobrious epithets; but the Seri outpass most, if not all, other tribes in dignifying themselves and derogating contemporary aliens.
>
> *McGee, 1898, p. 154*

McGee described extreme ethnocentrism among Seri Indians to consist of intense love for their own tribe, vanity, superiority, isolation, rejection of others, concern with blood purity, and strong intolerance, hatred, and even exaltation of the virtue of killing of people outside their tribe. This description of Seri Indians and their strong ethnocentrism can be found later in Sumner's (1906) writings on ethnocentrism.

Despite the term of ethnocentrism being used in various publications for at least 30 years, the US sociologist William Graham Sumner's (1906) book is widely credited with the introduction of the concept of ethnocentrism into the social sciences. This attribution is made in almost all publications in the English language, including some of the most important and widely cited contributions to the literature on ethnocentrism (e.g., Adorno et al., 1950; Brewer & Campbell, 1976; Tajfel, 1982). This attribution continues to this day (e.g., Brewer, 2016; Kinder & Kam, 2009). At the time of my writing of the paper on origins of the concept of ethnocentrism (Bizumic, 2014), I could find only a few publications in the English language that assumed that Sumner did not introduce the concept of ethnocentrism and that mentioned that the concept had previous usages, either in McGee's work (e.g., Simpson & Weiner, 1989, in the Oxford English Dictionary; van der Geest, 2005) or in Gumplowicz's work (e.g., Banton, 1998; Bracq, 1902). While researching for this book, I also found the attribution of Gumplowicz's writings in Gregor's (1969) work, who also argued that Gumplowicz's writings on ethnocentrism have had an important, though often overlooked, influence upon fascist theoretical literature.

Given their prominence, Sumner's writings (Sumner, 1906, 1911; Sumner et al., 1928) have had the strongest direct influence on the subsequent investigators of ethnocentrism. His definitions of ethnocentrism, however, correspond to what the other writers on ethnocentrism had been saying before him. His two explicit definitions of ethnocentrism follow:

> Ethnocentrism is the technical name for this view of things in which one's own group is the centre of everything, and all others are scaled and rated with reference to it. Folkways correspond to it to cover both the inner and the outer relation. Each group nourishes its own pride and vanity, boasts itself superior, exalts its own divinities, and looks with contempt on outsiders. Each group thinks its own folkways the only right ones, and if it observes that other groups have other folkways, these excite its scorn.
>
> *Sumner, 1906, p. 13*

> The sentiment of cohesion, internal comradeship, and devotion to the in-group, which carries with it a sense of superiority to any out-group and readiness to defend the interests of the in-group against the out-group, is technically known as ethnocentrism.
>
> *Sumner, 1911, p. 11*

As can be seen, ethnocentrism, according to Sumner, is a strong sense of ingroup cohesion, devotion, and loyalty, which brings with it superiority over other groups, rejection of other groups, and the view that ingroup interests are more important than outgroup interests. Sumner was strongly influenced by Gumplowicz – especially by his realpolitik perspective to war and conflict (Bannister, 1991). In fact, Sumner did cite Gumplowicz's (1883, 1892) two books that explicitly use the term ethnocentrism (Sumner, 1906, 1911, 1913; Sumner et al., 1928), denoting these and two other of Gumplowicz's publications as "exceptionally important sources" (Sumner et al., 1928, p. 1193). For example, Sumner et al. wrote: "The sentiment of 'belonging together' or 'syngenism' plus the allied sentiment of ethnocentrism, causes the conquerors and conquered to stand to each other in relation to hostility"

(1928, p. 528). Sumner used Gumplowicz's concept of syngenism as a related concept to ethnocentrism, and maintained that it predisposes groups to be in conflict with each other (Sumner et al., 1928).

Although Sumner did not coin the concept of ethnocentrism, it should be, nevertheless, noted that his writings on ethnocentrism were concise and potent. And in contrast to Sumner's writings, which discussed at length Gumplowicz's work on ethnocentrism, syngenism, and group conflict, almost all later books and publications on ethnocentrism completely overlooked Gumplowicz's contribution. As a result of Sumner's influence, the concept of ethnocentrism therefore started to be widely used in the early twentieth century among US social scientists (Bogardus, 1922; Boodin, 1918; Case, 1922; Keller, 1915; Park, 1914; Vincent, 1911). As mentioned above, it is, however, less often recognised that Gumplowicz's writings on ethnocentrism had a pronounced influence among Italian fascist social scientists, and contributed to the fascist ideology (Gregor, 1969).

The phenomenon and concept of ethnocentrism also held noticeable interest among anthropologists studying cultural relativism (Boas, 1940; Herskovits, 1948, 1972; Kroeber, 1948; Mead, 1928; Murdock, 1949). The central person in this area was Franz Boas, who strongly fought against ethnocentrism and racism. Boas (1931, 1934, 1940, 1928/1962), for example, opposed the view that certain ethnic groups are better than others, and questioned the prevalent views at the time in favour of biological underpinnings of many social and psychological phenomena, such as intelligence and ethnic prejudice.

Although Boas himself did not use the term ethnocentrism, his influential students and followers did. They mainly used it to describe a sense of superiority of and preference for one's culture, and using one's own culture as a reference point while judging other cultures. This is evident in the following explicit definitions of ethnocentrism: "that tendency to assume the universe as pivoted around one's particular people and to see one's in-group as always right and all out-groups as wrong" (Kroeber, 1948, p. 266); "the tendency to exalt the in-group and depreciate the other groups" (Murdock, 1949, pp. 83–84); and "the point of view that one's own way of life is to be preferred to all others" (Herskovits, 1948, p. 68). These theorists, however, did not focus on ethnocentric intragroup aspects, such as devotion, loyalty, and group cohesion, in their definitions of ethnocentrism, and ethnocentrism appeared primarily to be an intergroup phenomenon.

Common to Boas and his followers, who all had strongly influenced anthropology and the social sciences, is the condemnation of ethnocentrism. This was partly theoretical as they maintained that there is no evidence to justify the views that any ethnic group is inherently superior to others or to justify the views that mixing of ethnic groups weakens them. On another, more methodological, level, these researchers also argued that ethnic groups and cultures can be understood and studied only from within and not from outside, and that all cross-cultural comparisons are intrinsically ethnocentric.

Another line of work, however, was being developed at the same time and it became highly influential, especially in social psychology. This line of work principally focused on individual differences in ethnocentrism. Theodor Adorno, Else Frenkel-Brunswik, Daniel Levinson, and Nevitt Sanford (1950) published a book, titled *The Authoritarian Personality*, which was a seminal work that attempted to understand and explain individual differences in ethnocentrism. It investigated what personality characteristics predisposed people to ethnocentric and fascist ideologies. These researchers saw ethnocentrism as an ideology pertaining to groups and intergroup relations. The crucial part of their definition of ethnocentrism involved people's uniform consistency of reactions to other groups:

> Ethnocentrism is based on a pervasive and rigid ingroup-outgroup distinction; it involves stereotyped negative imagery and hostile attitudes regarding outgroups, stereotyped positive imagery and submissive attitudes regarding ingroups, and a hierarchical, authoritarian view of group interaction in which ingroups are rightly dominant, outgroups subordinate.
>
> *Adorno et al., 1950, p. 150*

Ethnocentric people are those who, as a result of internal psychodynamic conflicts, caused by punitive parenting, saw the world in a rigid way. They saw it to consist of virtuous ingroups, represented by virtuous authorities, and bad, dangerous, and inferior outgroups. To study ethnocentrism, Adorno et al. (1950) developed the Ethnocentrism Scale (E Scale). This scale measured anti-Jew, anti-African-American, anti-minority, and extremely patriotic or chauvinistic attitudes. An ethnocentric person would endorse all these attitudes.

According to Daniel Levinson (1949), who contributed to the psychometric work on ethnocentrism in this research programme, ethnocentrism could be seen as a bipolar dimension, with two extremes: strong ethnocentrism vs. strong anti-ethnocentrism (those in the middle region were described as uncertain, passive, or confused). Every person could score somewhere on this scale, with ethnocentric people being high-scorers and people rejecting ethnocentrism being low-scorers. The researchers also assumed that ethnocentric people have a generalised tendency to be "centred" on themselves and many ingroups (e.g., family, city, religion), and that this tendency would systematically correlate with having negative attitudes towards all those outside their ingroups.

Even though Adorno and colleagues considered various aspects of ethnocentrism, in the end their conceptualisation principally dealt with negativity towards many outgroups, and mainly ethnic minorities. With their work, a tradition in psychology was developed that saw ethnocentrism as mainly, or even exclusively, concerned with prejudice that is generalised across ethnic outgroups (e.g., Altemeyer, 2003; Pettigrew et al., 1997; Warr, Faust, & Harrison, 1967). This work has had a strong influence on the subsequent study of individual differences in ethnocentrism and prejudice, and strongly influenced several major areas of research in psychology: dogmatism and belief congruence (Rokeach, 1960), right-wing authoritarianism (Altemeyer, 1996, 2006), social dominance theory (Sidanius, Cotterill, Sheehy-Skeffington, Kteily, & Carvacho, 2017), and dual process cognitive-motivational theory (Duckitt, 2001;

Duckitt & Sibley, 2017). These theories will be discussed in more detail in subsequent chapters.

Another seminal work on ethnocentrism was conducted in the 1960s and the 1970s by Donald Campbell, Robert LeVine, and Marilyn Brewer (Brewer & Campbell, 1976; Campbell, 1965; Campbell & LeVine, 1961; LeVine & Campbell, 1972). First, these researchers wanted to investigate whether broad pro-ingroup and anti-outgroup attitudes that Sumner included in his writings on ethnocentrism do indeed represent a single dimension. They argued, drawing on Sumner, that ethnocentrism is a broad syndrome that includes 23 facets, which could be conceptualised as one dimension. This dimension included the association between various pro-ingroup and anti-outgroup attitudes and behaviours, such as: "See selves as virtuous and superior", "Cooperative relations with ingroup members", "See own standards of value as universal, intrinsically true. See own customs as original, centrally human", "Social distance", "Sanctions for outgroup murder or absence of sanctions against outgroup murder", and "Willingness to fight and die for ingroup" (LeVine & Campbell, 1972, p. 12).

LeVine and Campbell (1972) also revisited and described numerous existing theories of ethnocentrism, and systematised realistic group conflict theory based on the writings of conflict theorists (e.g., Coser, 1956; Sherif, 1966). This theory assumed that rather than because of irrational conflicts, as proposed by psychodynamic theorists, ethnocentrism emerges because it helps groups in conflict with each other over realistic resources. Empirical research with 30 ethnic groups in East Africa, conducted by Brewer and Campbell (1976), suggested that, contrary to Sumner and later Adorno and colleagues, positive attitudes towards ingroups were frequently independent of people's negative attitudes towards outgroups.

Another line of research and theorising, developed in experimental social psychology, and known as social identity theory, studied ethnocentrism as ingroup bias, which is "the laboratory analogue of real-world ethnocentrism" (Tajfel & Turner, 1986, p. 13). Social identity theorists studied this bias in artificially created groups in the laboratory, where participants do not know who the other members of the ingroup or outgroup are. Even in the absence of conflict between groups, studies found that people tended to often prefer ingroups to outgroups – by giving ingroup members more tokens or money, or by giving them more positive ratings. Ethnocentrism was here reduced to its experimental analogue of ingroup preferences, whereas the complex attitudes of ethnic ingroup devotion, group cohesion, purity, and exploitation were not seen as the core aspects of ethnocentrism. Further, ethnocentrism was also stripped of its ethnic connotations and could be applied to any group.

Mirroring the explanations of ethnocentrism by Zimmermann and Spencer, these theorists claimed that the process of categorising oneself as an ingroup member together with the need for positive self-esteem tended to underlie ethnocentrism. This tradition has had a strong impact on the social psychological study of ethnocentrism. Nevertheless, in a certain way, as a result of this tradition and a study of ethnocentrism in the laboratory, the concept became less popular, and psychologists have increasingly used the concepts of ingroup bias, intergroup bias, and ingroup favouritism. Although the idea that personal self-esteem predisposes people to ingroup bias, and therefore ethnocentrism, did not fare well (R. Brown, 2000), subsequent researchers paid a lot of interest to the idea of how categorisation, in interaction with social factors, causes ingroup bias. In fact, the most recent edition of the *Handbook of Social Psychology* devotes a whole chapter to the study of inter-group bias (Dovidio & Gaertner, 2010), suggesting that the study of ethnocentrism is still prominent in social psychology, even though the concept itself is not as widely used as in the past. Still, the concept is often mentioned in the literature, and various contemporary disciplines still study it. When it comes to psychology itself, authoritarian personality theory, realistic group conflict theory, and the social identity approach ended up being the three most influential perspectives on eth-nocentrism, and their influence is still very powerful, with almost all contemporary perspectives on prejudice and intergroup relations situated broadly within these three perspectives.

Summary and conclusions

This chapter presented a brief conceptual history of ethnocentrism across different areas. It is by no means an exhaustive historical review. It touched on certain, mainly forgotten, historical origins, and focused somewhat more on the coverage of the forgotten history and somewhat less on the more recent history. This is done to counterbalance the current emphasis in psychology on the historically near over the historically distant (the bias against which Vico, Ferguson, and Gumplowicz had warned us), and to give more prominence to the forgotten, but relevant, liter-ature on ethnocentrism. In addition, the more recent work will be discussed in the chapters that follow.

As a broader conclusion of the chapter, it is important to point out that psy-chology, like sociology (Agger, 2007; Steinmetz, 2013), suffers from "disciplinary amnesia", which means that it has largely forgotten its history. Why is the history of the concept important? Why is it important that people across ages and cultures observed ethnocentrism and explained it in similar ways? First of all, knowing what other people wrote on the same topic in the past should be an aspect of broad scholarship. Second, it is important to discuss the history because social scientists often devote a lot of time and resources to discovering something that has already been discovered, discussed, and perhaps explained (Andreski, 1972). Finally, the fact that people recognised ethnocentrism across societies and times, and that they had similar explanations of ethnocentrism, or the phenomenon that was to be called ethnocentrism, may point to the validity of this recognition and perhaps even these explanations. That people in different cultures and time periods provided similar descriptions and explanations of ethnocentrism may point towards the fact that the underlying phenomenon is real and recognised as an important characteristic of individuals and ethnic groups – across time periods and ethnic groups. Perhaps, the fact that these explanations, for example, invoked self-esteem to explain it (e.g.,

Dollard, 1937; Spencer, 1874; Tajfel & Turner, 1986; Zimmermann, 1758/1797) may suggest that there may be an underlying truth to these explanations. Nonetheless, before embarking further on explanations of ethnocentrism, it is important to discuss what ethnocentrism is because there has been a lot of confusion surrounding the concept in the literature.

2

THE CONCEPT OF ETHNOCENTRISM

The philosopher Ludwig Wittgenstein argued that psychology is characterised by "experimental methods and conceptual confusion" (Wittgenstein, 1953, p. 232). Psychologists themselves have also often criticised psychology for its vague concepts and conceptual confusion (Bredo, 2006; Harre & Tissaw, 2005; Wakefield, 2007). There is probably a direct relationship between the importance of a concept and the conceptual confusion surrounding it in psychology. This results in virtually no agreement on most psychological concepts, including the central ones such as the mind, personality, behaviour, mental health, identity, or even the concept of psychology itself. Often, in the words of Billig (2013), to understand the meanings of concepts in psychological theories, "You have to be on the inside to know these things: you cannot infer them simply from looking at the meanings of the words" (p. 183). In the presence of this conceptual confusion, empirical research itself may fail to settle debates in psychology. For example, much of the debate about whether people behave in line with their attitudes could be attributed to the conceptual confusion surrounding the terms behaviour and attitudes (Hill, 1981).

This state of affairs is not inevitable and other disciplines have benefited from systematic conceptual clarifications. Ernst Mayr (1982), a prominent evolutionary biologist, argued that most advances in biology have been caused by conceptual clarifications and improvements and not by empirical investigations. He also stated: "Our understanding of the world is achieved more effectively by conceptual improvements than by the discovery of new facts, even though the two are not mutually exclusive" (Mayr, 1982, p. 23).

Psychology itself, on the other hand, has rarely given attention to clarifications of its concepts in a systematic fashion. There are many reasons for this. For example, the more a concept is studied, the more perspectives are added to it as different theorists and researchers tend to be interested in different aspects of the concept and bring their own views on what that concept is. Other reasons are simply practical, such as external pressures on psychologists to generate numerous empirical articles at the expense of theoretical and conceptual work (Wachtel, 1980; Wakefield, 2007). In addition, psychologists usually do not like others to tell them what a particular concept is (Billig, 2013). So, psychological work focusing solely on conceptual clarification is rare. If, as Mayr pointed out, biology has been improved through conceptual improvements, then the lack of conceptual clarification that still exists in psychology has hampered the development of psychology as a science. The aim of the present chapter is to clarify ethnocentrism conceptually.

Ethnocentrism has been defined in many ways, and as seen in Chapter 1 different theorists and researchers have seen the concept differently, and certain researchers highly interested in ethnocentrism and influential in its study (e.g., Boas, 1931, 1940) have not used the term. This means that both a jangle fallacy, when different concepts are given the same name, and a jingle fallacy, when one concept is given different names (Block, 1996), have affected the study of ethnocentrism.

Tajfel (1983) described ethnocentrism as an umbrella concept – that is, a broad concept that has disparate concepts within itself. He was no doubt influenced by the many ideas included among the 23 facets of ethnocentrism in LeVine and Campbell's book (1972), and the argument that the different facets of ethnocentrism could not be reduced to one single dimension involving pro-ingroup and anti-outgroup attitudes and behaviours (Brewer, 1981; Brewer & Campbell, 1976; LeVine & Campbell, 1972). Similarly, others wrote of "the disutility of the ethnocentrism concept" (Heaven, Rajab, & Ray, 1985, p. 181) because certain conceptualisations of ethnocentrism comprise empirically unrelated concepts. Still, others questioned what, if anything, one can learn from all the work on ethnocentrism (Raden, 2003). These appear extreme views, caused by the conceptual confusion surrounding the term.

Accordingly, even though the concept itself is still widely used and studied in psychology and the social sciences, there is little agreement on what ethnocentrism is, and theorists and researchers who have studied and attempted to explain it have often addressed different phenomena. Chapter 1 showed that although the term ethnocentrism had been used before Sumner, it was, nevertheless, Sumner's work that researchers and theorists have read and consulted when writing on ethnocentrism. His early definitions of ethnocentrism were specific, but his descriptions and explanations (Sumner, 1906, 1911; Sumner et al., 1928) were much more wide-ranging. Although Sumner defined ethnocentrism primarily as ethnic group self-centredness, he also assumed that ethnocentrism would be inevitably associated with anti-outgroup attitudes. This has had a strong impact on subsequent theorists and researchers, who have, for the most part, uncritically accepted this idea and included outgroup negativity in their definitions, operationalisations, or measures of ethnocentrism. It is therefore not surprising that historically many have seen ethnocentrism as the association of various pro-ingroup and anti-outgroup attitudes (e.g., Adorno et al., 1950; Eisinga, Felling, & Peters, 1990; Scheepers, Felling, & Peters, 1989), with a strong emphasis on anti-outgroup attitudes (e.g., Altemeyer, 1998; Beswick & Hills, 1969; Warr et al., 1967). For example, Altemeyer (2003) described his Manitoba Ethnocentrism Scale as a measure of "prejudice against a wide variety of racial–ethnic minorities" (p. 18), whereas Pettigrew et al.'s (1997) measure of ethnocentrism included only outgroup negativity.

Theorists and researchers have criticised Sumner's ideas regarding ethnocentrism. For example, sociologists have criticised Sumner's ambiguous formulations and argued that he incorrectly presented a special case of intergroup relations as universal and that often certain outgroups are also ingroups in larger social organisations (Merton, 1957). Anthropological evidence, summarised by LeVine and Campbell (1972), suggested that ethnic outgroups may be positive reference groups for many ethnic groups, which may try to emulate and imitate the culture of these outgroups. Sumner's arguments, which were widely read, should therefore be seen as strongly influenced by an extreme version of the evolutionary theory that saw the world as a threatening place with unending conflicts between ethnic groups, and it appeared natural that in such a world hostility would coexist with ethnocentrism. This also appears to be the case with Gumplowicz's (1883) writings about the eternal conflict between ethnic groups.

The social identity tradition saw ethnocentrism primarily as preference for the ingroup over outgroups, with Tajfel and Turner (1986) referring to ingroup bias as "the laboratory analogue of real-world ethnocentrism" (p. 13). Proponents of this tradition have strongly argued against equating ingroup bias (and its real-world analogue) with outgroup negativity or prejudice (Brewer, 1979, 1999, 2007; Turner, 1978). It is, therefore, clear from this brief overview that there have been many conceptualisations of ethnocentrism. What is less clear is what conceptualisation we should rely on.

Main themes in definitions of ethnocentrism

To clarify conceptually the construct of ethnocentrism, I and John Duckitt (Bizumic & Duckitt, 2012) investigated how ethnocentrism has been defined by various authors. Appendix A presents these definitions. To illustrate the main underlying themes clearly, we separated some statements or merged them. Three broad major themes emerged in these definitions: (a) group self-centredness (i.e., giving strong importance to one's group); (b) outgroup negativity (i.e., hostility and contempt towards other groups); and (c) mere ingroup positivity (i.e., positive evaluation of one's own group). The definitions dealing with the theme of group self-centredness tended to deal either with a general concept or with specific facets. It appeared that those dealing with the more specific facets could be classified into six categories: strong devotion to the ingroup, the need for group cohesion, preference for the ingroup over outgroups, the perception of superiority of ingroup over outgroups, the wish to preserve the ethnic purity of one's own group, and exploitativeness (pursuit of ingroup interest without consideration for outgroups). Yet, numerous definitions of ethnocentrism included outgroup negativity and mere ingroup positivity as facets of ethnocentrism.

If one is to take a unidimensional approach, one would argue that ethnocentrism is a bipolar dimension (see Figure 2.1), whereby a person who is very positive about

rejection of group self-centredness,
outgroup negativity, ingroup positivity

high group self-centredness,
outgroup negativity, ingroup positivity

FIGURE 2.1 A unidimensional representation of ethnocentrism

their own group also endorses ethnic group self-centredness and negativity towards other groups. In contrast, a person who is low on ethnocentrism – or more precisely anti-ethnocentric or ethnically tolerant – would reject ingroup positivity, the view that their own group has a central place in the world, and outgroup negativity.

This unidimensional view is overly simplified, internally inconsistent, empirically not corroborated, and conceptually unclear. What is, nevertheless, clear is that different researchers and theorists were often thinking about different phenomena when they defined ethnocentrism. Thus, in light of the conceptual analysis, theoretical reasoning, and past empirical research, and to make it consistent with the original conceptualisations and with the origin of the term itself (an amalgam of the words "ethnos" and "centre"), ethnocentrism should be seen as ethnic group self-centredness and self-importance, which has six specific expressions. The term self-centredness is used here to denote centredness on one's own group (i.e., group self-centredness). Other researchers have similarly used the term "group self-hatred" (Rosenberg, 1979; see also Lewin, 1948) to refer to hating one's own group. The concept of group self-centredness implies being centred on the group that includes oneself and not other groups, and implies that it deals with the group, social, or collective self as opposed to the personal, individual, or private self (cf. Triandis, 1989).

Although, as seen in the definitions in Appendix A, many scholars have defined ethnocentrism as outgroup negativity, mere ingroup positivity, or the association of outgroup negativity and ingroup positivity, these constructs should be differentiated from ethnic group self-centredness, so that we can have a consistent and clear concept. One can draw a parallel here with narcissism, which can be seen as an individual-level analogue to ethnocentrism. Narcissism, that is, personal self-centredness, is different to misanthropy, that is, hostility to other people, and is different to self-esteem, that is, positive evaluation of oneself. In the same way, ethnocentrism, that is, ethnic group self-centredness, is different to outgroup negativity, that is, hostility to other groups, and mere ingroup positivity, that is, a positive evaluation of one's own group. A similar analogy can also be made in relation to anthropocentrism or human self-centredness (see Bizumic & Duckitt, 2007), in which anthropocentrism can be differentiated from hostility to other species and a positive evaluation of all humans.

Ethnocentrism is distinct from outgroup negativity

In contrast to many conceptualisations and measures, both theory and research suggest that ethnocentrism, that is, ethnic group self-centredness, and outgroup negativity, that is, prejudice, are distinct. For example, Allport (1954) assumed that preference, cohesion, and rejection of outgroups are not caused by outgroup neg-ativity, and can be much more easily explained by the fact that it is easier to deal with similar and familiar ingroups than with dissimilar and unfamiliar outgroups. He assumed that ingroup-outgroup segregation should not necessarily be attrib-uted to prejudice: "The fact is adequately explained by the principle of ease, least effort, congeniality, and pride in one's own culture" (Allport, 1954, p. 19). Although Allport assumed that outgroups are usually seen as less good, attitudes towards outgroups are not necessarily hostile. Similarly, Sherif and Sherif (1969) argued that outgroup hostility occurs only under certain conditions, and that people can often perceive outgroups as benign, friendly, and allies. Duckitt (1992) also points out that attitudes towards outgroups can range from liking to indifference to dislike and hatred. Accordingly, at least theoretically, it is possible that one can be ethnocentric and have indifferent attitudes towards outgroups, or even like them, but less than the ingroup.

Research mirrors these conclusions. For example, summarising the results of early experimental research, Turner (1978) said, "Not only is ingroup favouritism in the laboratory situation not necessarily related to outgroup dislike, it also does not seem causally dependent on denigration of the outgroup" (p. 249). Likewise, Brewer's (1979) review of early experimental research also showed that ingroup bias in the lab and outgroup dislike are independent of each other. A meta-analysis of studies that investigated the role of group memberships in cooperation showed that people tend to discriminate in favour of ingroup members over outgroup members because they favour their ingroups and not because they derogate outgroups, confirming that ingroup preference and outgroup derogation are distinct (Balliet, Wu, & De Dreu, 2014).

Anthropological work also confirms these assumptions. For example, Ross's (1983) analysis of political life in 90 ethnic groups showed that variables representing internal societal conflict and those representing outgroup hostility and external conflict loaded on two separate dimensions and were moderately positively, and not negatively, correlated, suggesting that intragroup conflict may translate into inter-group conflict and outgroup hostility. Cashdan (2001) analysed 186 ethnic groups and found that outgroup hostility and ingroup loyalty were virtually unrelated and that the two differentially predicted external variables, suggesting that these have different determinants.

Conclusions of experimental and field research are similar in that they suggest that ingroup preference and outgroup negativity can be differentially correlated and it is wrong to see them as equivalent (see Brewer, 1999, 2007). Although much of the work focused on ingroup preference or at times on ingroup superiority and how it is distinct from outgroup negativity and hostility, it is important to point out that all dimensions of ethnocentrism are distinct from it. The idea of centrality in ethnocentrism does not imply negativity towards those who are outside the centre, and ethnocentrism appears related to the process of ranking, whereby one's own group is placed at the top (Rose, 1966). This ranking and overly strong group self-focus may contribute to perceiving other groups as much less relevant and more distant from the self than one's ingroup. In the words of Gibbon (1788): "our sympathy is cold to the relation of distant misery" (p. 116). Accordingly, ethnocentrism may predispose people to be indifferent or neutral to the other ethnic groups. These attitudes are, however, distinct from outgroup negativity, such as hostility, hatred, and disparagement.

This is not to suggest that ethnocentrism is always unrelated to outgroup negativity. In fact, under specific circumstances, ethnocentrism could give rise to outgroup negativity. Ethnocentrism, with its focus on ingroup superiority and importance of ingroup interests over those of the outgroup, could easily predispose people to become negative to outgroups. Such circumstances could be when outgroups are perceived to be threatening to or in competition with the ingroup. This can also happen when outgroups are perceived to have very different norms, values, and beliefs – those that are highly incompatible with the ingroup's norms, values, and beliefs, and those that ingroup members perceive as illegitimate (cf. Mummendey & Wenzel, 1999).

It is therefore not necessary for ethnocentrism to lead to negativity to other ethnic groups, but ethnocentrism could more easily lead to negativity towards other ethnic groups than to attitudes of humanitarian concern for others. Nevertheless, ethnocentrism as group self-centredness is conceptually distinct from outgroup negativity and may have differential associations with it for different outgroups and circumstances. Similarly, research shows that narcissism is not necessarily related to negativity towards other individuals (Bizumic & Duckitt, 2008; Farwell & Wohlwend-Lloyd, 1998), unless these others threaten the narcissists' self-image (South, Oltmanns, & Turkheimer, 2002).

Ethnocentrism is distinct from mere ingroup positivity

Mere ingroup positivity (i.e., positive evaluation of one's own group) is also sometimes included in definitions or measures of ethnocentrism. It should be noted that those who include it invariably assume that ethnocentrism does not only involve mere ingroup positivity, but is coupled with other sentiments. Mere ingroup positivity is nevertheless conceptually distinct from ethnocentrism and under certain circumstances may not even be associated with it. It is possible, however, that people may have positive ingroup attitudes together with equally positive, or even more positive, outgroup attitudes. Furthermore, certain ethnocentric people may even have negative ingroup attitudes, as seems to be the case with extreme right-wing groups (e.g., in the US or in Nazi Germany) who derogate their actual ingroups, asserting that these have lost their true way (e.g., Ezekiel, 1995). More precisely, these extremist groups dislike the group as it is, but have an idealised vision for the ingroup that if satisfied would make the actual ingroup worthy of love.

Research on group identification appears useful for differentiating mere ingroup positivity and ethnocentrism. Given that identification, as usually measured in empirical research, is concerned with positively evaluating the ingroup (cf. R. Brown, 2000), ingroup identification can be seen as similar to mere ingroup positivity. (In fact, measures of identification frequently do not involve strong and passionate group identification, which are exemplified in Sumner's sentiments of "devotion, comradeship and cohesion.") A narrative review of laboratory and field studies of ingroup preference and ingroup identification found that the relationships between the two concepts were positive, negative, or non-significant (Hinkle & Brown, 1990). The average correlation was a relatively weak positive correlation. Thus, ingroup preference and identification appear empirically and conceptually distinct.

Additionally, nationalism, which deals with ingroup superiority and dominance, is similar to ethnocentrism, whereas patriotism appears to be primarily concerned with positively evaluating the ingroup (cf. Kosterman & Feshbach, 1989). Research has found that nationalism and patriotism are distinct (Blank & Schmidt, 2003; Karasawa, 2002; Kosterman & Feshbach, 1989) and predict external variables differentially (e.g., De Figueiredo & Elkins, 2003; Kosterman & Feshbach, 1989). For example, Blank and Schmidt (2003) found that German nationalism (measured primarily as national superiority) related to anti-Jewish and anti-foreigner attitudes, whereas patriotism (measured primarily as national allegiance) related to pro-Jewish and pro-foreigner attitudes.

Thus, there appear to be theoretical and empirical grounds to suggest that mere ingroup positivity is conceptually distinct from, and not necessarily related to, group self-centredness. Intense ingroup positivity, which involves a powerful sense of identification (see Duckitt, 1989) in the form of unconditional devotion to one's group, appears ethnocentric, but this should be differentiated from mere ingroup positivity, which is not necessarily ethnocentric. This is also exemplified in Adorno et al.'s (1950) distinction between patriotism, which appears to be primarily related to mere ingroup positivity, and pseudopatriotism, which is ethnocentric.

Ethnocentrism is not the association of ingroup positivity and outgroup negativity

There is a widely held belief that ingroup positivity and outgroup negativity together form ethnocentrism (see LeVine & Campbell, 1972). There are two versions of this. The first is that ingroup positivity and outgroup negativity form one dimension (LeVine & Campbell, 1972). The second is that, even if the two do not form one dimension, the instances when they do correlate will represent ethnocentrism (Phillips, Penn, & Gaines, 1993). Both views are difficult to justify.

The first view rests on Sumner's assumption that group self-centredness, mere ingroup positivity, and negative outgroup attitudes would be strongly intercorrelated and that they would form one dimension (pro-ingroup/anti-outgroup attitudes). As previously noted, research findings have shown that group self-centredness is distinct from, and may be differentially related to, outgroup negativity. In addition, mere ingroup positivity is empirically distinct from outgroup attitudes and ingroup positivity may in fact be positively related to outgroup positivity (e.g., Blank & Schmidt, 2003; De Figueiredo & Elkins, 2003). Furthermore, our own research in five countries (Bizumic et al., 2009; Bizumic, Smithson, & van Rooy, 2010) showed that the average correlation, corrected for measurement error, between mere ingroup positivity and outgroup negativity was only $r = -.11$, suggesting a weak negative correlation. This in essence means that people who were positive towards their ethnic group were *less, not more, likely* to be negative towards other groups. Therefore, ethnocentrism cannot be seen as the unidimensional association of pro-ingroup and anti-outgroup attitudes.

Another view can be exemplified by the assumption that ingroup positivity is not necessarily related to outgroup negativity, but when it is, this constitutes ethnocentrism (Phillips et al., 1993). This view is also problematic on conceptual, theoretical, and empirical grounds. First, it is problematic on conceptual grounds because it is difficult to justify a concept that consists of two distinct, and often unrelated, concepts. This is the reason Heaven et al. (1985) spoke about the uselessness of the ethnocentrism concept. Second, the view is problematic on theoretical grounds because it is unclear which causes and consequences relate to ingroup positivity and which to outgroup negativity. The view is also problematic on empirical grounds because if researchers combine two relatively independent constructs their findings may be confusing and unclear. For example, if a study finds that the overall construct changes as a result of time or experimental manipulation, researchers may not be certain that the change is due to changes in both constituent components or in only one. Accordingly, there are conceptual, theoretical, and empirical reasons against the view that ethnocentrism is an association of ingroup positivity and outgroup negativity.

Facets of ethnocentrism

The review of the definitions of ethnocentrism suggested six specific facets of ethnocentrism, all of which reflect the view that one's own group is of central importance. The following section will define, describe, and illustrate the six specific facets.

1. Devotion

This facet of ethnocentrism represents a strong, ardent, and unconditional loyalty, attachment, and dedication to one's own ethnic group and its interests. This strong commitment is caused by the view that one's ingroup is of central importance to the group members. They should, therefore, offer blind and uncritical support for the group's actions and even be prepared to sacrifice their lives for it. These ideas are present in certain definitions of ethnocentrism, such as Sumner's (1911), Adorno et al.'s (1950), and the American Psychological Association's (2001) definition. The sentiment of devotion is also central to Gumplowicz's concept of syngenism, which overlaps with the concept of ethnocentrism (Gregor, 1969).

Adorno et al. (1950) differentiated simple love for the ingroup (akin to mere ingroup positivity) from ethnocentric ingroup love, which "involves blind attachment to certain national cultural values, uncritical conformity with the prevailing group ways" (p. 107). The idea of blind patriotism (see Schatz & Staub,

1997; Schatz, Staub, & Lavine, 1999; Staub, 1997), building on Adorno et al.'s ideas, also deals with ingroup devotion. Blind patriots are those people who feel intensely attached to their national groups and are uncritically supportive of the group's practices. Any criticism of the group is seen as disloyalty. American blind patriots are likely to accept statements such as "I would support my country right or wrong" or "The United States is virtually always right". A study by Schatz et al. (1999) showed that in contrast to constructive patriots, blind patriots are uncritically attached to the group and tend to believe in ingroup superiority and rightful dominance over outgroups. They are also less supportive of individual rights and freedoms, such as free speech (Parker, 2010). Although blind patriotism is concerned with nationality, it can be related to ethnicity, and therefore to ethnocentrism.

2. Group cohesion

Group cohesion involves the view that high levels of integration, unity, and cooperation should pervade one's ethnic group, with the needs of the ingroup taking precedence over the needs of its individual group members. The perception that the ingroup is of such high importance is, in this facet, reflected in the view that for the sake of one's ethnic group and its unity all group members must reject individual freedoms, disagreements, and differences. Although many definitions do not include group cohesion as an aspect of ethnocentrism, the term cohesion was explicitly included by Sumner (1911) as a major facet of ethnocentrism and had already been part of Gumplowicz's concept of syngenism, which as mentioned above overlaps with ethnocentrism (Gregor, 1969). Similarly, a number of prominent theorists and researchers have seen group cohesion as a central aspect of ethnocentrism (e.g., Brewer & Campbell, 1976; Campbell, 1965; LeVine & Campbell, 1972; Seeyle & Brewer, 1970).

Darwin (1875) argued that group cohesion appears necessary for any group to function successfully. In the chapter on patriotic biases, Spencer (1874) wrote of the opposition and antagonism between the sentiments of individuality and of nationality, and argued that if one is overly focused on one of these two, then the other one is suppressed. Group cohesion may increase when groups are threatened, and therefore realistic group conflict theorists (see LeVine & Campbell, 1972) argued that conflict with outgroups promotes group cohesion. This idea of a functional relationship between conflict, external threat, and group cohesion has been widely mentioned in the literature (see LeVine & Campbell, 1972; Tajfel, 1982). Although it appears that group cohesion is a product of categorisation of the self with the group and is not necessarily caused by threat, group cohesion can nevertheless increase as a result of threat (Turner, Hogg, Oakes, Reicher, & Wetherell, 1987).

3. Preference

Preference is an inclination to like and prefer one's own ethnic group, including its individual members, over other groups and their members. The term preference assumes that people have a subjective liking for and favour the ingroup over outgroups, but it does not necessarily involve seeing the ingroup as superior to outgroups or advocating ethnic purity. Brewer and Gaertner (2001) argued that ingroup preference is the primary process underlying intergroup discrimination. According to them, preference consists of positive affect, such as trust and liking, aimed at ingroup members but not at outgroup members. People prefer their ingroups, because trusting them is less risky than trusting outgroups (Brewer, 1981). Within ingroups there appears to be a "reciprocity" pact of interpersonal trust and cooperation, which is not extended to outgroup members (Brewer, 1997; see also Foddy, Platow, & Yamagishi, 2009).

Numerous studies have shown that both artificial and real-world groups exhibit ingroup preference. For example, Sherif's (1966) studies suggested that in the absence of group differentiation participants used personal preferences when choosing friends, whereas once groups were formed they were much more likely to choose friends from their ingroups than outgroups. Social identity theory (Tajfel & Turner, 1986) was originally developed to account for the findings that people show ingroup preference (which these authors equated with ethnocentrism in the real world) even in minimal groups, that is, artificially constructed groups where there is no interaction between group members, who do not know who the other group members are.

4. Superiority

According to the definitions of ethnocentrism reviewed, superiority appears to be the most widely emphasised facet of ethnocentrism. (It is, however, intriguing to note that most existing scales that measure ethnocentrism do not include this facet.) This facet is related to the belief that one's own ethnic group is better than or superior to others on certain dimensions, which are usually of central significance to the ingroup, such as morality, history, spirituality, sociability, economy, development, military might, and so forth. This process may often involve social creativity, through which ethnic groups choose dimensions of comparisons that would bring about relative superiority (see Tajfel & Turner, 1986). Past research has suggested, however, that positive evaluation of groups is primarily based on the morality dimensions rather than on those related to ingroup competence or sociability (see Leach, Ellemers, & Barreto, 2007).

A belief in ingroup superiority is widespread. Most examples of ethnocentrism put forward by early writers on ethnocentrism (e.g., Evans, 1894; Gumplowicz, 1881, 1887, 1892, 1895; Sumner, 1906; Sumner et al., 1928) indicate that ethnic groups frequently believe themselves to be superior to all other ethnic groups. For example, many non-industrial societies believe that the world originated with their group or that they are in some way "chosen people" (e.g., Bogardus, 1922; Cox, 1948; Evans, 1894; Gumplowicz, 1881, 1895; Sumner, 1906). These ideas also feature prominently in different kinds of contemporary nationalisms, such as among the Afrikaners (Templin, 1999) and Hindus (van der Veer, 1999). Empirical research shows that beliefs in the superiority of large-scale groups, such as ethnic and national groups, are widespread (e.g., Brewer & Campbell, 1976; Koomen & Bahler, 1996).

5. Purity

The purity facet of ethnocentrism involves a desire to maintain the "purity" of one's ethnic group and reject mixing with outgroups. Group self-importance is expressed here in the sense that one should associate primarily or even exclusively with ingroup members, whereas outgroup members should be kept at a distance or should even be completely shunned. In addition to Sumner et al. (1928), many other authors have implicated purity as a central component of ethnocentrism. For example, Adorno et al. (1950) believed that ethnocentric people espouse various strategies (i.e., outgroup liquidation, subordination, or segregation) to preserve ingroup purity. Referring to Adorno et al.'s (1950) Ethnocentrism Scale, Allport (1954) indicated that a better name for the scale would be "isolationism" because an "island of safety" (p. 72) outlook pervades the items. Ethnocentric people, therefore, feel threatened and build various defences, and consequently they find an island of safety in ethnic purity (Allport, 1954). In fact, in certain conceptualisations of ethnocentrism, purity is the primary dimension (Berry & Kalin, 1995).

Ethnic purity possibly comes close to the concept of outgroup negativity, and it can be assumed that rejection of outgroups is evidence of negative affect, such as hostility and hatred. This is not infrequently mentioned in the literature. Indeed, when members of one ethnic group hate another they certainly engage in social distance towards that group. Nevertheless, ethnic purity and outgroup negativity are not the same, and people can hate, dislike, and derogate other ethnic groups without necessarily espousing the belief that their own ethnic group should be ethnically pure. In fact, misanthropic people may have generalised hatred towards every human being: they can, therefore, hate, dislike, and derogate other ethnic groups, while also hating, disliking, and derogating other people within their own group and therefore not espousing ethnic purity.

Similarly, as has been recognised for a long time, people can reject outgroups, not because they dislike or hate them, but because of a lack of common experiences or goals (Banton, 1967), difficulties in dealing with those who are seen as strangers (Allport, 1954), or because of social norms prescribing avoidance of other groups (Chein, 1946). In fact, for much of human history only a small number of human societies have fully approved of miscegenation (Murdock, 1949), which does not mean that individuals in these societies are full of hatred for all other ethnic groups.

6. Exploitativeness

The exploitativeness facet of ethnocentrism expresses ethnic group self-centredness through the belief that one's own ethnic group's interests are of foremost importance and that in pursuing them little or no consideration should be given to the views and feelings of outgroups. It is acceptable to rob, enslave, kill, and exploit outgroups in any way as long this is in one's ingroup interests. Exploitativeness appears to be a central component of ethnocentrism, and Sumner (1911), in his definition of ethnocentrism, argued that groups tend to pursue their self-interests against any outgroup. Exploitativeness seems to represent "A frequent and perhaps perennial tendency of members of one ethnic group to exploit members of another" (Harding, Proshansky, Kutner, & Chein, 1969, p. 56). Widespread exploitativeness between ethnic groups led Gumplowicz to propose the idea of permanent so-called "racial struggle" between different ethnic groups.

Exploitativeness has negative connotations, but it is not the same as outgroup negativity, and in fact it sometimes may not necessarily involve it. Exploitativeness may be accompanied by indifference to outgroups or even outgroup liking. Jackman (1994) has argued that dominant groups may often like the exploited outgroups. Such exploited outgroups may be seen as childish, cheerful, endearing, and careless, and *noblesse oblige* can pervade the ingroup's relationship with the exploited outgroup (van den Berghe, 1967). The exploited ethnic outgroup can, therefore, be seen as children who need to be taken care of by a more competent adult. So, this sense of liking may be accompanied also by the perception of low competence in an ethnic outgroup (Fiske, Cuddy, Glick, & Xu, 2002). Exploitativeness, however, appears to be related to outgroup negativity when the exploited groups attempt to change the status quo (Harding et al., 1969; van den Berghe, 1967) or when outgroup negativity is used to justify exploitative behaviours (Bar-Tal, 1990, 2013).

Reconceptualised ethnocentrism

The six proposed facets of ethnocentrism are, therefore, six intercorrelated and mutually reinforcing expressions of *ethnic group self-importance*. It should, however, be noted that there is an important conceptual difference between two groups of facets of ethnocentrism. Certain facets (devotion and group cohesion) involve the idea that the ingroup as a whole is more important than separate individual ingroup members, whereas others (preference, superiority, purity, and exploitativeness) involve the idea that the ingroup is more important than other groups. This suggests two kinds of ethnocentrism: intragroup and intergroup.

Accordingly, stronger relationships may be expected within the intragroup facets of devotion and group cohesion, and within the intergroup facets of preference, superiority, purity, and exploitativeness, than between the two major kinds of ethnocentrism. This should be the case because the two kinds of facets seem to have different functions. It is likely that the main function of intergroup facets is to instil the idea that the ingroup is more important than outgroups, whereas the function of intragroup facets is to instil the idea that the ingroup is more important than its individual members.

Measurement of reconceptualised ethnocentrism

Together with several colleagues, I developed a new measure of ethnocentrism, the Ethnocentrism Scale 1, which measures reconceptualised ethnocentrism (Bizumic et al., 2009). The measure went through rigorous scale construction where we developed a large item pool, and tested it with expert judges for content validity and fidelity to the construct definitions of each of the positive and negative poles of ethnocentrism. Table 2.1 presents a slightly updated version of the construct definitions. We then tested an initial version of the measure in New Zealand, and conducted numerous tests of each item and each subscale of ethnocentrism using the procedures of classic item analysis and factor analysis. In addition, we validated the measure against relevant correlates, causes, and consequences. Subsequently, we refined the measure by deleting poorer items and creating new items in the United States, Serbia, and France (in the latter two countries we used translated versions of the measure), and subsequently conducted analyses similar to those in the initial scale construction study. The final measure consisted of 58 items.

Confirmatory factor analysis (CFA) on this measure showed that ethnocentrism consisted of the six intercorrelated first-order factors, which corresponded to the six ethnocentrism expressions. Higher-order CFA, however, showed that the six dimensions of ethnocentrism could be further organised as the two higher-order dimensions of intergroup and intragroup ethnocentrism, which in turn were organised into one third-order factor of ethnocentrism. Ethnocentrism, as a broad construct, is therefore like many other psychological constructs that are hierarchically organised (F. J. Frank & Widaman, 1995; Reise, Waller, & Comrey, 2000), and that exist at several levels of breadth, such as at the broad level, middle level, or narrow level (Clark & Watson, 1995).

These cross-cultural studies supported the model of reconceptualised ethnocentrism, with the six facets of ethnocentrism being distinct dimensions of ethnocentrism, with intragroup and intergroup ethnocentrism being two distinct second-order dimensions, and with the total ethnocentrism being a broad and distinct third-order dimension. Our research has also demonstrated that the measure of ethnocentrism correlated with expected correlates, causes, and consequences. For example, intergroup ethnocentrism was primarily associated with outgroup negativity, high social dominance orientation (SDO), and warlike attitudes, whereas intragroup ethnocentrism was primarily associated with mere ingroup positivity, ethnic identification, and the perception of non-specific threat to the ingroup. Both kinds of ethnocentrism were related to ethnic pride and right-wing authoritarianism.

Subsequently, and using both item analysis and CFA of the data from the cross-cultural research, I have reduced the number of items to 36 (see Appendix A), with each dimension of ethnocentrism being measured with three positive items (i.e., those representing higher ethnocentrism) and three negative items (i.e., those representing lower ethnocentrism, anti-ethnocentrism, or ethnic tolerance). The 36-item version has been extensively tested on the website YourMorals.Org with 4187, mainly US, participants. The website has been developed by Ravi Iyer, Jonathan Haidt, and researchers working on moral foundation theory, and it has been collecting data from participants in exchange for giving them information about their values, personality, attitudes, and other psychological constructs.

The third-order CFA model using individual items from the 36-item version of the scale in the YourMorals.Org dataset is presented in Figure 2.2. The fit of the

TABLE 2.1 Ethnocentrism dimensions with descriptions of higher and lower levels

Subscale	Higher ethnocentrism	Lower ethnocentrism
Devotion	An attitude in favour of a strong, ardent, and uncritical dedication and loyalty to one's ethnic group, and its ways and values, and readiness to suffer any kind of sacrifices for the sake of one's group interests.	An attitude in favour of a lack of strong dedication and uncritical loyalty to one's ethnic group, and its ways and values, and lack of willingness to sacrifice for the sake of one's group interests.
Group cohesion	An attitude in favour of integration, cooperation, and unity within one's own ethnic group over independence, dissent, and individual expression.	An attitude in favour of independence, dissent, and individual expression within one's own ethnic group over integration, cooperation, and unity.
Preference	An attitude in favour of preferring, liking, and trusting one's own ethnic group and its members and their cultural ways over other ethnic groups and members of other groups.	An attitude in favour of not preferring one's own ethnic group to others'; of not liking, trusting people from other groups as much as people from one's own; of not being as comfortable with people from other ethnic groups as with people from one's own group.
Superiority	An attitude in favour of a belief that one's own ethnic group is special and unique, and is objectively better than or superior to others on the dimensions of comparison important to that group.	An attitude in favour of a belief that one's own ethnic group is quite ordinary and average and not better than or superior to other groups.
Purity	An attitude in favour of a desire to maintain 'purity' of one's ethnic group, intolerance of cultural diversity, and a desire to maintain social distance from other peoples to the extent that they are culturally different from the ingroup.	An attitude in favour of an expression of the wish to mix, live, work, and interact with people from different ethnic groups and to appreciate their differences.
Exploitativeness	An attitude in favour of a belief that one's ethnic group interests are always of the first and foremost importance without any respect for the views and positions of human beings in other groups and consequences for their welfare.	An attitude in favour of a belief that one's ethnic group actions should be carried out with respect for the welfare of human beings from other ethnic groups, avoiding any negative consequences for them, such as harm, manipulation, or exploitation.

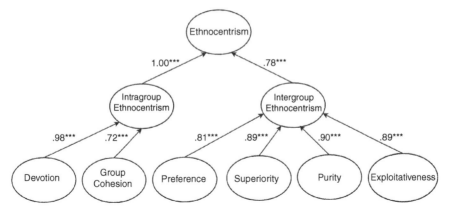

FIGURE 2.2 A third-order factor model of ethnocentrism ($N = 4178$)

model was appropriate given the model's complexity, $\chi^2(587) = 10590.74, p = .001$, CFI = .89, RMSEA = .064 (95% CI = [.063,.065]), SRMR = .058, with each item's factor loadings being higher than .50 and all the factors strongly loading on their higher-order factors. In this model, intragroup ethnocentrism appeared to be a purer expression of the total ethnocentrism with the loading of even 1.00. This model is in line with the analyses in the cross-cultural research using the full 58-item scale (Bizumic et al., 2009). Similarly, this version of the scale and its subscales had excellent psychometric properties in this large sample. For example, all reliability coefficients, Cronbach's alphas, were larger than .80, and mainly in the high .80s. In addition, the measure correlated with the expected validity criteria, including relevant values and morality dimensions. Some of these findings will be presented in later chapters. Histograms of the six subscales from the 36-item version of the Ethnocentrism Scale 1 are in Figure 2.3. These show that participants in the YourMorals.Org sample tended to generally reject ethnocentrism (though somewhat less the dimensions of preference and group cohesion), which is not surprising given that most participants in the sample were liberals. The results also show that there was a large variety of individual responses. It is important, however, to note that participants' scores on interval scales, which this measure uses, cannot be interpreted in an unequivocal way. In fact, countless measures in psychology have arbitrary metrics stemming from the fact that psychological phenomena are typically unobservable (Blanton & Jaccard, 2006). Still, these measures are useful for testing psychological theories about the structure, causes, and consequences of psychological phenomena. It is, therefore, unclear where on the dimension of high ethnic tolerance to high ethnocentrism participants' scores stop indicating ethnic tolerance and start indicating ethnocentrism, and it is not particularly useful to attempt to guess this. For example, a person who slightly disagrees with the statement "It is better for people from different ethnic and cultural groups not to marry" does reject ethnocentrism, but is also unlikely to be seen as an ethnically tolerant person.

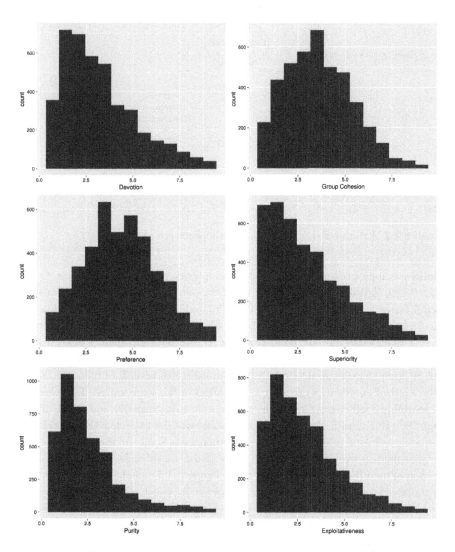

FIGURE 2.3 Histograms for the six subscales of the 36-item version of the Ethnocentrism Scale 1 ($N = 4187$)

Note: Ethnocentrism was measured on a 9-point scale with 1 indicating very strong rejection of ethnocentrism and 9 indicating very strong acceptance of ethnocentrism.

Although the measure has usually worked well in the student and more educated populations (e.g., such as those completing the measure on YourMorals.Org), it did not always work perfectly well with community samples. Two problems appeared. The first is related to the infrequent finding that the items in the Group Cohesion Subscale did not always produce a clear factor which correlated strongly with the other factors. For example, one published study that used the Ethnocentrism Scale 1 in a relatively small sample of participants (154 Australian participants from the general population) failed to find support for the view that group cohesion is part of ethnocentrism (McWhae, Paradies, & Pedersen, 2015). The problem with the sub-scale in certain community samples appeared to be readability: although the other subscales had readability indices suitable for the general population, this subscale did not, and it required more schooling from participants to complete it. For example, the Flesch Kincaid Reading Ease for the subscale was low, 36.7, suggesting that it required more education from participants, whereas the Flesch Kincaid Reading Ease indices for the other scales were much higher, and mainly in the .60s, with only the Devotion Subscale's index being less than 60, that is, 55.2. It is usually required that scales developed for use in the general population have a Flesch Kincaid Reading Ease of around 60–70 (lower numbers indicate poorer readability). Another problem of the measure was mentioned by certain participants, mainly in the US, who com-pleted the measure on YourMorals.Org, telling us that they were confused by the usage of the terms cultural group and ethnic group in the items.

These kinds of criticism do have merit, though they do not invalidate the findings with the scale. The scale works well in many samples, but it can certainly improve. Accordingly, in 2016, I revised the 36-item scale and slightly rewrote items focusing primarily on ethnicity and the ethnic group. In addition, I improved the readability of items measuring group cohesion and slightly improved those measuring devotion. Readability indices, using the Flesch Kincaid Reading Ease, were acceptable, with the lowest being 64.2 (the new Devotion Subscale), suggesting that each subscale could be used in community samples. This 36-item scale, named the Ethnocentrism Scale 2, was tested in two community samples of CrowdFlower participants, one an international sample of 654 participants, and the other a US community sample of 302 participants. CrowdFlower is a website (www.crowdflower.com) that enables researchers to study large community samples for financial compensation. The first study included 16 items measuring group cohesion, but only the best three positively keyed and negatively keyed items were selected for the final scale. The final scale was then tested only in the US. That final 36-item measure is included in Appendix C.

The 36-item scale worked well in both samples, and demonstrated high reli-ability coefficients for each subscale and the total scale. In addition, it also replicated the structure of the original Ethnocentrism Scale 1, and correlated, as expected, with important validity criteria. The model representing the three levels of eth-nocentrism using the Ethnocentrism Scale 2 in the US sample is presented in Figure 2.4. I used item pairs in this analysis because the model was complex with items relative to the sample size, but fit indices were mostly also good for the item-level model. In addition, item analyses showed that all the items correlated strongly with their own scales, and all reliability coefficients were excellent (the lowest being .78, and all others in the .80s or .90s).

The fit of the third-order model was again excellent, $\chi^2(128) = 378.83, p = .001$, CFI = .94, RMSEA = .081 (95% CI = [.071,.090]), SRMR = .065. All the factor loadings were strong and higher than .65, with all factors loading on their respective higher-order factors. Again, as in Figure 2.2, intragroup ethnocentrism appeared to be a purer expression of the higher-order ethnocentrism factor as it had a stronger

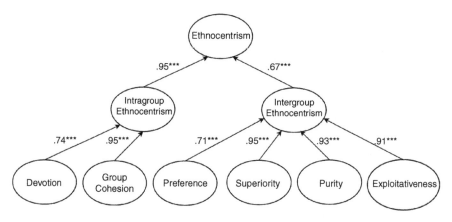

FIGURE 2.4 A third-order factor model of ethnocentrism (N = 302)

standardised loading. Finally, it should be noted that I also tested in subsequent studies a 12-item version of the scale (see Appendix C) and a 6-item version of the Ethnocentrism Scale 2, and that both shortened scales had good psychometric properties across samples (see Table 2.2 for items).

Accordingly, the findings from the cross-cultural research with the 58-item Ethnocentrism Scale 1, the findings from many participants from YourMorals.Org using the 36-item version of the Ethnocentrism Scale 1, and the findings with the 36-item version of the Ethnocentrism Scale 2 all show that ethnocentrism is a complex expression of ethnic group self-centredness, which is, like many other psychological constructs, hierarchically organised. At the broad level, there is general ethnocentrism; at the mid-level, there are intragroup and intergroup ethnocentrism; and at the narrow level, there are the six dimensions of ethnocentrism. Certainly, ethnocentrism can be found even at the narrower levels, such as more specific instances of ethnocentric preference, superiority, or group cohesion, but my purpose here is to focus on more general aspects of the construct. Any further fragmentation, however, threatens the parsimony of explanations, which science values (cf. Fabrigar & Wegener, 2012; Reise et al., 2000; Wegener & Fabrigar, 2000). Consequently, any further refinement of these constructs would require clear discriminant validation of their usefulness.

Furthermore, in addition to conceptual and theoretical arguments presented above, there was also no support for the view that intergroup ethnocentrism, intragroup ethnocentrism, outgroup negativity and mere ingroup positivity represent one construct. In fact, the best CFA model was the one positing the conceptual distinction between the four constructs – as reported in more detail in Bizumic and Duckitt (2012). The average correlations, corrected for measurement error, between the four variables were much lower than 1, suggesting a degree of relationship, but never so strong to indicate that any of the dimensions should be merged with another. Furthermore, related regression analyses presented in detail in Bizumic et al. (2009) showed that ethnocentrism was associated with most external

TABLE 2.2 A 6-item version of the Ethnocentrism Scale 2

Preamble:	The following statements deal with various ways in which you may think, feel about and relate to the ethnic group you see yourself belonging to or are most closely identified with. Some statements also pertain to your relationship with other ethnic groups. Please assume that the term "we" relates to your ethnic group.
Item 1 (Devotion)	No matter what happens, I will ALWAYS support my ethnic group and never let it down.
Item 2 (Group cohesion)	It is absolutely vital that all members of our ethnic group think and behave as one.
Item 3 (Preference)	In general, I prefer doing things with people from my own ethnic group than with people from other ethnic groups.
Item 4 (Superiority)	I don't believe that my ethnic group is any better than any other.
Item 5 (Purity)	I like the idea of a society in which people from completely different ethnic groups mix together freely.
Item 6 (Exploitativeness)	We should always be considerate for the welfare of people from other ethnic groups even if, by doing this, we may lose some advantage over them.

Note: A 9-point Likert-type scale is used to measure participants' agreement with these items: 1 (*Very strongly disagree*), 2 (*Strongly disagree*), 3 (*Somewhat disagree*), 4 (*Slightly disagree*), 5 (*Unsure/neutral*), 6 (*Slightly agree*), 7 (*Somewhat agree*), 8 (*Strongly agree*), 9 (*Very strongly agree*). To find out an individual's score, one adds up one's scores on items 1, 2, and 3; then one adds up one's reversed scores on items 4, 5, and 6 (using the following formula: 10 minus the score on each item); and finally one adds them all up and divides by 6.

criteria over and above mere ingroup positivity and outgroup negativity, further supporting the view that ethnocentrism is distinct from these concepts.

Ethnocentrism is a latent variable that causes people to accept or reject certain items on a questionnaire, such as those in the Ethnocentrism Scale, but ethnocentrism can also predispose people to express this attitude in many other ways. Ethnocentrism, therefore, cannot be seen – at least with current technology – but it exists as an unobservable entity in people's mind. It is important to attempt to explain what causes ethnocentrism, and this will be explored in the chapters to follow. It is, however, also important to add certain clarifications to the present conceptualisation of ethnocentrism. These relate to the link between ethnocentrism and ethnic groups, the importance of ethnicity, and what the opposite of ethnocentrism represents.

Additional clarifications

Ethnocentrism, ethnic groups, and the importance of ethnicity

Possibly, because Sumner used the term "group" in defining ethnocentrism, ethnocentrism has often been seen and studied as a potential characteristic of any group, even gender groups (e.g., Grant, 1993) or artificial groups (e.g., Crocker & Schwartz, 1985). There is certainly confusion whether ethnocentrism primarily relates to ethnic relations, or whether it relates to all intergroup relations (D. E. Brown, 2000). The broader context of Sumner's work, however, suggests that he referred primarily to ethnic groups when writing about ethnocentrism. Similarly, Gumplowicz also referred to ethnic groups while writing about ethnocentrism. That ethnocentrism refers to ethnic groups is also evident in the term *ethnos*. This reconceptualisation of ethnocentrism, therefore, sees ethnocentrism as a characteristic of ethnic groups. Perhaps the six expressions of ethnocentrism may in some form relate to many kinds of groups, primarily those that are structured around specific ideologies (e.g., political, national, religious), but also to many other groups that possess a distinct way of life or culture (even if only an inchoate culture), or that are coalitions (see Kurzban & Leary, 2001). The existence and structure of the proposed expressions of ethnocentrism in other groupings are, however, not the topic of this book.

Although it is difficult to precisely define the term ethnic group (Allport, 1954; Zagefka, 2009), there appears to be broad agreement on what it involves. According to Schermerhorn (1970), an ethnic group is "a collectivity within a larger society having real or putative common ancestry, memories of a shared historical past, and a cultural focus on one or more symbolic elements defined as the epitome of their peoplehood" (p. 12). Ashmore (1970) and Blalock (1982) saw ethnic groups to be distinct from others on the basis of certain cultural characteristics, and the term culture has been defined as "a *relatively organized* system of shared meanings" (P. B. Smith & Bond, 1998, p. 39, italics in original). Thus, ethnic group can be defined as the real-world groups that their members perceive as having a unique "system of shared meanings" (e.g., distinct customs, mores, norms, language, or dialect), the perception of common historical past and future, and most often belief in a common origin. Ethnic groups, defined in such a way, have existed since the time of early human groups (cf. Mihalyi, 1984), and have characteristically been highly self-involving kinds of groupings both historically and cross-culturally. This is in part because of specific cultural patterns, but also because, unlike many other groupings, ethnic groups tend to have an imposed membership that is difficult, or even impossible, to change, and that tends to include one's own immediate family and kin as well as one's own ancestors and descendants.

Likewise, Worchel (1999) claimed that not all groups are equally important to people – that even groups such as national and religious groups do not have as much importance to humans as ethnic groups have. His reasoning why ethnicity is so unique and special to humans is summarised in the following paragraph.

> It is unique because it touches so many aspects of human existence, including biology, religion, culture, communication, and personality history. It is unique because we become permanent members of this group and never need fear excommunication. It is unique because membership is not a matter of personal or group choice. Because of these characteristics, ethnic identity

becomes the bedrock of our personal identity, and as such it plays a major role in human relations, especially war and conflict.

Worchel, 1999, p. 19

McCauley (2001, 2008) maintained that ethnic groups are immensely important to humans and have a special place because they satisfy a number of psychological conditions: entitativity, essentialism, and immortality. Campbell (1958) introduced the concept of entitativity to explain when a collection of stimuli are likely to be perceived as one entity. Using four gestalt principles (similarity, proximity, common fate, and pregnance), Campbell asserted that a collection of stimuli is likely to be seen as one entity if the stimuli are similar to each other, close to each other, move in the same direction, and have clear boundaries from others. Ethnic groups satisfy the four principles well: ethnic group members often look similar to each other; ethnic group members usually live in proximity to each other; ethnic group members have a common fate (and have had it in a distant past); and ethnic group members have, over many generations, created clear boundaries from other ethnic groups (such as norms, values, beliefs, customs, mores, and practices, and, perhaps most importantly, a specific language). For example, this may explain why ethnicity has been historically so important to humans – and more important than other social groups. An attempt by communists to unite people from the proletariat social class failed in part because social classes are not easy to perceive as unique entities. In fact, it is very difficult to think of another large-scale group that satisfies the four principles as well as ethnicity does.

Second, essentialism relates to the belief that objects have deeper essences that make them what they are (Medin, 1989). Social groups can also be essentialised – in the sense that people tend to believe that there is something deeper, possibly genetic and biological, which makes social groups distinct from each other. Ethnic groups are particularly likely to be essentialised because they tend to be self-reproducing – both biologically and socially (Hirschfeld, 1996). Accordingly, people may believe that ethnic groups are more likely than most other groups to be perceived as real, having immutable membership. For example, membership in religious groups or nations is not immutable because people can often change their membership of these groups.

Finally, McCauley also asserted that ethnic groups are immensely important to us because they can help us satisfy our need for immortality. He relied on terror management theory (Solomon, Greenberg, & Pyszczynski, 1991), which assumes that people tend to value their own culture more than other cultures when reminded of death because their culture may provide them with a sense of immortality. This is because cultural groups most often survive individual group members, and also because people may feel that they will continue to live through their group even when they die as individuals. According to McCauley, the belief and perception that one's own ethnic group and its culture has existed for many generations assure an individual group member that it will exist in the future for many generations, and that, therefore, one part of the individual will continue to exist perhaps forever.

Additionally, theorists in favour of evolutionary and biological explanations of ethnicity have assumed that ethnicity, in addition to being strongly concerned with cultural, geographic, and religious similarity, is also strongly concerned with the genetic similarity of ethnic group members. Rushton (2005) contended that ethnicity has a powerful influence on humans because there is a particularly strong genetic similarity within the ethnic group, which fundamentally stems from kinship relationships. Further, evolutionary theorists have argued that theories that focus exclusively on social and cultural explanations of ethnicity and ethnocentrism cannot explain the persistence of ethnic groups in the world – despite modernisation (van den Berghe, 1981). Accordingly, evolutionary theorists argue that ethnicity persists and holds powerful sway over humans because it relies on fundamental processes underlying kin-based selection and is based on strong kinship ties (Bayar, 2009; MacDonald, 2001; van den Berghe, 1981).

To sum up, ethnocentrism should be exclusively related to ethnic groups and not any kinds of groups. Ethnocentrism and ethnicity have had a particularly firm hold of the human mind over millennia. This is possibly because ethnicity strongly resonates with human psychology and most likely with human biology.

Opposites to ethnocentrism

Ethnocentrism is conceptualised as an attitude related to a belief in the immense importance of one's own ethnic group. So, possible opposites to ethnocentrism are: (1) ethnic tolerance and acceptance of all ethnic groups; (2) a positive evaluation of the transcendence of ethnicity and identification with all humanity (McFarland, Webb, & Brown, 2012); and (3) an attitude in favour of foreign ethnic groups over one's own ethnic group, also called xenophilia (Perlmutter, 1954, 1956) and xenocentrism (Kent & Burnight, 1951). As mentioned previously, I conceptualise ethnocentrism as a dimension ranging from high ethnocentrism to very low ethnocentrism, or anti-ethnocentrism, which involves ethnic tolerance and rejection of ethnocentrism. People who reject ethnocentric statements on the Ethnocentrism Scale 1 and 2 tend to strongly accept statements in favour of ethnic tolerance, such as "I'd like to live in a neighbourhood where there are many people from all sorts of quite different cultural and ethnic groups to mine" or "I like the idea of a society in which people from completely different ethnic groups mix together freely".

I therefore believe that neither identification with all humans nor xenophilia/ xenocentrism are the polar opposites of ethnocentrism. People who identify with all humans may not necessarily be tolerant of other ethnic groups and may often wish for ethnic memberships to disappear. For example, many communists, such as Leninists, appeared anti-ethnocentric because they wanted to suppress and destroy ethnic identities (Tuschman, 2013). Nonetheless, wanting to destroy ethnic identities and identifying with all humanity are not necessarily opposed to ethnocentrism. They are, for example, not opposed to the view that one's own ethnic group is superior to others. In a way, one's ethnic group may be seen to be prototypical of all humanity and should enforce its culture on all humans. For example, Richard

Rorty (1986, 1989) appears to espouse this kind of approach when he argued that there are certain values, norms, and beliefs that are better than others – such as those in Western liberal democracies because these benefit humans everywhere – and that these are better than values, norms, and beliefs that can be found in other ethnic groups, which may harm humans. Similarly, Stanley Hoffmann said that "there are universal values, and they happen to be mine" (as quoted by Taruskin, 2009, p. 91). These views are versions of ethnocentrism, and they primarily deal with its superiority and preference dimensions. It is, therefore, expected that people who identify with all humanity may, but at times may not, reject ethnocentric statements, and may not necessarily accept ethnic tolerance and fully appreciate cultural diversity.

Similarly, people who engage in xenophilia or xenocentrism may dislike their ethnic group and prefer foreigners, and by definition do not accept all ethnic groups. Spencer (1874) contrasted the patriotic bias with the opposite, which he calls "anti-patriotism", and which he thought should also be avoided. Anti-patriotism is a lack of appreciation of one's own ethnic group or culture and, according to Spencer, may arise because people reject patriotic biases, because of pretentiousness, or because of ignorance. In fact, Spencer argued that, like patriotic bias, it also biases judgement and leads to incorrect knowledge.

Thus, the opposite to ethnocentrism is ethnic tolerance and appreciation of ethnic diversity – as well as the diversity within one's own ethnic group. In contrast, identifiers with humans, xenophiles/xenocentrics, and anti-patriots may not necessarily be ethnically tolerant. Later in the book, I will present how ethnocentrism relates to a measure of identification with humanity (McFarland et al., 2012).

Summary and conclusions

To sum up, this chapter clarified the concept in line with already published work (Bizumic & Duckitt, 2012; Bizumic et al., 2009) which showed that ethnocentrism connotes a strong sense of ethnic or cultural importance and self-centredness, including intragroup dimensions, such as devotion and group cohesion, and intergroup dimensions, such as superiority, preference, purity, and exploitativeness. The chapter also discussed what ethnocentrism is not, and why it is important to disentangle ethnocentrism from other concepts, such as prejudice and mere ingroup positivity.

In general, there has not been much effort expended on how the usage of the term ethnocentrism in one theory applies to the usage in another. People often start with their own, often vague, definition and understanding of the concept and then they develop a theory to explain their own concept. For example, Turner, Hogg, Oakes, Reicher, and Wetherell (1987) define ethnocentrism as "ingroup members' positive evaluation of the group as a whole" (p. 57), whereas Altemeyer (2003) sees it as "prejudice against a wide variety of racial–ethnic minorities" (p. 18). It is not, therefore, surprising that a theorist who sees ethnocentrism principally as a positive evaluation of any ingroup may have a different explanation of ethnocentrism to the one who sees it principally as prejudice and hatred against ethnic minorities. This does not help us understand the concept and may confuse us about its causes and consequences. Certainly, factors that predispose people to hate ethnic minorities may be very distinct from those that predispose people to prefer their own ethnic group over others. The material presented in this chapter can therefore help us better understand ethnocentrism. Knowing what ethnocentrism is and is not, we can now review and discuss its causes and consequences.

3

THE CAUSES OF ETHNOCENTRISM

Fear and self-aggrandisement

Why is there ethnocentrism? Why do people prefer ethnic ingroups over outgroups, see ethnic ingroups as better than ethnic outgroups, exploit and reject ethnic outgroups, and sacrifice their individuality, their personal freedoms, and at times even their lives for their ethnic groups? To respond to these questions, social scientists have developed diverse theories. This and the next chapter will critically review these various, primarily psychological, theories of ethnocentrism. The focus will be on the theories that have been widely studied in psychology, although theorising from other disciplines will also be covered. In addition, it is important to note that the focus will be on the theories that deal with ethnocentrism, and not on those specifically developed to explain prejudice (defined as outgroup hostility). As was argued above, prejudice is a correlate, and not part, of ethnocentrism.

One should point out that there are two widely studied groups of proximal explanations of causes of ethnocentrism. One group is related to different kinds of fears and threats. The other group is related to different kinds of self-aggrandisement. Although social scientists have come up with many other possible proximal causes, these could all be largely reduced to these two groups of causes. In addition, there are also two groups of distal causes of ethnocentrism. One group relates to the idea that ethnocentrism is ultimately the product of biology and evolution, and therefore can be best understood through understanding human biology and evolution. The other group relates to the idea that ethnocentrism is mainly the product of social factors, and can be understood and explained through social scientific analysis, and our knowledge of biology and genetics does not help us explain ethnocentrism.

Many of the theories cannot be fully categorised into a single broad approach to ethnocentrism, and certain explanations overlap each other. For example, explanations focusing on proximal causes may overlap with those focusing on distal causes: certain theorists may assume that self-aggrandisement or fears in relation to ethnic groups are biological instincts, whereas other theorists may assume that self-aggrandisement or fears are entirely socially learned. A number of these explanations are also complementary to each other, and they focus on different processes that generate ethnocentrism. This chapter will focus on the more proximal explanations of ethnocentrism: fear and self-aggrandisement.

Ethnocentrism originates in fear

Numerous explanations propose that people are ethnocentric because they are afraid, threatened, and insecure, and find security in their ethnic group and ethnocentrism. I use the term fear here not just as a specific emotion, but as a broader concept that generally relates to the perception that something bad can happen to oneself, including one's own personal interests, and one's own ethnic group, including its interests. I will also be using the terms fear and threat interchangeably. Additionally, I will assume that conflicts between groups tend to generate the perception of fears and threat in group members. The most widely studied fears pertaining to ethnocentrism are realistic (LeVine & Campbell, 1972; Sherif, 1966) as these relate to obvious fears surrounding the material well-being of the group and its members (Coser, 1956; Gumplowicz, 1885/1963; LeVine & Campbell, 1972; Sumner, 1906). Other fears that relate to ethnocentrism are fears surrounding beliefs and values (Rokeach, 1960; Rokeach & Mezei, 1966), and intrapsychic, psychodynamic fears (Adorno et al., 1950; S. Freud, 1930/1961; Solomon et al., 1991; Volkan, 1997). It should be noted that many other theorists have implicated fears and threats in intergroup phenomena, although their focus has often been exclusively on prejudice (e.g., Hovland & Sears, 1940). Such theories will not be discussed here.

Explanations invoking realistic fears

It is interesting to note that the person who was probably the first to use the concept of ethnocentrism, Ludwig Gumplowicz, is also called "the father of conflict theory" (Horowitz, 1991, p. 281) because he proposed a broad theory of realistic conflicts and their role in intragroup and intergroup attitudes. One of his chief publications, *Racial Struggle* (Gumplowicz, 1883), presented realistic conflict theory that focused on ethnic groups. He assumed that ethnic groups are frequently in conflict because of realistic, such as economic, group interests. He also theorised that strong intragroup attitudes predispose ethnic groups to exploit, subordinate, and hate other groups. Sumner's (1906) theory was also an early realistic conflict theory because he also assumed that ethnic groups are in realistic conflicts with each other. Finally, another well-known early theory focusing on conflict was proposed by Marx and Engels (1846/1970). In contrast to Gumplowicz and Sumner, this theory has not focused on conflicts between ethnic groups, but on conflicts between social classes over the means of production. This theory, nevertheless, has had a significant influence upon later conflict theorists, such as Sherif.

Realistic group conflict theory

The role of realistic group fears and conflicts in ethnocentrism and prejudice has been systematised in a broad theory, titled realistic group conflict theory by LeVine and Campbell (1972). These realistic and rational fears and conflicts were contrasted with non-realistic and irrational fears and conflicts, which psychodynamic theorists assumed to lead to intergroup conflicts and intergroup attitudes. As will be noted later in the chapter, psychodynamic theorists proposed that intergroup conflicts are to a large extent caused by intrapsychic defence mechanisms, such as displacement or projection, which in turn attempt to protect individuals from intrapsychic conflicts, anxieties, and threats.

LeVine and Campbell's (1972) book, titled *Ethnocentrism: Theories of conflict, ethnic attitudes, and group behavior,* summarised the principles of realistic group conflict theory, most of which were proposed by other theorists (Coser, 1956; Sherif, 1966; Sumner, 1906). Realistic group conflict theory proposes that the whole syndrome of ethnocentrism stems from competition or conflict over resources, such as territory, employment, and material benefits, or threat to the ingroup's access to or possibility of attainment of these resources. This theory assumes that group conflicts are rational in the sense that groups often have incompatible goals and compete for scarce resources. These are realistic conflicts because the sources of the conflict are realistic; but they do not have to be real and often can be manufactured by leaders. As pointed out by Kinder (1998), a common factor of group conflict is imagined threat. Threat can be imagined or minor, but its reality and magnitude could be exaggerated by leaders and group members. For example, the threat of Jews in Germany in the thirties was unreal, but Nazi propagandists manufactured both the threat and its magnitude – which in turn made Germans fearful of Jews and in such a way enhanced German ethnocentrism.

This theory proposes that real threat originates in the present or past conflicts of interests between groups and perceptions that outgroups are antagonistic and compete with the ingroup. This real threat has numerous consequences. First, it causes groups to perceive threat. As a result of real threats, ingroup members engage in ingroup solidarity, which appears functional in surviving the conflict. They also become increasingly aware of group identity, which includes group norms, values, and customs. As a result of real threats, group members emphasise and exaggerate positive aspects of ingroup identity and negative aspects of outgroup identity.

Real threat also results in tightening of ingroup boundaries, so that it becomes difficult for people to enter or leave the ingroup (e.g., it is often hard to leave, or get into, the countries involved in wars), and ingroup members develop increasing social distance towards all outgroups. It also predisposes ingroup members to be less likely to want to desert or leave the ingroup, and makes ingroup members more likely to punish those who do attempt to desert or leave the ingroup. In addition, as a result of real threats, ingroup members become more punitive of those who deviate from group norms, such as nonconformists and individualists. Real threat causes ingroup members to become hostile towards those groups that cause threat, and the more threat the group experiences, the more hatred there is towards the group or groups that cause the threat. So, real threats cause outgroup hostility or prejudice. According to LeVine and Campbell (1972), all 23 facets of ethnocentrism that they identified in Sumner's writings tend to increase as a result of real threat.

Realistic group conflict theory is functionalist, arguing that ethnocentrism is useful for reaching a group goal. If intergroup competition is essential for reaching the group goal, then ethnocentrism and outgroup hostility would emerge in the groups that compete. Yet, if intergroup cooperation is essential for reaching the goal, then ethnocentrism and prejudice would disappear, and intergroup positivity would emerge.

Research generally confirms the basic tenets of the realistic group conflict theory. Field experiments (Sherif, 1966; Sherif, Harvey, White, Hood, & Sherif, 1961; Sherif & Sherif, 1969) showed that when there is negative group interdependence, that is, when groups compete for a goal that can be achieved by only one group at the expense of the other, certain aspects of ethnocentrism, such as group cohesion, preference for ingroups over outgroups, and overestimation of ingroup accomplishments, increase rapidly. Reviewing experimental studies, J. C. Turner (1981) argued that intergroup competition increases aspects of both intragroup and intergroup self-centredness. Thus, people tend to give more importance to their groups when their group is in competition and threatened. A meta-analysis of numerous correlational and experimental studies (Riek, Mania, & Gaertner, 2006) showed that realistic threats do have a considerable effect on both outgroup attitudes and ingroup preferences – although the effect on ingroup preferences seems to be weaker than the effect on outgroup attitudes.

Although underemphasised in LeVine and Campbell's theorising, realistic threats can also be aimed at less tangible resources, such as group rank, prestige, status, or political power (Blumer, 1958; Bobo, 1988, 1999; Tajfel, 1982). Research confirms this by showing that threats to less tangible resources, involving group status and position, also effect increases in certain aspects of ethnocentrism, such as rejection of contact with ethnic outgroup members or stronger devotion to the ethnic ingroup (Bobo & Zubrinsky, 1996; Craig, Rucker, & Richeson, in press; Green, Abelson, & Garnett, 1999; J. S. Jackson, Brown, Brown, & Marks, 2001; Outten, Schmitt, Miller, & Garcia, 2012; C. Smith, 2013). For example, Bobo and Zubrinsky (1996) showed that US Anglo/White attitudes towards ethnic residential segregation appeared driven by people experiencing threat to their traditional relative status and prestige. More recent research recently summarised by Craig et al. (in press) suggests that ethnic majority participants in Western countries, such as the US and Canada, tend to see the growth of ethnic minority groups and rising ethnic diversity in these countries as threatening to their status and prestige, and tend to react with increasing ethnocentric attitudes and behaviours.

Applying realistic group conflict theory to the present conceptualisation of ethnocentrism suggests that the six dimensions of ethnocentrism are all functional responses to threat and conflict. If an ethnic group was impartial in a zero-sum competition over scarce resources, showing full consideration for the outgroups, or allowing ingroup members individual freedoms, defection, or disloyalty, it would be less likely to compete successfully against outgroups that were partial, inconsiderate, and cohesive.

A critique of explanations invoking realistic fears

There is no doubt that ethnocentrism is a kind of group defence mechanism (Mihalyi, 1984), and there is much support for the view that realistic threats pre-dispose people to ethnocentrism. These explanations, however, also face a number of difficulties. Evidence shows that not all realistic threats increase ethnocentrism and certain threats may even lead to outgroup preference and perception of out-group superiority. For example, Bettelheim (1947) described how many prisoners in Nazi concentration camps, because of outgroup threats, often identified with the powerful outgroup, that is, the German guards, and felt these were superior. Similarly, low-status or minority groups, in response to threat from a high-status or majority outgroup, may show preference for the high-status or majority outgroup and may dislike the ingroup (see Lewin, 1948). In fact, it is not infrequent in history that ethnic groups disappear, lose their culture, language, and identity, as a result of conflicts with other ethnic groups. For example, the German community in the US used to be very large and for several generations had attempted to preserve its unique culture, language, and identity. The Germans were, however, pressured to assimi-late into the dominant Anglo-American culture and denounce their culture and language as a result of the American conflict with Germany in the twentieth century (Kirschbaum, 2014). In fact, the process of ethnic groups losing their identity as a result of threats from stronger ethnic groups is still present in the globalised world in which languages and traditional cultures constantly disappear. Thus, certain outgroup threats may over time erase or reverse ethnocentrism. Accordingly, an important criticism of the theory is that it does not differentiate well between different kinds of group threats and sees threats too broadly. The theory does not tell us how much and what kind of realistic threat would increase or decrease levels of ethnocentrism.

Another problem, which led to the formation of social identity theory, was that threat to resources appears not to be central for the development of certain aspects of ethnocentrism, such as preferences for ingroup members over outgroup members. Even Sherif's research discussed above (Sherif, 1966; Sherif et al., 1961; Sherif & Sherif, 1969) showed that after group formation, but before intergroup competition, participants felt preferences for the ingroup over the outgroup. As will be discussed later in the chapter, social identity researchers showed that the simple process of categorisation into ingroup and outgroups, together with the universal need for relative group superiority, appears to be sufficient for ingroup preferences to develop (Tajfel & Turner, 1986). Nevertheless, research does suggest that under most circumstances realistic threats could often increase levels of ethnocentrism in already established groups.

It should be noted that Stephan, Ybarra, and Morrison's (2009) integrated threat theory maintained that realistic threats predispose people to prejudice and intergroup attitudes. This theory also argued that it is important to distinguish between threats to the group (e.g., its resources, power, well-being) and threats to the individual. Threats related to groups have already been covered above in the discussion of realistic group conflict theory. Threats to the individual are related to individual group members facing material harm or physical harm, including suffering, painfulness, and death. These individual threats may also include the individual losing resources, being economically deprived, becoming ill, and feeling insecure. These threats have been, however, much less studied than those affecting the whole group – even by Stephan and colleagues. One possibility is that it is because researchers have often assumed that realistic fears tend to be felt by all or most group members and that it is difficult to separate purely personal from group threats. Finally, integrated threat theory also maintained that in addition to realistic threats, there is another group of threats, called symbolic threats, which are responsible for the development of intergroup and intragroup attitudes.

Explanations invoking symbolic fears

Many fears may stem from perceiving other groups as different to one's own ethnic group. These differences can be considered to predispose people to fears surrounding the more symbolic aspects of ethnic group memberships, such as those concerned with deeply held values, beliefs, and worldviews that are shared by members of one's own ethnic group. Probably the most influential theory to propose the role of symbolic fears is belief congruence theory, but many theories have invoked the role of conflicting values, beliefs, and worldviews between different ethnic groups as sources of symbolic fears that lead to ethnocentrism.

Belief congruence theory

A classic psychological theory that proposed the role of differences in values and beliefs in ethnocentrism is belief congruence theory (Rokeach, 1960; Rokeach & Mezei, 1966). This theory proposed that people prefer those who have similar values and beliefs to themselves over those who have different values and beliefs. According to Rokeach (1960), "*insofar as psychological processes are involved*, belief is more important than ethnic or racial membership as a determinant of social discrimination" (p. 135, italics in original). Other people who have similar values, beliefs, and attitudes to oneself tend to validate one's own values, beliefs, and attitudes, whereas other people who have different values, beliefs, and attitudes to oneself tend to threaten them. According to this theory, people prefer their ethnic group members over outgroup members because they perceive ethnic ingroup members to have more similar values, beliefs, and attitudes to themselves than ethnic outgroup members do. Accordingly, it is not a category, such as ethnicity, that influences ethnocentrism, but perceived differences on important issues between those categorised as ethnic ingroups and those categorised as ethnic outgroups. According to this theory, when people encounter a person from another ethnic group who has similar beliefs to them and a person from their own ethnic group who has dissimilar beliefs to them, they will prefer the outgroup person over the ingroup person.

Research has generally confirmed certain propositions of the theory (Rokeach, 1960; Rokeach & Mezei, 1966; Silverman, 1974). For example, studies by Rokeach and Mezei (1966) showed that participants in their study tended to choose for partners two people (one ethnic ingroup and one ethnic outgroup member) who agreed with them rather than two ethnic ingroup members when one disagreed with them. Nevertheless, a literature review by Insko, Nacoste, and Moe (1983) of research testing the theory suggested that belief congruence may be particularly important when general liking is involved, whereas group membership may still be more important when one is choosing marriage or dating partners. It is important to point out that belief congruence theory seems to be primarily related to inter-group aspects of ethnocentrism, principally preference, which deals with differential liking. Thus, there is evidence that people will like ethnic ingroup members more than outgroup members because they see the ingroup members as having more similar beliefs to themselves than outgroup members do.

Other theories invoking symbolic fears

Belief congruence theory is not the only theory that has proposed that symbolic fears predispose people to ethnocentrism. For example, symbolic racism theory argues that Anglo/White-Americans in the US discriminate against African-Americans based on the perception that African-Americans violate traditional American values (Kinder & Sears, 1981). Similarly, Berger and Luckmann (1966) claimed that the mere existence of another symbolic universe, which is another culture, can predispose people to reassert the superiority of their own symbolic universe, that is, their own culture, and to denigrate, even dehumanise, the rival symbolic universe. Terror management theory also assumes that clashes between competing cultural worldviews may lead to ethnocentrism (Solomon et al., 1991). Likewise, moral foundations theory (Graham, Haidt, & Nosek, 2009; Haidt, 2012), although often used to explain dislike between ideological groups, such as conservatives and liberals, is relevant to explaining what happens when individuals belonging to different groups emphasise different moral values. Accordingly, ethnic group members who strongly favour particular moral values may feel threatened when they observe that another ethnic group does not give much importance to those moral values. For example, Haidt (2012) wrote that Westerners who strongly value fairness, often perceiving it as the dominant moral value in interpersonal relations, may frown upon Indians from the upper castes who, while interacting with people from the lower castes, tend to more strongly value purity and authority as moral values than they value fairness.

According to integrated threat theory, in addition to realistic threats, which as mentioned affect the group's resources, power, and well-being, there is a broad category of symbolic threats that also affect prejudice and intergroup attitudes

(Stephan et al., 2009). Symbolic group threats include threats to values, ideologies, worldviews, and beliefs, and are particularly likely to predispose people to reject, morally exclude, and show reduced empathy for outgroups, while also predisposing them to become more conformist with ingroup values and norms. Thus, symbolic threats to important values and beliefs may produce both intergroup ethnocentrism and intragroup ethnocentrism, but also outgroup prejudice.

A meta-analysis (Riek et al., 2006) showed that the effects of symbolic threats on outgroup attitudes and ingroup preferences in correlational and experimental studies tend to be as large as the effects of realistic threats. Nonetheless, these effects were stronger for outgroup attitudes than for ingroup preferences. Additionally, as with realistic threats, Stephan and colleagues maintained that symbolic threats can be both group and individual. Symbolic individual threats are related to losing face or honour, or threatening one's personal self-esteem, and may be caused by lack of respect or even dehumanisation by another group. These threats, however, have not been much studied by researchers.

A critique of theories invoking symbolic fears

Theories linking intergroup differences with ethnocentrism have a number of problems. The exact nature of the link between intergroup difference and ethnocentrism is not straightforward, and researchers still grapple with these issues (Costa-Lopes, Vala, & Judd, 2012; Jetten, Spears, & Postmes, 2004; Mummendey & Wenzel, 1999). It appears that difference plays a role mainly when it is perceived as challenging and threatening, that is, when it becomes a symbolic threat. Nonetheless, although dissimilarity can often be threatening, so can similarity and it is often the case that a similar outgroup may be perceived as a realistic threat to the ingroup. Empirical research (Esses, Dovidio, Jackson, & Armstrong, 2001) suggests that similar outgroups (e.g., competent and educated immigrants) may be perceived by the host country to be more threatening to the ingroup than dissimilar outgroups (e.g., less competent and educated immigrants). So, the experience of threat, and not difference on its own, appears to cause ethnocentrism. When the differences in beliefs and values are so large that outgroup beliefs and values may be completely incompatible with the beliefs and values of ethnic ingroup members, and when the difference challenges one's own deeply held beliefs and values (cf. Mummendey & Wenzel, 1999), which are associated with fundamental values of one's own ethnic group, then the difference may be seen as threatening and would lead to increases in ethnocentrism. This appears to be the case with strong symbolic threats to the group.

Almost all the work in the area has focused on symbolic group threats and there is almost no work to explicitly investigate the role of symbolic individual threats. They are possibly less widely studied because, as with realistic individual threats, it is difficult to disentangle when these threats affect individuals on their own and when they are aimed at the group on its own. For example, if a person feels dehumanised by a member of another ethnic group, this dehumanisation is most likely perceived to relate to the whole ethnic ingroup and not just one individual.

Explanations invoking intrapsychic fears

Psychodynamic theorists assume that ethnocentrism, which they often term group narcissism, is caused by various intrapsychic fears, conflicts, and insecurities. Various defence mechanisms, such as externalisation, displacement, projection, or splitting, are invoked to defend against these fears, causing ethnocentrism. According to Moses (1982), these tend to have narcissistic origins because their goal is to protect the self. Classic psychodynamic theories saw defence mechanisms as unconscious intrapsychic processes, the role of which is to defend the person from experiencing anxiety generated by intrapsychic conflicts between different parts of the personality (A. Freud, 1936/1993).

The main argument of the theories proposing intrapsychic threats is that idealising the ingroup and derogating and exploiting the outgroup are defences against intrapsychic threats that generate deep and unconscious individual anxiety. Psychodynamic theories, therefore, tend to see ethnocentrism as consisting of the association of a sense of group self-centredness, notably devotion, group cohesion, superiority, or purity, with negative attitudes towards outgroups. They suggest that this sense of group self-importance is functional in defending against these intrapsychic fears.

Defence mechanisms

The founder of the psychodynamic theory, Sigmund Freud, used the defence mechanism of displacement to explain ethnocentrism (S. Freud, 1932/1950, 1921/1955, 1930/1961). He assumed that people's natural inclination towards aggression is prohibited in groups because it is threatening to group life. Accordingly, this aggression is displaced onto outgroups, so that love and solidarity can pervade the ingroup. As Freud stated, "It is always possible to bind together a considerable number of people in love, so long as there are other people left over to receive the manifestations of their aggressiveness" (S. Freud, 1930/1961, p. 114).

The thirteenth-century Muslim poet Rumi wrote, "how many an evil that you see in others is but your own nature reflected in them! ... You do not see clearly the evil in yourself, else you would hate yourself with all your soul" (as quoted in Miller, O'Neal, & McDonnell, 1970, p. 267). This idea that people tend to deny their own negative threatening aspects and attribute them to others has found expression in certain psychodynamic theories of ethnocentrism. According to Erikson (1968), people project negative ingroup characteristics onto outgroups, facilitating the ingroup members to exploit the outgroups. According to Kakar (1994), the defence mechanism of splitting, whereby the world is split into positive or negative parts, is used by Hindus to idealise themselves and derogate Muslims. Volkan (1997) used the defence mechanism of externalisation, where both positive and negative aspects are externalised outside, to argue that children, reinforced by parents and other significant others, tend to externalise unintegrated positive aspects of themselves onto a large-scale ingroup and negative aspects onto large-scale outgroups.

Similarly, another psychodynamic theorist argued: "When we externalize upon others that which we cannot bear in ourselves, we feel good, pure, and just, whereas the enemy seems bad, polluted, and evil" (Falk, 1992, p. 225).

Authoritarian personality theory

None of the theories described above, however, have achieved the popularity of authoritarian personality theory (Adorno et al., 1950), which also used several defence mechanisms to explain ethnocentrism. According to this theory, harsh, strict, and punitive parenting predisposes people to develop an authoritarian personality, which in turn predisposes them to hold ethnocentric attitudes. This personality is characterised by nine traits, such as submissiveness to authority, rigid conventionalism, cynicism, superstition, and preoccupation with power. Children who are exposed to this kind of parenting experience ambivalent feelings because they love, fear, and hate their parents at the same time. Such internal conflicts cause anxiety, which defence mechanisms resolve in a certain way. These children repress fear and hatred, externalise them outside, and displace them against weak outgroups, such as ethnic minorities. They also develop a particular thinking style that leads them to see the world in terms of dichotomies or, more precisely, polar opposites. This results in the idealisation of parents and other authority figures, including the whole ethnic group, and the derogation of other ethnic groups and other kinds of minorities. These authors wrote: "the prejudiced subject's ambivalence toward his parents, with a repression and externalization of the negative side of this ambivalence, may be a factor in determining his strongly polarized attitudes, such as his uncritical acceptance of the ingroup and violent rejection of the outgroup" (Adorno et al., 1950, p. 482).

Adorno and colleagues did find support for the view that authoritarianism tends to be strongly related to ethnocentrism, and the link between the two concepts held across many studies – regardless of the way in which both concepts were measured (e.g., Adorno et al., 1950; Altemeyer, 1996, 1998, 2006; Duckitt, 2000; Heaven, 1976; Lambley, 1973; McFarland, Ageyev, & Abalakina-Paap, 1992; Meloen, Van der Linden, & De Witte, 1996; Scheepers, Felling, & Peters, 1990; Van Ijzendoorn, 1989). Studies using different versions of the Ethnocentrism Scale 1, described in Chapter 2, have also always found strong correlations between authoritarianism and each of the six dimensions of ethnocentrism (e.g., Bizumic et al., 2009). Thus, regardless of how authoritarianism or ethnocentrism is measured, the two constructs are empirically related.

Yet, no study has found support for the role of the proposed defence mechanisms in the development of authoritarianism and ethnocentrism in children. So, the theory of the childhood origins of authoritarianism, ambivalence, and displacement has not been unequivocally supported (R. Brown, 1965; Duckitt, 1992). Research findings have suggested that different kinds of fears appear to be involved in the development of authoritarianism. These tended to be societal threats (Duckitt & Fisher, 2003; Feldman & Stenner, 1997; Sales, 1973), of which the most important are threats to one's own ethnic group (Shaffer & Duckitt, 2013), and not personal threats, including deep psychodynamic threats. Altemeyer (2006) rejected the psychodynamic explanation of authoritarianism and based his explanation on social learning theory. His argument is that people become authoritarian as a result of growing up in authoritarian families, which emphasise to children that the world is a dangerous place, and as a result of having particular, and perhaps restricted, life experiences (e.g., being brought up in patriarchal families; interacting only with patriotic or heterosexual individuals; always following rules).

Altemeyer's (1981, 1996, 1998, 2006) work also showed that authoritarianism consists of only three facets (i.e., authoritarian submission, conventionalism, and authoritarian aggression) of the original nine proposed by Adorno and colleagues. He argued that these three facets form one general and unidimensional personality construct ranging from low to high authoritarianism. More recent research, however, gives support to the view that authoritarianism is not unidimensional and consists of three separate dimensions, which do not always necessarily correlate, and which differentially relate to external variables (see Duckitt & Bizumic, 2013; Duckitt, Bizumic, Krauss, & Heled, 2010; Dunwoody & Funke, 2016; Funke, 2005; Mavor, Louis, & Sibley, 2010). Another criticism is that authoritarianism is not a personality disposition as Adorno and colleagues and Altemeyer argued, but that it is an ideological social attitude (Duckitt, 2001; Stone, Lederer, & Christie, 1993), which, in contrast to personality variables, may change with contextual influences, such as societal threats (Duckitt & Fisher, 2003).

Terror management theory

There is another theory, terror management theory, which has been widely tested in the literature, and which also proposed that psychodynamic intrapsychic mechanisms play a role in the development of ethnocentrism. Terror management theory originated in the ideas of the anthropologist Ernest Becker (1962, 1973, 1975) and was developed by Greenberg, Solomon, Pyszczynski, and their colleagues (Greenberg et al., 1990; Greenberg & Arndt, 2012; Pyszczynski, Greenberg, & Solomon, 1999; Pyszczynski, Solomon, & Greenberg, 2015; Solomon et al., 1991). Becker's main argument was that people feel terror because they are aware of their own mortality and use different intrapsychic mechanisms, such as reasserting the value of their own culture, in an attempt to manage this awareness and the resulting terror.

Terror management theory explicitly argues that ethnocentrism, like many other psychological phenomena related to self-esteem and worldview defences (e.g., attitudes to animals, creativity, individual ideology, support for authorities, attachment styles, religiosity), is caused by this intrapsychic threat of mortality. Cultural value systems serve as buffers against death anxiety, and whenever people are reminded of their own death they experience intrapsychic threats, which they try to overcome by unconscious defence mechanisms, whereby they reassert their cultural worldview and exhibit ethnocentrism (i.e., by emphasising the importance of their ingroup and worldview in relation to other groups and other worldviews).

This can be explained by the compensatory need to confirm one's own cultural values, and to disconfirm different and contradictory cultural values. The belief that one's own culture will survive even after the death of the individual suggests to the individual that one part of them may also survive. In addition, certain religious and cultural systems offer the hope of blissful immortality to group members, as long as they behave in the way prescribed by the desirable standards of the culture or religion. A person, therefore, prefers the other ingroup members over outgroup members because the ingroup members validate the person's cultural worldview.

Research has been indirectly supportive of the theory in relation to ethnocentrism by showing that participants are more likely to prefer their ingroups, including national and ethnic, over outgroups if participants are experimentally reminded of death (e.g., Arndt, Greenberg, & Cook, 2002; Arndt, Greenberg, Pyszczynski, & Solomon, 1997; Castano, Yzerbyt, Paladino, & Sacchi, 2002; Gailliot, Schmeichel, & Maner, 2007; Greenberg et al., 1990; Nelson, Moore, Olivetti, & Scott, 1997). For example, Nelson et al. (1997) demonstrated that reminding US participants of their mortality induced them to prefer the US over Japan. The participants who were reminded of their death were more likely to blame a Japanese car manufacturer than an American car manufacturer for a car accident. Furthermore, the participants were less likely to blame the driver for the car crash if they believed that the car was made in Japan than when they believed that it was made in the US. A meta-analysis of many studies testing this theory did support the proposition that reminding people of their mortality, but keeping these reminders outside one's own conscious awareness, may significantly affect a variety of variables proposed by the theory, including ingroup preferences (Burke, Martens, & Faucher, 2010). Effect sizes, however, appear to be smaller and results more inconsistent in studies conducted in non-Western cultures (Martin & van den Bos, 2014; Yen & Cheng, 2010, 2013).

A critique of theories invoking intrapsychic fears

The major criticism of psychoanalytic explanations of ethnocentrism is that they are rarely testable and cannot be falsified because any finding can be interpreted to support the theory. The refutability criterion asks scientists to state explicitly in their theories what observational data are possible and what observational data are not possible (Popper, 2002). Altemeyer (2006) notes that the original explanation of the authoritarian personality, in which unconscious mechanisms of repression, ambivalence, and displacement are at play, cannot be empirically tested and refuted because whatever the study finds could be interpreted in support of the theory. For example, if a study finds positive attitudes towards parents in authoritarians, the theorist can state it is because the genuine negative attitudes are repressed; if a study finds negative attitudes towards parents in authoritarians, the theorist can state it is because the genuine attitudes have resurfaced; and if a study finds ambivalent attitudes, that is, both positive and negative attitudes towards parents, in authoritarians, the theorist can state that the theory of the role of ambivalent, that is, both negative and positive, attitudes has been supported.

In fact, researchers have criticised even the more widely tested terror management theory for being impossible to falsify. Martin and van den Bos (2014) wrote: "the theory allows researchers to generate predictions, but it also allows them to generate theory-consistent interpretations when those predictions are not supported" (p. 53). For example, if one becomes more ethnocentric as a result of mortality salience, a terror management theorist could state that this is due to the reassertion of one's own cultural worldview. Yet, if one becomes less ethnocentric as a result of mortality salience, the theorist could state that this is due to the reassertion of the person's dominant value system of being ethnically tolerant (cf. Greenberg & Arndt, 2012). If there is no effect of the manipulation of mortality salience on variables, the theorist could still justify the results by suggesting that the manipulation itself was not strong enough to elicit mortality salience, or that the sample consisted of both ethnocentric and ethnically tolerant individuals and the effects in these two groups cancelled each other out. The dominant paradigm among psychologists is that psychological theories should be scientific theories and should be falsifiable (Popper, 2002). Theories that invoke intrapsychic threats, which exist at an unconscious or preconscious level, cannot at present be easily – or at all – falsified.

Ethnocentrism originates in self-aggrandisement

Another broad group of theories of ethnocentrism assumes that it is caused by personal self-aggrandisement or group self-aggrandisement. The basic idea is that people are motivated to see themselves or their groups as superior to others and may want to exploit outgroups for their own or their group's selfish needs. The major theories dealing with these ideas are the social identity approach, elite theory, and social dominance theory. In addition, the dual process cognitive-motivational theory also incorporates this idea, but also argues that threat is equally important for understanding ethnocentrism.

Many theories assume that humans use ethnocentrism to increase their own or their group's importance, esteem, prestige, power, and wealth. There are two main groups of explanations that assume that self-aggrandisement leads to ethnocentrism. The first group relates to the role of ethnocentrism in satisfying psychological needs for self-esteem and relative superiority over others. The second group relates to instrumental processes, whereby people are ethnocentric because of chiefly material benefits to themselves.

Explanations invoking self-esteem

The first group of explanations assumes that ethnocentrism has origins in self-esteem: people engage in ethnocentrism because they want to feel good about themselves and this is achieved through a sense of superiority of one's ingroup over others. There are many theorists who have invoked the role of self-esteem in explaining ethnocentrism (Dollard, 1937; S. Freud, 1930/1961; Spencer, 1874;

Tajfel & Turner, 1986; Zimmermann, 1758/1797). For example, the psychologist Dollard (1937) explicitly invoked it when he was explaining ethnocentrism among Whites in the South of the US. He argued that a sense of inborn superiority among Whites in the South increases their self-esteem:

> ... one has prestige solely because one is white. The gain here is very simple. It consists in the fact that a member of the white caste has an automatic right to demand forms of behavior from Negroes which serve to increase his own self-esteem. To put it another way, it consists of an illumination of the image of the self, an expansive feeling of being something special and valuable. It might be compared to the illusion of greatness that comes with early stages of alcoholization, except that prestige is not an illusion but a steadily repeated fact. It gives not only the sense of a sweet submissiveness on the part of other, but also a gratifying sense of mastery.
>
> *Dollard, 1937, p. 174*

Superiority and self-esteem in various variants of this approach can relate to the individual, but also to their group. This means that ethnocentrism might be driven by individual self-esteem or individual need for superiority, but also by group self-esteem or group need for superiority. Nonetheless, most explanations assume that the individual and group are somehow merged, and, given the overlap, self-aggrandisement relates to both. The social identity approach is the most influential example of this theoretical approach as it explicitly argues that group identity is a fundamental aspect of each person, and that needs for self-esteem and relative group superiority underlie ethnocentrism.

The social identity approach

The social identity approach, which includes social identity theory (Tajfel, 1981; Tajfel & Turner, 1986) and self-categorisation theory (Turner, 1991, 1999; Turner et al., 1987), has been applied to many areas of group processes and intergroup relations, including ethnocentrism. In a way, it is similar to terror management theory, which was discussed in the previous section, in that it has emerged as a broad social psychological approach that attempts to explain a wide variety of phenomena. The approach is both motivational and cognitive, with social identity theory emphasising motivational processes and intergroup relations, and self-categorisation theory emphasising cognitive processes and the psychological significance of being in a group. Although somewhat different, these two theories are treated here as a single approach, because they share meta-theoretical assumptions, and social identity theory can be seen as a subset of self-categorisation theory (Abrams & Hogg, 2004; Turner, 1999).

The main assumption of this approach, following Koffka's (1935) distinction of sociological and psychological groups, is that social groups can be sociological and psychological. Sociological groups are collections of people grouped together, usually by others, such as institutions. In contrast, psychological groups are more important to people because people identify with them and feel a sense of "togetherness" and "we-ness" (Turner, 1982). This approach is mainly interested in psychological groups, that is, the groups that are important to individuals and where people feel a sense of belonging. Initially, the theorists in this approach claimed that each individual has two key identities: personal and social. Personal identity deals with individuals' unique characteristics and traits, and social identity is "that part of an individual's self-concept that derives from his knowledge of his membership of a social group (or groups) together with the value and emotional significance attached to that membership" (Tajfel, 1981, p. 255). Social identity, however, is seen as central to group processes and ethnocentrism. Later developments in the theory proposed that in addition to the two levels of self-definitions, there are countless other self-definitions, including those lower than personal identity (e.g., the ideal me, the real me) and those higher than social identity (e.g., human identity) (Turner, Reynolds, Haslam, & Veenstra, 2006). This approach, however, has been principally focused on social identity (Turner, 1999) – and these other levels, although legitimate levels of individual identification, have been much less studied by social identity researchers.

This theoretical approach was initially developed to explain ingroup preference in minimal groups, which are artificially constructed groups where there is no interaction between group members and group members do not even know who the other group members are. As discussed above in the section on realistic group conflict theory, theorists had assumed that threat is responsible for ethnocentrism, but laboratory research has shown that even without threat there is ingroup bias, which Tajfel and Turner (1986) called an analogue to ethnocentrism. Tajfel and Turner accepted that realistic threats do lead to ethnocentrism, and, as acknowledged by Turner (Turner & Reynolds, 2010), the two saw themselves as Sherifians, but, finding ingroup bias in minimal groups (Tajfel, Billig, Bundy, & Flament, 1971), where there is no realistic threat, they attempted to explain it using psychological concepts.

Although the proponents of this approach have proposed different variables that could affect ingroup preference and ethnocentrism (e.g., similarity, threat, group norms), the two central psychological variables, as stated by the founders of social identity theory, Tajfel and Turner (1986), are group categorisation and the need for positive self-esteem, which involves self-aggrandisement. It is essentially self-aggrandisement that is the motivational core of social identity creating ethnocentrism, and simple categorisation into ingroups on its own, and without self-aggrandisement, appears insufficient to create ethnocentrism and group preferences.

When people categorise themselves as members of a group, their social identity is made salient, and they experience depersonalisation, perceiving "themselves as relatively interchangeable with other ingroup members" (Brown & Turner, 1981, p. 39). Thus, their personal identity and individual differences disappear, their personal self-interest transforms into group self-interest, and they act as members of a group, not separate individuals. As mentioned, social categorisation is not enough to trigger ingroup preferences, and it works together with the need for positive self-esteem to predispose people to favour their ingroups over outgroups. People tend to discriminate in favour of the ingroup because they want to achieve a sense of positive group distinctiveness. The need for positive self-esteem and the overlap between the individual and the group had already been implicated in ethnocentrism (or more specifically, the phenomenon that was to be called ethnocentrism), but in this theory these two concepts have been systematically integrated. The need for group superiority derives from people's basic need for positive self-esteem (Tajfel & Turner, 1986). This led researchers in this tradition to argue that ingroup preference should lead to higher self-esteem and that lower self-esteem should lead to ingroup preference (Abrams & Hogg, 1988; Hogg & Abrams, 1990).

The overall approach, therefore, appears relevant to the present conceptualisation of ethnocentrism, with self-categorisation theory related to intragroup ethnocentrism and social identity theory more clearly related to intergroup ethnocentrism. Categorisation alone, which leads to depersonalisation, should lead to intragroup aspects of ethnocentrism. As Turner (1999) stated, depersonalisation changes personal self-interest into a group interest, enhancing ingroup cohesion. Accordingly, as a result of categorisation, people tend to perceive their group as more important than individual group members. Additionally, once people categorise themselves as ethnic group members, and they perceive that other groups exist, they tend to see their ethnic group as more important than these other groups, because they are motivated by self-aggrandisement in these situations. Perceiving one's own ethnic group to be more important than others then leads to a tendency to prefer one's own ethnic group, to see it as superior, to reject outgroup members from one's own group, and to see ingroup interests as more important than outgroup interests, leading to exploitation.

A critique of explanations invoking self-esteem

The relationship between self-esteem and ingroup bias has not been convincingly demonstrated (R. Brown, 2000), and at times is mentioned as a misunderstood aspect of social identity theory (Turner, 1999). Nevertheless, a review of the literature suggests that there is generally more empirical support for the proposition that state self-esteem is enhanced as a result of engaging in and demonstrating ingroup preferences than for the proposition that lower self-esteem leads to ingroup preference (Rubin & Hewstone, 1998). This led researchers to recently conclude that the global self-esteem hypothesis in its original form is not supported, but that people do experience a certain amount of temporary self-enhancement following engagement in ingroup preferences (Fiske & Taylor, 2017). In short, there is certain evidence that people feel better about themselves when they favour their ingroup members over outgroups. Meta-analytic research, however, suggests that self-esteem does appear in some forms relevant to ethnocentrism, but the relationship is complex and affected by different conceptualisations of ingroup preferences and self-esteem (Aberson, Healy, & Romero, 2000). It should be pointed out that much of the research on self-esteem and ethnocentrism does not deal specifically with ethnocentrism as a real-world phenomenon and as conceptualised in this book.

In fact, research appears to suggest that it is narcissistic self-esteem that relates to ethnocentrism – but primarily the intergroup dimensions, and may even be opposed to the two intragroup dimensions of ethnocentrism (Bizumic & Duckitt, 2008, 2009). Narcissistic people like to see themselves and everything connected to themselves as being superior, special, and particularly important, and this evidently predisposes narcissistic people to also assume that their ethnic group is more impor-tant than others. Nonetheless, this personal self-aggrandisement may also predispose people to become less likely to sacrifice themselves and submit their uniqueness to group unity – making narcissism opposed to devotion and group cohesion.

When it comes to the role of categorisation in ethnocentrism, there is no doubt that for ethnocentric attitudes to occur, people need to categorise themselves with their own ethnic group. The exact process of how categorisation with one's ethnic group leads to ethnocentrism is still being contested. For example, a number of researchers have also argued that when people fuse with their group, that is, when their personal and social identities significantly overlap, they become particularly likely to engage in extreme behaviours on behalf of the group, such as fighting other groups or even dying for their group (Swann et al., 2014; Swann, Gómez, Dovidio, Hart, & Jetten, 2010; Swann, Gómez, Seyle, Morales, & Huici, 2009; Swann, Jetten, Gomez, Whitehouse, & Bastian, 2012). Accordingly, it may not be just social identification, as social identity theorists would assume, but the fusion of social and personal identities that predisposes people to ethnocentrism.

It is also important to point out that the social identity approach has largely ignored the role of individual differences and personality in the development of ethnocentrism, focusing instead almost entirely on situational determinants of intergroup attitudes (R. Brown, 2010; Duckitt, 2014). Its main arguments are that intergroup relations and ethnocentrism are affected by the social context and salient social identities, influencing people to act purely as interchangeable group members, whereas individual differences are important only when personal iden-tity is salient (Turner, 1999). Thus, the proponents of this approach would argue that ethnocentrism is not a stable, or even a relatively stable, characteristic of an individual, but purely the product of a specific social context (Huang & Liu, 2005; Schmitt, Branscombe, & Kappen, 2003), and that it is relatively easy to change eth-nocentrism with changes in the social context.

There are certain problems with this aspect of the social identity approach. People do differ in the extent to which they hold ethnic attitudes. For example, research demonstrates that people who are prejudiced against one ethnic outgroup tend to be prejudiced against most ethnic outgroups, even fictitious ones (Hartley, 1946). This uniformity of ethnic attitudes within the individual cannot be explained purely by the immediate situation and social context, but points to important per-sonality and individual differences. Further, longitudinal research with monozy-gotic and dizygotic twins suggests that, at the individual level, ingroup preferences, including ethnic preferences, are exceptionally stable over a period of 10 years, and the stability appears to be due to genetic, and not social, influences (Lewis & Bates, 2017).

In addition, although underemphasised, individual difference variables are actually present in the social identity approach. For example, social identity processes are frequently related to a person's strength of group identification (Hinkle & Brown, 1990) and readiness to categorise, which is affected by "a person's past experience, present expectations and current motives, values, goals, and needs" (Turner, 1999, p. 12). These are individual difference variables because people differ in the strength of group identification, experiences, values, and goals. Different individuals, therefore, seem to bring with themselves a different repertoire of personal characteristics to intergroup relations. This, of course, does not mean that the social context is unimportant. It can undoubtedly increase or decrease an individual's levels of ethnocentrism (i.e., produce mean-level changes), but it does not appear to strongly affect people's relative standing on ethnocentrism (i.e., rank-order stability). Unfortunately, there has not been much work in this theoretical framework on individual differences, whether they are relatively stable or change with situations, and how they can be conceptualised, measured, and investigated.

Explanations invoking exploitation and dominance

There are two theoretical approaches in the second version of explanations invoking self-aggrandisement. The first assumes that ethnocentrism is caused by elites in ethnic groups when the elites use ethnocentrism to dominate or exploit the rest of the ethnic group, as well as other ethnic groups, for the elites' self-aggrandising purposes. The value of ethnocentrism is instrumental: ethnic subgroups, such as the elites, and at times the whole ethnic group may benefit from ethnocentrism because it enables them to exploit and dominate others. The second approach, social dominance theory, argues that there are individual differences in how much people endorse group inequalities and group-based dominance, and that these can explain the phenomenon of ethnocentrism.

Elite theory

Elite theory is usually associated with the Italian sociologists Mosca (1939) and Pareto (1935), and the US sociologist Mills (1956). This theory is also influenced by Marx's writings about the ruling class (e.g., Marx & Engels, 1846/1970). Interestingly, and again less frequently mentioned, Gumplowicz's writings had also profoundly influenced the work on this theory (Gregor, 1969; Scott, 2007). James Gregor noted:

> All the ideas that significantly influenced Mussolini and Fascism are found in the books of an Austrian scholar whose work was certainly known to Mosca and in all probability to Pareto as well—Ludwig Gumplowicz (1838–1909). Intimations of those ideas, as well as some of the ideas themselves, are to

be found in the writings of Henri Saint Simon, Hippolyte Taine and Karl Marx, among others. However, they are fully developed only in the work of Gumplowicz. The extent of Gumplowicz' influence on Fascist theory construction has been little appreciated. It appears almost certain that he was the initial source of almost all of Mosca's ideas and, at least indirectly, those of Pareto. And their ideas provided much of the initial intellectual substance of Fascism.

Gregor, 1969, p. 38

The main idea of elite theory, and this can be found in the works of Gumplowicz, Mosca, and Pareto, is that there is an elite, which is always a minority group in a society, and this elite rules over the rest of the society. According to this approach, this is a characteristic of all organized groupings, where the elites use various mechanisms to rule over the rest of the society.

The writers who have applied this theoretical approach to ethnocentrism (e.g., Lanternari, 1980; van Dijk, 1993) assumed that ethnocentrism is one such mechanism. According to Lanternari (1980), ethnocentrism presumes "an ideological function, i.e., the 'false consciousness' imposed from above by the ruling class" (p. 57). He argued that the elites impose ethnocentrism on the subordinated societal groups, and in such a way dominate them, while at the same time the subordinated groups, which are exploited by the elites, could also feel important and superior. For example, one of the purposes of ethnocentrism in colonial societies was to comfort the disadvantaged ethnic ingroup members, who inhabited these colonies and lived in unfavourable circumstances. These disadvantaged ethnic group members, therefore, still felt important and superior to others – but they were, in fact, exploited and dominated by the elites, who benefited economically from the work of the colonialists. According to this theory, therefore, ethnocentrism – and all six expressions of ethnocentrism are relevant – could be used by elites to preserve the societal status quo and to mobilise the whole ethnic group for the elites' projects.

Van Dijk (1993) argued that ethnocentrism and related phenomena, such as racism and prejudice, are principally top-down phenomena, that is, they are mostly enforced, usually in subtle ways, by societal elites, such as politicians, corporate managers, and academics, on the rest of the ethnic majority population to legitimise the ethnic ingroup dominance. He analysed parliamentary, political, corporate, academic, educational, and media discourses, and showed that these discourses often present the ethnic ingroup, which is the ethnic majority group, as more important, better, and rightly dominant. In contrast, the societal ethnic minorities and the ethnic outgroups tend to be presented as less important, less good, and at times deviant or threatening to the ingroup (and therefore rightly subordinate within the society). This kind of dominance is in place today in many national states, where ethnic majority groups dominate immigrants and other ethnic minorities.

A case study about the role of elites in the development and reinforcement of ethnocentrism is ex-Yugoslavia, where virulent ethnocentrism took place in the

1990s, and where the most deadly European conflict since the Second World War took place. There is no doubt among most scholars that increased ethnocentrism was to a large extent caused by selfish personal self-aggrandisement of the elites in the ethnic groups. For example, many commentators on wars in ex-Yugoslavia have assumed that the elites propagated ethnocentrism (ethnocentric superiority, devotion, purity) as well as violence for their own self-aggrandisement (Bennet, 1995; Gagnon, 2004; Glenny, 2001; Mueller, 2000; Pesic, 1993). Glenny (2001) argued that the real intentions of the elites in ex-Yugoslavia, primarily in Serbia and Croatia, were their own "economic and/or political consolidation or aggrandizement" (p. 158). Gagnon (2004) even argued that the main reason why Serbian and Croatian elites manipulated ethnocentric sentiments, as well as creating ethnic wars and engaging their ethnic groups in violence, was to demobilise the forces that were against them, such as the liberal political opposition. Self-aggrandisement among the elites was generally unrelated to the elites' intragroup expressions of ethnocentrism, as the elites were unlikely to intend to sacrifice themselves for the ethnic group projects (see Djilas, 2005). Furthermore, Gagnon (2004) argued that in ex-Yugoslavia the elites only pretended to care about the ethnic ingroups, and they were ready to sacrifice many ingroup members for the selfish purposes of the elites.

It should be noted that these explanations have mainly focused on economic and material advantages of ethnocentrism, but there might be other related advantages, such as the sexual exploitation of another ethnic group (Dollard, 1937). For example, it was argued that the sexual exploitation of ethnic outgroups was a potent driver of British ethnocentric imperialism, and that it was possibly as important for imperialism as economic exploitation was (Hyam, 1990). Sexual exploitation has also been historically a prominent aspect in relations between Anglo/White-Americans and African-Americans (Dollard, 1937).

Social dominance theory

Social dominance theory (Pratto, Sidanius, & Levin, 2006; Sidanius et al., 2017; Sidanius & Pratto, 1999) proposes an individual difference variable, social dominance orientation (SDO), to describe individual variation in endorsement of group inequalities. According to this theory, because of evolutionary influences, people have developed a "basic human predisposition to form group-based social hierarchies" (Sidanius & Pratto, 1999, p. 38). People who are characterised by this individual difference, that is, those who are high in SDO, support ideologies that promote group inequalities, and have attitudes, values, and attributions that assign differential values to social groups (Pratto, 1999; Sidanius, Pratto, & Rabinowitz, 1994). People high in this individual difference variable tend to agree with items on the SDO Scale, such as "Some groups of people are simply inferior to other groups", "Some groups of people must be kept in their place", and "We shouldn't try to guarantee that every group has the same quality of life" (Ho et al., 2015). In contrast, people low on this variable tend to prefer equality between groups and reject the idea that any group should dominate in a society.

Social dominance theory argues that different constructs that justify intergroup inequality (e.g., ethnocentrism, militarism, sexism, nationalism) would be positively intercorrelated because they are driven by SDO (Sidanius & Liu, 1992). Accordingly, given that ethnocentrism involves giving more value to the ethnic ingroup than to outgroups and that it can be used to justify inequality, it is theoretically linked to SDO. This appears to be especially the case in high-status ethnic groups because ethnocentrism is a kind of "legitimising myth" that justifies and maintains intergroup hierarchies (i.e., "our ethnic group deserves to be on top because it is better and superior to other ethnic groups"). Ethnocentrism, which gives more social value to the ethnic ingroup than to ethnic outgroups, would be higher among the members of more powerful or higher-status ethnic groups because they promote and benefit from intergroup hierarchy among different groups (Federico, 1999; Rabinowitz, 1999; Sidanius et al., 1994). Research generally supports the linking of SDO to various measures of ethnocentrism (Altemeyer, 1998; Duckitt, 2001; Pratto, 1999), including the Ethnocentrism Scale 1 (Bizumic et al., 2009).

More recent research on this theory (Ho et al., 2012, 2015) suggests that SDO consists of two main dimensions, which differentially relate to external variables. The first is called SDO-Dominance, and it involves preferring certain groups to actively and forcefully dominate and oppress others. The second is called SDO-Egalitarianism, and it involves opposing intergroup equality between groups and enforcing in subtle ways inequality between groups. Despite certain differences between the two, they are strongly intercorrelated, and it is expected that both would strongly correlate with ethnocentrism, as conceptualised in this book.

This theory assumes that people from low-status groups may show less SDO and, by extension, low-status ethnic groups may show less ethnocentrism, pursuing egalitarian or hierarchy-attenuation solutions, or even showing outgroup favouritism. This phenomenon of the differential bias is called "asymmetric ingroup bias" (Sidanius et al., 1994). These ideas in relation to ethnocentrism had been discussed by Kurt Lewin (1948), who argued that each society has ethnic groups with different status and that higher-status groups tend to have more opportunities and fewer difficulties than lower-status groups do. As a result, in contrast to higher-status groups, which often rate central aspects of their ingroups (e.g., values, traditions, habits) highly, lower-status groups may dislike and devalue their ethnic groups.

Research suggests that group self-aggrandisement is not only a characteristic of high-status groups. Cross-cultural research with ethnic groups in East Africa (Brewer & Campbell, 1976), for example, showed that ethnic groups of higher status and those of lower status tended to have a much more positive self-regard than groups of intermediate status – possibly because of the influence of defensive self-esteem in lower-status groups. Other relevant research, in both labs and real groups, suggests that low-status groups often exhibit favouritism on the dimensions that are not relevant to status, whereas high-status groups exhibit favouritism on the dimensions relevant to status (e.g., Ellemers & Van Rijswijk, 1997; Poppe & Linssen, 1999; Reichl, 1997; Sachdev & Bourhis, 1987, 1991). A comprehensive meta-analysis testing these ideas, however, showed that high-status groups tend to exhibit ingroup bias on both status-relevant and irrelevant dimensions, whereas low-status groups tend to exhibit ingroup bias only on the dimensions relevant to low-status groups (Bettencourt, Dorr, Charlton, & Hume, 2001). According to these authors, the general findings are that high-status groups exhibit more ingroup bias, but also identify more strongly with their groups, than low-status groups do.

A related point put forward by Sidanius and colleagues (1994) is that being male predisposes people to SDO. According to this theory, as a result of biological influences males are more likely to become socially dominant and, by extension, ethnocentric. Indeed, there is a large body of evidence in favour of the argument that males tend to be higher on both SDO and ethnocentrism than females (Bizumic et al., 2009; Ho et al., 2015; Sidanius et al., 1994).

Social dominance theory appears relevant to how this book conceptualised ethnocentrism. Individuals who are high in SDO may use ethnocentrism, that is, the ideas that their own ethnic group is of extreme importance, to justify ethnic intergroup hierarchies, dominance, and exploitation of other ethnic groups, especially when the ingroup is high in status and power. Although all six aspects of ethnocentrism might be relevant for this, intergroup dimensions appear particularly strongly related to SDO. In support of this, research across cultures suggests that SDO tends to correlate more strongly with intergroup ethnocentrism than with intragroup ethnocentrism (Bizumic et al., 2009).

A critique of explanations invoking exploitation and dominance

There is considerable support for the view that elites manipulate their ingroups for the elites' own selfish needs. Although elite theory appears useful for explaining influences on ethnocentrism that are often overlooked by social psychologists, it can be criticised for underemphasising the influence of non-elites, who are rarely the passive recipients of ethnocentrism (cf. A. D. Smith, 2010). Aly (2005/2016) argued that many Germans were, for example, not only complacent in German ethnocentrism and violence in the Second World War, but actively and willingly drawn to it because they economically benefited from large-scale German thefts, exploitation, and slavery. Germans were open to Nazi propaganda not because they were easily manipulated by the elites, but because they had vested interests in Nazi Germany. Accordingly, ethnic group members, rather than being indoctrinated and docile, may often actively and willingly accept and propagate ethnocentrism because it may also satisfy their own self-aggrandising motivations.

Another related potential problem of the elite theory of ethnocentrism is related to the attraction that ethnocentrism has for people. For example, Brexit in the UK in 2017 showed that even though most elites (e.g., the media, major political parties, universities) attempted to convince people that remaining in the European Union is more advantageous than Brexit, most people still relied on ethnocentric sentiments and voted for Brexit. Similarly, after the fall of the Soviet Union, people in most ex-communist countries wanted to live in nations consisting primarily of their ethnic groups (e.g., different ethnic groups in Yugoslavia and the Soviet Union; the Czechs and the Slovaks in Czechoslovakia), preferring ethnocentric politicians over those who were more cosmopolitan, socialist, and liberal. Accordingly, questions can be asked about the extent to which elites are creating ethnocentrism, and why it is often much easier for them to make people attached to their ethnicity, and therefore ethnocentric, than to make them attached to other social groups.

There has been a considerable argument about the origins of SDO, and the extent to which SDO is shaped by social, and not necessarily evolutionary and biological, processes (Schmitt et al., 2003; Turner & Reynolds, 2003; M. S. Wilson & Liu, 2003). For example, as mentioned above, there is a large body of evidence linking males to SDO and ethnocentrism. Nevertheless, whether the cause of these findings is in biology or socialisation has been debated. For example, Johnson and Marini (1998) assumed that males are more intolerant of cultural diversity than females because males are socialised to be self-oriented (and therefore prone to self-aggrandisement), whereas females are socialised to be other-oriented (and less prone to self-aggrandisement).

Discussion

A number of theories have emphasised either fears or self-aggrandisement as the main causes of ethnocentrism. Certain theories, such as the social identity approach, acknowledged the role of threats and fears, but tended to focus on self-aggrandisement as the main underlying motivation for ethnocentrism. Nevertheless, a number of theoretical frameworks can be used to further integrate both kinds of explanations.

The dual process cognitive-motivational model

Duckitt's dual process cognitive-motivational theory builds on theories of authoritarianism and social dominance to argue that both threat and self-aggrandisement motivations are equally responsible for prejudice and ethnocentrism (Duckitt, 2000, 2001, Duckitt & Sibley, 2010, 2017; Duckitt, Wagner, du Plessis, & Birum, 2002). This theory proposes two processes that run in parallel, largely independently of each other, and cause ethnocentrism. One process starts with punitive socialisation that produces conforming personalities. Such people tend to perceive the world as a dangerous place. In addition, a dangerous and threatening social context may also predispose people to perceive the world as a dangerous place. This worldview then activates people's need for security, which leads to authoritarianism, which in turn predisposes people to primarily intragroup ethnocentrism.

The other process starts with unaffectionate socialisation that produces tough-minded personalities. These people are likely to see the world as a competitive jungle. Similarly, a competitive social context may also predispose people to see the world as a competitive jungle. This worldview then activates the need for dominance and superiority, expressed in high SDO, which in turn predisposes people to primarily intergroup ethnocentrism. This model has been extensively tested across cultures and the data generally supported the model (Duckitt & Sibley, 2010, 2017). Empirical research with the Ethnocentrism Scale 1 suggests that SDO is primarily related to intergroup ethnocentrism, though authoritarianism appears to be related equally to intragroup and intergroup ethnocentrism (Bizumic et al., 2009).

This theory is unique in the sense that it gives equal importance to the role of threat and self-aggrandisement in causing ethnocentrism, whereas the other theories discussed thus far have tended to emphasise either fears or self-aggrandisement as the major influence on ethnocentrism. In addition, the theory attempts to account for a number of distal and indirect influences on ethnocentrism. As mentioned in the discussion of the theories invoking fears and threats, it appears that all six dimensions of ethnocentrism could be caused by fears. There appears to be support for the view that the four intergroup dimensions are directly related to self-aggrandisement. Intragroup dimensions, however, may at times be opposed to self-aggrandisement.

Value-based frameworks

Related frameworks concerned with values also appear to be relevant to the views that there are two main and broad underlying general categories of explanations that appear to underlie ethnocentrism. Although many theoretical models of values have been developed, the two most prominent today are Schwartz's (1992, 1994, 1999, 2012; Schwartz et al., 2012) model of personal values and Haidt's (2012) model of moral values. Schwartz's model is broader, and concerns everything that people may value in life, and is not explicitly concerned with morality, whereas Haidt's model is explicitly concerned with moral values. Nevertheless, certain values that pertain to morality are not present in Schwartz's model, such as the values of purity and fairness, whereas certain of Schwartz's values, such as achievement, stimulation, and hedonism, do not appear to have moral underpinnings. Accordingly, although the models overlap each other, both appear relevant and complement each other.

Schwartz's model proposes 10 groups of personal values, with each having specific motivational goals. In the most recent version of the model, Schwartz also argues that there are certain subdimensions within the values (Schwartz et al., 2012). The 10 groups and their motivational goals are: (1) conformity, with the goal of restraining actions that transgress norms and hurt people; (2) tradition, with the goal of respecting traditional ways; (3) security, with the goal of preserving the safety of oneself and other people in one's society; (4) self-direction, with the goal of acting and thinking independently; (5) stimulation, with the goal of engaging in novel and exciting experiences; (6) hedonism, with the goal of sensual gratification; (7) power, with the goal of controlling others and resources; (8) achievement, with the goal of attaining success as defined by society; (9) universalism, with the goal of advancing the welfare of all people and nature; and (10) benevolence, with the goal of advancing the welfare of people close to oneself.

Schwartz conceptualised values as people's guiding principles in life. Values are generalised, broad, and transcend situations. Schwartz assumes that values are part of our human nature, and exist to facilitate societal functioning and positive social relations, but also satisfy individual needs. They also underlie attitudes and behaviours. The 10 basic groups of values can be further organised at the broadest level of generalisation into: (1) the values of conservation (consisting of conformity, tradition, and security) versus the opposing values of openness to change (consisting of self-direction, stimulation, and hedonism); and (2) the values of self-enhancement (consisting of power, achievement, and also hedonism) versus the opposing values of self-transcendence (consisting of universalism and benevolence). His model of values has been widely studied across over 80 countries and has excellent empirical support.

Haidt's model (see Graham et al., 2011, 2013; Haidt, 2012; Haidt & Joseph, 2004; Iyer, Koleva, Graham, Ditto, & Haidt, 2012) proposes five basic moral values, or moral foundations. Although Haidt and his collaborators have used various terms for these values, I will use the following five because they have been used widely in the literature: (1) purity (which concerns valuing cleanliness, primarily in a religious sense), (2) ingroup loyalty (which concerns valuing allegiances to one's own group), (3) authority (which concerns valuing legitimate hierarchies and authorities), (4) harm (which concerns valuing the avoidance of harming others, especially those who are vulnerable), and (5) fairness (which concerns valuing proportionality and reciprocity in relationships with others). These moral foundations could be organised as two broad dimensions of values. The first broad dimension relates to binding values (purity, ingroup loyalty, and authority), and is concerned with effective communal functioning. This dimension appears closely linked to human evolution as group members. The second dimension relates to individualising values (harm and fairness), and is concerned with reducing suffering and promoting individual rights and justice. This dimension appears closely linked to the evolution of empathy and cooperation with other individuals. This model is, therefore, evolutionary, and assumes that evolutionary factors have shaped humans to adopt these moral values across all societies. Nevertheless, although moral values are seen as innate, they also respond to environmental influences. Although people are aware of these values, they usually operate at the unconscious level. Finally, there are also important differences in how much people espouse these values – across both individuals and groups. This model has also been extensively studied and has excellent support.

Both Schwartz's model and Haidt's model have been related to authoritarianism and SDO, and were linked to the dual process model (Cohrs, Moschner, Maes, & Kielmann, 2005; Duckitt & Sibley, 2010; Federico, Weber, Ergun, & Hunt, 2013). They in fact appear to have a lot in common with fear and self-aggrandisement. First, Schwartz's values of conformity, tradition, and security (and these can be contrasted with the values of self-direction and stimulation, and somewhat with hedonism) appear to be related to fears as they emphasise and value certainty and protection against different kinds of threats (threats of changes, deviance, disagreements, and general insecurity and uncertainty). Secondly, the values of power and achievement, and partly hedonism, are in service of self-aggrandisement as they are about pursuing self-interest, dominance, and success, and these can be contrasted with the values of universalism and benevolence, which are about self-transcendence. Schwartz (2012) argues that values underlie attitudes and that we hold attitudes that allow us to advance and reach the goals that we have.

Thus, ethnocentrism, which is an attitude related to strong ethnic group self-importance, is likely to have a basis in particular values. First, if people value tradition, security, conformity, purity, authority, and ingroup loyalty, they are likely to positively evaluate ethnocentrism (and mainly its intragroup expressions), because ethnocentrism may help them reach important goals. In contrast, if people value self-direction and stimulation, they are likely to negatively evaluate ethnocentrism (and mainly its intragroup expressions) because it may prevent them from reaching important goals. In the same way, if people value power and achievement, they are likely to positively evaluate ethnocentrism (and mainly its intergroup expressions), but if they value benevolence, universalism, fairness, and harm/care (i.e., avoidance of harming others), they are likely to negatively evaluate ethnocentrism (and mainly its intergroup expressions). Still, these theoretical approaches need to be explicitly related to the dimensions of ethnocentrism because it is possible that a more complex picture may emerge. I will attempt to do that in Chapter 6.

Summary and conclusions

This chapter reviewed a number of theories linking fears and self-aggrandisement to ethnocentrism. There is strong support for the theories that propose that realistic and symbolic fears affect ethnocentrism, whereas there is much less support for the role of unconscious intrapsychic fears in ethnocentrism. All six dimensions of ethnocentrism may increase as a result of both realistic and symbolic fears. It is, however, also important to point out that it is rare that only one fear operates in intergroup relations. For example, Green, Abelson, and Garnett (1999) studied two extremist groups of individuals who are strongly opposed to interethnic mixing and immigration in the US: perpetrators of hate crimes and white supremacists. These groups perceived that ethnic outgroups invade and threaten the dominant ethnic group's realistic resources, such as territory and societal position, but also its symbolic meanings, such as culture, and these perceptions had a particularly strong effect on ethnocentric attitudes.

There is also considerable support for the propositions that both personal and group self-aggrandisement affects ethnocentrism, even though there appears more support for group self-aggrandisement being more important for ethnocentrism than personal self-aggrandisement. Personal self-esteem appears weakly, if at all, relevant to ethnocentrism, but narcissistic self-esteem appears more relevant. Although self-aggrandisement theories may be relevant to all six dimensions of ethnocentrism, they appear most directly relevant to the four intergroup dimensions.

4

THE CAUSES OF ETHNOCENTRISM

Social factors, biology, and evolution

The previous chapter focused on a variety of explanations of ethnocentrism that invoked fears and self-aggrandisement. The present chapter will look into explanations of ethnocentrism that focus on social factors, and those that focus on biological and evolutionary factors. Both groups of explanations have been prominent in psychology and the social sciences, and both have had passionate proponents and critics. The idea of the causal role of social factors can be broadly summarised in the following way: people are ethnocentric because they learn and are influenced by social factors, such as social norms, to become ethnocentric. An assumption is that ethnocentrism is mainly a social phenomenon that can disappear with changes in these social factors. The idea of the causal role of biology and evolution in ethnocentrism can be broadly summarised in the following way: the human species has evolved to be ethnocentric and ethnocentrism is wired into human biology and is unlikely to disappear because it is part of our genetic makeup, which is shaped by evolutionary factors. Most of the theories, of course, cannot be so easily categorised into either of the two groups of explanations, and many assume different kinds of interactions between social and biological factors in producing ethnocentrism.

Explanations invoking social factors

A report by the Woodrow Wilson Center accused Japanese textbooks of causing ethnocentrism in Japanese school-children ("Japan textbooks may give rise to ethnocentrism: U.S. report", 2000). The reason behind this accusation is a study that demonstrated that a dominant focus of the textbooks in Japan is often on the Japanese ethnicity and the views that the Japanese are unique and different in comparison to other ethnic groups. Such textbooks, according to the writers of the report, may make the Japanese school-children ethnocentric. Many social psychologists, sociologists, anthropologists, and political scientists would have agreed with this causality as many have assumed that humans are not wired for ethnocentrism, but that they learn ethnocentrism through socialisation and are directly or indirectly pressured to conform to it.

There are different influences upon the view that ethnocentrism is primarily shaped by social factors. Explanations that focus on social factors have at times been extreme in their attempt to explain all behaviours as products of social factors. Such explanations have been influenced by a broader set of explanations that assume that there is no fixed human nature, such as empiricist philosophy (Locke, 1689/1825), behaviourist psychology (Watson, 1925), Marxism (Marx & Engels, 1846/1970), cultural relativist anthropology (Boas, 1940; Mead, 1928), and a widely accepted sociological dogma of environmentalism and sociocultural determinism (see van den Berghe, 1990). Indeed, the central idea of liberal and socialist explanations of ethnocentrism is that it is caused by social, and not biological, factors and that it would wither away over time (cf. Singer, 2000). All these ideas have also had a profound influence on social psychological approaches to ethnocentrism that focus on social factors as determinants of ethnocentrism.

In the following section, I will review major theories that saw the main cause of ethnocentrism in broad social factors. There are many theories that assume that ethnocentrism is shaped by social factors, and my presentation is not exhaustive. What appears common to many of these theories is the assumption that ethnocentrism is learned, conformed to, and internalised, as well as the assumption that in the same way that humans learn, conform to, and internalise ethnocentrism, they can also learn, conform to, and internalise ethnic tolerance and humanitarianism.

Socialisation and social norms

In a certain way, the process of socialisation in every ethnic group includes learning about what is right and wrong and what is good and bad. People are influenced by the culture of their ethnic groups from the moment of birth, and possibly even before they are born, and culture has an enormous influence throughout people's lives (Bohannan, 1993). People learn about important cultural values within their ethnic group, and they learn its cultural norms, roles, and standards. These include the right ways to think, feel, and behave, and they also show what the wrong ways to think, feel, and behave are. Through the process of socialisation people learn about what it means to be a good member of their own ethnic group. Accordingly, it is not surprising that when people observe other ethnic groups they may perceive them to be less good. Thus, people are socialised into a specific kind of ethnocentrism by others. For example, when people interact with others on an everyday basis across contexts, they may be exposed to many socialisation routes that reinforce ethnocentrism (Siamagka & Balabanis, 2015). In contemporary societies, this may include family and peer-group contexts, educational institutions, religious institutions, the media, and so forth. These influences can often be explicit, but most of the time they appear subtle and banal (cf. Billig, 1995).

Social psychologists have in particular focused on the concept of social norms to explain a variety of behaviours whereby people submit to their important groups, including their ethnic groups. What exactly are social norms? There have been many definitions in the literature. One better-known definition sees social norms as "customs, traditions, standards, rules, values, fashions, and all other criteria of conduct which are standardized as a consequence of the contact of individuals" (Sherif, 1936/1973, p. 3). This is a widely accepted – though broad – definition of social norms. Another popular definition distinguishes between two types of norms: descriptive and injunctive (Cialdini et al., 2006). Descriptive norms (the norms of "is") are about what people commonly do, and injunctive norms (the norms of "ought") are about behaviours that people approve or disapprove of. Both types of norms guide people's behaviours, but they operate through different mechanisms. Whereas descriptive norms indicate to people what is efficient and adaptable behaviour, injunctive norms indicate which behaviours bring about informal rewards and which informal punishment. Through the processes of socialisation or adaptation to a particular culture, people often internalise social norms (Sherif, 1936/1973), and these internalised norms do reflect attitudes. Nevertheless, even when there is no internalisation, people feel pressured to conform to the norms (Harding et al., 1969).

There are different explanations of how exactly people internalise and learn social norms and create attitudes such as ethnocentrism. First, based on the behaviourist principles of operant conditioning, people may learn to behave in accordance with ethnocentric social norms, and potentially develop ethnocentric attitudes, because they may be rewarded by other people for expressing ethnocentrism and punished when they do not express ethnocentrism or express ethnic tolerance. As a result of that, people's ethnocentrism may reflect their learning history. Similarly, Bandura's social learning theory, now termed social-cognitive theory (Bandura, 1999), assumes that through observational learning, which includes imitation, children and adults learn attitudes and behaviours from important other people. Self-categorisation theory argues that when people identify with specific groups, they internalise group norms as part of their identity, and these then impact significantly on their attitudes and behaviours (Turner, 1982). These mechanisms assume that ethnocentrism is then something outside the individual, which can be picked up from the environment.

A concept similar to social norms is Serge Moscovici's concept of social representations, which can be largely considered as beliefs, ideas, and practices shared within a social groups, and these help people act within groups and communicate with each other (Farr & Moscovici, 1984; Moscovici, 1973). Van Dijk (1993) argued that these social representations are distinctly group properties and should be distinguished from the more personal representations (e.g., personal beliefs, opinions, attitudes). He argued that phenomena such as racism, ethnocentrism, and discrimination can largely be seen as social representations. Related research, though not directly concerned with ethnocentrism, showed for example how social representations of one's group as tolerant or intolerant affect xenophobia (Billiet,

Maddens, & Beerten, 2003; Maddens, Billiet, & Beerten, 2000). Similarly, work by Liu and colleagues (Liu, 1999; Liu, Lawrence, Ward, & Abraham, 2002; Liu, Wilson, McClure, & Higgins, 1999) showed that groups' social representations of history have implications for both intragroup and intergroup ethnic attitudes. For example, a study with Maori and European New Zealanders demonstrated that certain social representations of the history of New Zealand, such as how well Maori honoured the historical Treaty of Waitingi in comparison to European New Zealanders, were associated with present attitudes towards ethnic issues, such as teaching the Maori language in schools (Liu et al., 1999). According to this theoretical approach, ethnocentrism is shaped by a group's broad social representations.

If we are to apply these approaches to our conceptualisation of ethnocentrism, it would appear that when people socialise within ethnic groups that are ethnocentric or within specific ethnic subgroups (e.g., family, religious group, friendship group) which have ethnocentric norms and representations, people become more ethnocentric. So, socialisation in or conformity to groups with the norms and representations that reflect the view that one's ethnic group is immensely important could lead to all six dimensions.

Ignorance and lack of contact

Closely related are explanations dealing with ignorance and lack of contact. If people are socialised into insular groups that have little contact with other ethnic groups and do not comprehend the others, then they may be ethnocentric. Early writers on ethnocentrism have recognised this. For example, Zimmermann (1758/1797) claimed that when people are ignorant of the world and lack contact with other cultures, they become self-complacent and self-conceited, and they then despise people from other cultures. In contrast, when people have knowledge about and contact with other cultures, they become friendly and warm towards people from other cultures. Similarly, McGee (1900) assumed that ignorance about the world leads to ethnocentrism: "Knowing little of the external world, tribesmen erect themselves or their groups into centers about which all other things revolve" (pp. 830–831). In fact, a long time ago, Plato related lack of knowledge to ethnocentrism, and he referred to the corrective role of knowledge in reducing perceptions that other cultures are wrong because their social norms appear different: "For anyone will say in answer to the wondering stranger who looks upon something contrary to his habits: 'Do not wonder, stranger. This is our *nomos*; perhaps you in such matters have a different one'" (Plato, Laws, 637C, as quoted by Redfield, 1985, p. 99).

Psychologists have recognised for a long time that knowledge about outgroups relates to both ethnocentrism and prejudice (e.g., Allport, 1954; LeVine & Campbell, 1972; Murphy, Murphy, & Newcomb, 1937; Rosenblatt, 1964; Stephan & Stephan, 1984). Although Stephan and Stephan's (1984) review of research showed that knowledge about outgroups improves intergroup attitudes and decreases prejudice, simple knowledge of and familiarity with outgroups are not enough (Allport, 1954, 1960; Duckitt, 1992; Proshansky, 1966). According to Allport's (1954) contact hypothesis, social factors need to be arranged in a particular way to bring about real and potentially long-lasting change in intergroup attitudes: people need to experience optimal contact with outgroups to enhance intergroup relations. This contact is characterised by equal status of the participants, institutional support for the contact, common group interests, and intergroup cooperation. Confirming this, a meta-analysis by Pettigrew and Tropp (2006) of numerous studies of intergroup contact showed that samples experiencing optimal forms of contact were more likely to improve attitudes towards other groups than other samples. Decades of research into intergroup contact have shown that different varieties of intergroup contact have numerous outcomes, including positive attitudes towards groups with which one has contact, but also towards other groups with which one does not have contact, and may lead to so-called deprovincialised thinking (Hodson, Crisp, Meleady, & Earle, in press), which can be seen as non-ethnocentric and more cosmopolitan thinking about humans.

Most studies dealing with the role of knowledge and contact in influencing ethnic attitudes have dealt primarily with outgroup prejudice, though they would at times focus on measures pertaining to ethnocentrism, such as discrimination in favour of members of one's own group over others. Nonetheless, despite this work's focus on prejudice, ignorance and lack of contact are relevant to the present conceptualisation of ethnocentrism. People may prefer ingroup members because of familiarity and may espouse superiority because they see outgroup differences as limitations. They may avoid mixing with outgroups because of the fear of the unknown and may approve of exploiting outgroups because the plight of unknown people is less likely to arouse sympathy. Finally, ignorance and fear of the unfamiliar may cause people to cling to the familiar (their ingroup and its ways), be devoted to it, and reject ingroup changes or innovations.

Social categorisation

Aboud (1988) argued that external social factors interact with children's own social-cognitive development in causing ingroup preference. In fact, much of the work on ethnocentrism and prejudice in social psychology, especially since the 1970s, focused on how social categorisation interacts with social factors and learning to make humans more favourable towards their groups and unfavourable towards other groups.

Humans simplify the world because they are unable to properly process its complexity (Allport, 1954; R. Brown, 1995). As a result, they form categories, which involve objects, other living beings, and humans (i.e., social categories). The process of forming social categories for simplifying the world can be related to ethnocentrism, because it involves two easily manageable categories: us/ingroup and them/outgroup. Whereas the ingroup is perceived as important, trustworthy, or desirable, the outgroup is perceived as less important, less trustworthy, or less desirable. Social categorisation is, however, seen to be content-free in the sense that people do not automatically categorise the world into ethnic ingroups and outgroups, and they can categorise themselves and others in an infinite number of ways (Turner et al., 2006).

The social identity approach, which was discussed in the previous chapter, is a central approach to propose that social categorisation underlies ethnocentrism. This approach assumes that categorisation into social groups and positive group distinctiveness are social psychological phenomena, being the product of social comparisons and social values (Turner & Reynolds, 2010). In addition, it assumes that under certain conditions ethnocentrism is not a necessary outcome of social categorisation because social groups provide relevant values for comparisons and differentiation. Reicher and Hopkins (2001) asserted that "one could also differentiate oneself by being more charitable or more generous or more caring towards the other" (p. 34). Consequently, if the dominant norms and values in an ethnic group are related to ethnic tolerance, then people who categorise as ingroup members may in fact internalise ethnic tolerance, and when they self-aggrandise, they may do so by being even more tolerant than other ethnic groups. Although this may rarely happen in interethnic relations, the theory is not opposed to the view that the world may consist of ethnic groups who compete with each other in ethnic tolerance, generosity, and caring for each other. The theory, therefore, assumes that broad social factors may create an ethnocentric world, but also a non-ethnocentric world. It has just happened that historically ethnocentrism has become prominent, but a world in which ethnocentrism may not exist is plausible and not opposed to human psychology. This theory, however, does not attempt to explain why ethnocentrism, with its continual tendency to exploit people from other ethnic groups (Harding et al., 1969), has been so widespread across history and ethnic groups. Nevertheless, given that categorisation into ethnic ingroups and outgroups has become prominent and that ethnocentrism is so pervasive, other approaches and related interventions have been developed to ameliorate this categorisation in order to reduce ethnocentrism and prejudice.

These approaches assume that with a rearrangement of social factors, ethnocentrism may decrease and disappear. Certain theorists have argued that social factors that predispose people to perceive others as individuals and not group members, such as ethnic group members, may reduce ethnocentrism because these factors remove the categorisation process behind it, and previously perceived ethnic ingroup and outgroup members may be perceived as unique and separate individuals (Brewer & Miller, 1984). Other theorists have argued that social factors that predispose people to cross-categorisation, that is, to focus on ways in which outgroup members may be ingroup members on certain dimensions, may also mitigate ethnocentric biases (Crisp, Ensari, Hewstone, & Miller, 2003; Migdal, Hewstone, & Mullen, 1998). For example, when gender is made salient, females in an ethnic group may perceive increased self-categorisation with females in another ethnic group, and this should theoretically lead to decreased ethnocentrism.

The common group identity model (Dovidio & Gaertner, 2010; Dovidio, Gaertner, & Saguy, 2009) has argued that ingroup preferences are reduced or may disappear under the social conditions that induce people to perceive a common group identity. This happens when people recategorise themselves and members of other groups as members of a higher-order group. For example, when different ethnic groups within a country identify with the country, and stop identifying with these separate ethnic groups, ethnocentric biases may disappear. A related model, the ingroup projection model (Mummendey & Wenzel, 1999; Waldzus & Mummendey, 2004; Waldzus, Mummendey, Wenzel, & Weber, 2003; Wenzel, Mummendey, & Waldzus, 2007), assumes, however, that when groups share a higher-order ingroup category, such as citizens of one country, and when one ethnic group within that category assumes that it is more prototypical of this category than any other ethnic subgroup, then ethnocentrism and intergroup discrimination against other ethnic groups may emerge. This theory explicitly assumes that intergroup tolerance emerges with manipulating social factors that prevent people perceiving this relative ingroup prototypicality, and this can be achieved by diffusing the prototype or making it more complex.

All these theories have substantial empirical support and tend to show that intergroup attitudes, such as ethnic attitudes and ingroup preferences, can change as a result of experimental manipulations. They are explicit about the role that social factors have when it comes to categorisation and ethnocentrism, and assert that social factors interact with basic categorisation processes to influence ethnocentrism. Moreover, they assume that if social conditions are right, then changes in categorisation may produce ethnic tolerance and not ethnocentrism. Almost all research in this area, however, is experimental and finds evidence for momentary changes to attitudes, but the assumption is that if effects of social factors on social categorisation are repeated across different situations, they will produce enduring changes in attitudes (e.g., see Crisp & Turner, 2011).

A critique of theories invoking social factors

A general criticism of socialisation, normative, and social representation explanations of ethnocentrism is that they do not really explain why and how ethnocentric socialisation, norms, and social representations came about (Duckitt, 1992; Pettigrew, 1991). It is not clear why ethnocentric norms and representations have been developed so widely across cultures and time periods, and why so many people are being socialised to become ethnocentric. In addition, although early normative theorists (e.g., Cantril, 1941; Sherif, 1936/1973) stressed the role of individual differences, these are usually underemphasised. Finally, it has been argued that neither children (Aboud, 1988) nor adults (Duckitt, 1992) are passive recipients of group attitudes.

Further, much of the work in this area of social psychology is based on experimental research. Many experimental studies of ethnocentrism, however, have important problems. First, experiments tend to suffer from demand characteristics, whereby the methods of an experiment may produce particular findings, such as when participants may consciously or unconsciously conform to the experimenters. Second, social psychological experiments often ignore the role of individual differences, which in statistical analyses are often treated as error variance (Cronbach,

1957). Next, experiments often present highly artificial situations and therefore have problems with ecological validity, and it is uncertain whether their findings translate to the real world. Finally, most experiments in social psychology place participants, usually undergraduate students, in brief situations and it is unclear whether recorded changes are transitory or may extend over longer periods of time.

One idea that is undeveloped and appears unappreciated in much of the work on social factors on ethnocentrism is why ethnicity has become such a potent force and not some other group identity. Many theorists have assumed that with changes in social factors, ethnocentrism would lose its importance and would disappear over time. This thesis is not new. In fact, the thesis was popular – especially in the first half of the twentieth century. For example, writing at that time, Max Weber and other social scientists assumed that ethnicity and ethnic phenomena would disappear within a modernised and industrialised world (Eriksen, 2010). Many of these thinkers also drew on Marx's ideas about the inevitability of progress in history and about human nature. Marx, in his sixth thesis on Feuerbach, wrote that there is no fixed human nature, but that human nature "is the ensemble of the social relations" (Engels & Marx, 1888/1976, p. 63), and that if one changes this ensemble one can change human nature (Singer, 2000). As noted by Singer:

> Belief in the malleability of human nature has been important for the left because it has provided grounds for hoping that a very different kind of human society is possible. Here, I suspect, is the ultimate reason why the left rejected Darwinian thought. It dashed the left's Great Dream: The Perfectibility of Man. Since Plato's *Republic* at least, the idea of building a perfect society has been present in Western consciousness. For as long as the left has existed, it has sought a society in which all human beings live harmoniously and cooperatively with each other in peace and freedom.
>
> *2000, p. 24*

Ethnocentrism, therefore, according to this approach, can be escaped from with a change in social circumstances. Humans can be perfected to the point where they would not be ethnocentric at all. This was a guiding idea of many people on the left and, therefore, by extension, of many social scientists who have studied ethnocentrism. The idea can still be seen in modern works. Suffice to say, and contrary to Weber and others, ethnocentrism has not disappeared, but has had an extreme and violent resurgence in the twentieth and twenty-first centuries. Even in the communist countries, ruled by the elites that attempted to change people according to Marxist principles, ethnicity has remained prominent, and even in previously relatively tolerant multicultural societies such as ex-Yugoslavia, ethnic divisions have persisted and exploded into ethnic wars (Djilas, 2005; Sekulic, 2004). A recent investigation of identities among young people in ex-Yugoslavia showed that ethnic identities are still exceptionally salient, even 20 years after these wars (Pratto, Zezelj, Maloku, Turjacanin, & Brankovic, 2017). Further, ethnocentrism is now also having a resurgence in many Western countries, such as the US and Europe, where politicians promoting ethnocentrism and anti-immigration sentiments have become increasingly popular. For example, Donald Trump has become US president largely based on his support for ethnocentric policies. It appears that the powerful force of ethnicity and ethnocentrism has been thoroughly underestimated by both Marxists and Western liberals (cf. Gellner, 1994). The thesis that social factors can fully ameliorate ethnocentrism appears to have been falsified thus far.

There are, however, many theorists who have assumed that ethnocentrism is an aspect of human nature and is almost universally found across ethnic groups, and complete ethnic tolerance is difficult, if not impossible, to achieve. Many of the theorists who have claimed that ethnocentrism is most likely to be with humans for a very long time have emphasised the role of biology and evolution in creating ethnocentrism. I will discuss these explanations in the next section.

Explanations invoking biology and evolution

It is often assumed that the widespread prevalence or even universalism of ethnocentrism is due to its origin in the human evolutionary and biological makeup (D. E. Brown, 1991, 2000, 2004; D. Jones, 2000; MacDonald, 2001; Salter, 2007; van den Berghe, 1978, 1999). Not only does ethnocentrism exist across cultures, but early forms of ethnocentrism appear in infants, even newborns, who can discriminate between native and foreign languages, and show a certain amount of ethnocentrism reflected in preferences for their own native language over foreign languages (Kinzler, Dupoux, & Spelke, 2007; Mehler et al., 1988; Moon, Cooper, & Fifer, 1993).

D. E. Brown (2000) wrote: "Any pattern that might on the surface appear possibly to be sociocultural and that occurs in unrelated societies raises the question of whether its multiple occurrences are coincidental or whether some nonsociocultural causation is at work" (p. 163). He argued that it is improbable that complex universals, such as ethnocentrism, are coincidental, and maintained that they are more likely to be part of human nature, that is, that they are part of our genetic makeup. D. E. Brown (2004) argued that many universals, given their complexity, do not have an individual, but a group, referent. For example, although not every person dances, dancing is universal across human groups. The same can be said for ethnocentrism: although ethnocentrism has existed across societies for a long time, not every person who has ever lived has been ethnocentric and many individuals may have completely rejected ethnocentrism. This may explain why ethnocentrism appears to be found across groups and time periods even though many individuals may strongly reject ethnocentrism.

In the first part of this section, I will discuss biological approaches to ethnocentrism. These are unified in the assumption that ethnocentrism has different biological underpinnings, such as genes, hormones, and brain regions. The personality trait approach will also be discussed here because it assumes that personality traits are inherited and genetic. Subsequently, I will discuss evolutionary approaches to ethnocentrism.

Biological approaches

A number of researchers have assumed that genetic differences in ethnocentrism underlie expressions of ethnocentrism. This research, when it comes to ethnocentrism, is still in its infancy. There are two main bodies of research that have investigated this. The first is indirect, and based on twin research, which shows that monozygotic twins, who share 100% of genes, tend to be more similar in their ethnocentric attitudes than dizygotic twins, who share 50% of genes (e.g., Lewis & Bates, 2017; Lewis, Kandler, & Riemann, 2014; Orey & Park, 2012). A study (Lewis & Bates, 2017) using a 10-year longitudinal twin research design has demonstrated that there is a lot of stability in ingroup, including ethnic ingroup, favouritism. Furthermore, this research suggested that the stability was mostly due to genetic influences, whereas changes in these attitudes were mostly due to non-shared environmental influences. This research implies that temporal stability in ethnocentrism at the individual level may be primarily because of biological factors, that is, genes, and not because of stable social environments.

The body of research using twin designs is, however, indirect because it does not explicitly study genes. There is, unfortunately, little research that connects genes with ethnocentrism. One such study (Dutton, Madison, & Lynn, 2016) has shown that at the national level, frequencies of DRD4a dopamine receptor gene repeats of seven and seven-or-eight times were associated with a measure of ethnic purity (i.e., rejection and avoidance of immigrants and racial outgroups), whereas CAG repeats on the AR gene were associated with a measure of devotion (i.e., readiness to fight for one's country).

Researchers have also attempted to link neurochemistry to ethnocentrism. The main candidate for causing ethnocentrism appears to be oxytocin, which acts as a hormone and neurotransmitter. Theorists have assumed that oxytocin has been essential for human evolution, especially the evolution of human cortex, bonds with other humans, and complex sociality (Carter, 2014). It is also argued that evolution, possibly through the effects of oxytocin, has influenced people to become accepted and respected members of social groups that they serve (De Dreu & Kret, 2016).

Oxytocin has numerous functions, many of which are pro-social. However, it has limits in its pro-social effects. Research suggests that oxytocin administration can predispose people to pro-social behaviours (including personally costly or unethical behaviours) and attitudes towards ingroup, but not outgroup, members (e.g., preferences for the Dutch over Arabs and Germans among Dutch participants) – though it can also predispose people to outgroup negativity in threatening contexts (De Dreu, 2012; De Dreu, Greer, Kleef, Shalvi, & Handgraaf, 2011; De Dreu & Kret, 2016). It appears, however, that oxytocin does not lead to indiscriminate preferences for the ingroup. One study in China (Ma et al., 2014), for example, found that oxytocin administration led Chinese participants to prefer social stimuli and the Chinese flag over social stimuli and flags of several other Asian countries, but not to prefer non-social stimuli, such as Chinese buildings, monuments, money, and cars. It has been argued that oxytocin appears to enhance positivity towards the ingroup because it reinforces positive interactions, which are more likely to be with ingroups than with outgroups (Bethlehem, Baron-Cohen, van Honk, Auyeung, & Bos, 2014).

Researchers have also attempted to link different brain regions to intergroup biases. One study (Baumgartner, Schiller, Rieskamp, Gianotti, & Knoch, 2014) showed that a larger volume in the temporal-parietal junction (TPJ) and the dorsomedial prefrontal cortex (DMPFC) related to less intergroup bias. A follow-up study (Baumgartner, Nash, Hill, & Knoch, 2015) showed that increased white matter integrity at the right TPJ and its stronger connectivity with the DMPFC related to decreased intergroup bias, possibly because these brain regions predisposed people to equally mentalise ingroup and outgroup members. Research also yields support for the view that the amygdala may be involved in ingroup preferences, but its exact effects are not yet clear (Cikara & Van Bavel, 2014).

Personality traits

When it comes to biological approaches to ethnocentrism, it may well be that personality traits mediate the impact of genetic and other biological influences upon ethnocentrism. Allport (1937), the father of trait theory, argued that personality traits exist as biological structures within the nervous system and cause people's behaviour across a variety of situations. Although there are many potential personality traits (Allport & Odbert, 1936), at present the most influential view is that there are five basic (also called the Big Five) personality traits which can explain the variation in personality traits across all humans (John, Naumann, & Soto, 2008). These are: (1) neuroticism, which is an individual tendency to experience negative and uncomfortable emotions; (2) extraversion, a tendency to be energetic, sociable, assertive, and action-oriented; (3) openness to experience, a tendency to be curious, imaginative, intellectual, appreciative of art and beauty, and open to change and different kinds of emotions; (4) agreeableness, a tendency to be willing to cooperate, get along with others, help others, compromise with others, be honest, considerate, and helpful; and (5) conscientiousness, a tendency to be self-disciplined, achievement-oriented, hard-working, careful, organised, and reliable. These five traits are conceptualised as higher-order, broad, and general personality traits, but each also consists of numerous lower-order, narrow, and specific traits.

Although there is disagreement among psychologists about the origins of personality traits, many theorists and researchers have claimed that personality traits have origins in biological and genetic processes. This is especially the case in the Five-Factor Model of personality, which explains the nature, characteristics, causes, and consequences of the five basic personality traits (Costa & McCrae, 1992; McCrae, 2010; McCrae & Costa, 2008). This theory argues that these five basic traits are endogenous basic tendencies, caused by genetic and biological factors. The theory argues that personality traits are highly resistant to change, and that they may change only when the biological bases of the traits change. Theorists who subscribe to this view cite evidence from twin studies, which consistently show much larger correlations between personality traits for monozygotic than dizygotic twins (Bouchard & Loehlin, 2001), which suggests that personality traits are inherited. In addition, they also claim that cross-cultural replicability of the five-factor model confirms its biological origin in the human species (McCrae & Costa, 2008).

Research has also shown that different areas of the brain relate to different personality traits. For example, researchers have shown that participants' Big-Five personality scores related significantly to the relative volume of their specific brain regions (DeYoung et al., 2010). For example, conscientious participants tended to have a more developed left lateral prefrontal cortex, which is responsible for planning and decision-making. Moreover, the findings that personality traits are highly consistent over time – especially in adulthood – point to their biological basis (McCrae & Costa, 2008).

So, how do personality traits relate to ethnocentrism? There is a lot of evidence in fact that they do relate to a variety of attitudes, including social, political, and ethnic attitudes (e.g., Akrami & Ekehammar, 2006; Ekehammar & Akrami, 2007; Jost, 2006; Kandler, Bleidorn, & Riemann, 2012; Sibley & Duckitt, 2008). Possibly the personality trait most relevant to ethnocentrism is openness to experience, because people who are low on this trait tend to lack curiosity, are closed to change, and are generally less interested in a variety of experiences. Accordingly, people with these personalities may be less likely to appreciate the diversity of individuals within and between ethnic groups. In addition, people who are low on openness to experience are likely to simplify their social world, to be cognitively rigid and intolerant of ambiguity, and these variables tended to be related to variables that resemble both intergroup and intragroup facets of ethnocentrism (Budner, 1962; Stangor & Thompson, 2002). Further, low agreeableness, with its uncooperativeness and lack of consideration for other people, appears likely to predispose people to higher levels of intergroup ethnocentrism. It is also plausible to expect that higher conscientiousness, with its focus on achievement, reliability, and organisation, may predispose people to ethnocentrism. These findings and expectations suggest that personality traits may, at least in part, mediate the impact of biological factors, such as genes and brain regions, on ethnocentrism. Researchers assume that biological factors, including personality traits themselves, are shaped by evolutionary factors (Penke, Denissen, & Miller, 2007). These will be discussed in the next section.

Evolutionary approaches

Original writings on ethnocentrism were influenced by Darwin's evolutionary theory, and the concept of ethnocentrism was explicitly related to anthropocentrism, or the belief that humans are special and the most important species (Gumplowicz, 1881), which evolutionary theorists heavily criticised. Darwin (1875) himself was writing on the origins of ethnocentrism when he argued that intergroup competition makes people more cooperative with ingroup members and that cooperative groups are more likely to prosper in competition with noncooperative groups. Other early evolutionary theorists have argued that ethnocentrism enhances the survival of ethnic groups. Herbert Spencer (1892a), usually categorised as a social Darwinist, argued:

> A life of constant external enmity generates a code in which aggression, conquest, revenge, are inculcated, while peaceful occupations are reprobated. Conversely, a life of settled internal amity generates a code inculcating the virtues conducing to harmonious cooperation – justice, honesty, veracity, regard for other's claims.
>
> *p. 471*

These two moral codes have evolved because they helped groups survive, and exist in both modern and non-industrial societies. Sumner (1906) also accepted these ideas in his discussions of ethnocentrism. Though belonging to a different evolutionary tradition to social Darwinists, who emphasised that competition is at the core of human nature, Kropotkin (1902), who emphasised that cooperation is at the core, also argued that this double morality has existed in humans for a long time. Most early theorists of ethnocentrism were generally less concerned with the cooperative nature of humans than Kropotkin was, and assumed that intergroup competition and conflict are essential for survival. These ideas, however, became unpopular because of generally poor scientific support and even more because of the real-world consequences of such beliefs, such as the perceived meaningless-ness of world wars and the atrocities committed by the Nazis, who subscribed to a crude version of social Darwinism. One of the rare theorists still espousing these ideas in the mid-twentieth century was Keith (1948), who argued that group sur-vival is possible only when intragroup cooperation and intergroup competition are combined and in balance. Otherwise, Keith assumed, too much cooperation or too much competition is detrimental to group survival. Evolutionary explanations of ethnocentrism, however, started to gain more prominence in the 1970s, and they are still popular. I will outline several prominent explanations here.

Recently, using computer simulations of evolution, researchers have attempted to find out whether ethnocentrism appears to be an evolutionarily useful strategy for people. For example, Hammond and Axelrod (2006) produced an evolu-tionary simulation model that showed that ethnocentrism, operationalised as in-group favouritism, which involves cooperating with an agent of the same colour (an ingroup member), but defecting from agents of a different colour (outgroup members), tends to be selected as the preferred strategy. The other strategies were defection against both ingroup and outgroup members, indiscriminate coop-eration, or defection against ingroup members, but cooperation with outgroup members. These researchers showed that ethnocentric strategies appear particu-larly useful while interacting with others, and argued that these sustain cooperation with ingroup members when there are no other external mechanisms to sustain it, such as social norms and institutions. Bausch's (2015) agent-based simulation that modified Hammond and Axelrod's model showed that interactions with closely related people from the same ethnic group, and not group membership as such, leads to ethnocentrism. Another simulation (De, Gelfand, Nau, & Roos, 2015) replicated the original findings of Hammond and Axelrod, but showed that with increased mobility, agents are more likely to treat other agents as individuals than group members, indicating a lack of ethnocentrism. The research supplements these findings by showing that US states with more mobile populations tend to be less ethnocentric. All these models suggest that ethnocentrism has been an evolution-arily useful strategy for humans, but the last model questions its inevitability.

Another prominent explanation that draws attention to evolutionary causes of ethnocentrism assumes that ethnocentrism is caused in part by avoiding dis-ease, pathogens, and parasites (Faulkner, Schaller, Park, & Duncan, 2004; Fincher & Thornhill, 2012; Navarrete & Fessler, 2006; Navarrete, Fessler, & Eng, 2007). The main idea is that in human ancestral environments humans would find interactions with outgroups more risky than interactions with ingroups because ingroup members are more likely to have the antibodies towards pathogens that exist in ingroup members than towards those in outgroup members. Accordingly, the threat of infection and disease is greater when interacting with outgroup members. A related, complementary explanation is that ill people are more likely to receive help and care from ingroup members than from outgroup members. Consequently, as a result of pathogen threat, people may reject outgroups and become more focused on the ingroup (Navarrete & Fessler, 2006).

Research shows that participants who report that they are susceptible to illnesses, and those who are primed with susceptibility to illnesses, tend to oppose immigra-tion of people from subjectively perceived foreign ethnic groups (Faulkner et al., 2004). Related research (Navarrete & Fessler, 2006) showed that participants who report that they are susceptible to illness also tended to score highly on an ethno-centrism scale. The same research also found that after being primed with disgust sensitivity, which makes pathogen threat salient, participants became more positive towards the ingroup member who praised the ingroup. Finally, research has also shown that pregnant women's intergroup bias appeared to be highest in the first tri-mester, when there is most threat of disease to the developing offspring, and that it becomes reduced in the second and third trimester (Navarrete et al., 2007). All these findings appear to suggest that the link of pathogen threat to ethnocentrism may have evolutionary roots. It should be noted, though, that there is more support for the view that pathogen threat may predispose people to intergroup avoidance, and less that it can directly make people more loyal to their ingroup (Cashdan, 2012).

Sociobiological theory

Possibly the most elaborate attempt to explain ethnocentrism using evolutionary principles is based on sociobiological theory (E. O. Wilson, 1975), proposing that ethnocentrism is an extension of the basic mechanism underlying kin selection. Van den Berghe's sociobiological theory applied to ethnocentrism illustrates this approach well (van den Berghe, 1978, 1981, 1995, 1999). He relied on the ideas that it is beneficial for animals to cooperate with each other and that the major genetic mechanism for cooperation is the kin selection that maximises inclusive fitness. The theory of inclusive fitness (Hamilton, 1964) proposes that genes can be transmitted to descendants through both direct and indirect reproduction. Indirect reproduction is the reproduction of relatives, who have the same genes. Animals tend to cooperate with those genetically related to them and tend to favour their kin over non-kin. Altruism towards non-kin is perceived to be biologically pointless, and humans, as animals, also tend to behave in this way, preferring those who are more genetically related to them over those who are less related to them. This theory explains altruistic acts that humans perform on behalf of other biologically related humans. Evolution has favoured individuals who have engaged in kin-based preferences, and therefore kin-based selection has become part of our biological nature.

Van der Berghe, however, also claimed that humans have extended their kinship groups to their ethnic groups. So, the central thesis, here, is that ethnicity is the extension of kinship and that ethnic sentiments are fundamentally extensions of sentiments surrounding kin selection. Van den Berghe (1978) noted that "ethnocentrism evolved during millions, or at least hundreds of thousands of years as an extension of kin selection" (p. 404). It was evolutionarily useful to extend kin groups to ethnic groups, and ethnocentric societies were more likely to survive than non-ethnocentric societies. Ethnic groups are to a certain extent human super-families: they are breeding populations and include kin groups that intermarry (van den Berghe, 1999). So, ethnocentrism could be seen as an extension of kin selection, in the sense that ingroup cooperation, self-sacrifice, and group selfishness all stem from the same processes of nepotism, kin selection, and inclusive fitness.

Van den Berghe (1995) maintained that the myth of common descent of ethnic groups, though a myth, is still based on the fact that members of ethnic groups share certain biological features. Furthermore, the widespread prohibitions against intermarriage with other ethnic groups have enhanced biological interrelatedness within an ethnic group. Ethnic groups tend to stress cultural differences, such as language, and not biological differences, because they want to differentiate from similar-looking neighbours (van den Berghe, 2012). Finally, van den Berghe (1995) claimed that though nepotism is weaker and more diluted in large-scale groups (because there is less kinship in such groups) than in nuclear or extended families, its principle is still present.

There is another theory, which more strongly emphasises the genetic basis of ethnocentrism than the theory proposed by van den Berghe. Genetic similarity theory (Rushton, 1989, 2005) proposes that at the core of human nature is preference for the genetically similar. People tend to prefer those who are similar to themselves at the phenotypical level because that level signifies that people are similar at the genetic level. Accordingly, people are more likely to prefer, cooperate with, and help others who appear similar to themselves in both physical and psychological features because they assume that those are genetically similar to themselves. Rushton claimed that people maximise inclusive fitness when they engage in ethnocentrism, and that ethnic identity is based on altruistic biology because of a larger genetic similarity within than between ethnic groups. Rushton (2005) writes: "If a fellow ethnic looks like you, then on average, he or she is genetically equivalent to a cousin" (p. 499). As people have particularly strong genetic interest in their ethnic group, they tend to particularly value that group over other ethnic groups. This theory finds support in a large body of research showing that similarity is extremely important for human preferences, and that people are even more likely to prefer others who are more similar to themselves on more heritable traits than on less heritable traits.

Similarly, MacDonald (2001) assumed that those processes that lead people to favour ingroups over outgroups benefit people not only socially, but also genetically. He claimed that the natural sense of "we-ness" is more likely to exist in ethnic groups than in other groups because of genetic similarities, and possibly because there may be an evolved racial/ethnic module which makes people more likely to categorise people into racial/ethnic groups. These are, according to MacDonald, reasons why ethnic groups are still with us and unlikely to disappear.

Finally, it is important to point out that although Edward O. Wilson's work has influenced work on kin selection, he later proposed a different theoretical approach, group selection, which is also relevant to ethnocentrism (E. O. Wilson, 2012). The idea of group selection is old and can be found in Darwin's writings. The main idea is that natural selection can also work at the group level and that the characteristics that benefit groups can be selected for. For example, although altruistic cooperation and self-sacrifice may not benefit the organism, they may benefit the organism's larger group. For example, a group that is united, cohesive, and cooperative benefits from individuals who are altruistic and self-sacrifice for their group, and therefore would be more likely to survive than other groups without these characteristics. Accordingly, traits that benefited the group (e.g., in competition with other groups) would be more likely to be passed on to future generations. E. O. Wilson (2012) claimed that due to group selection, certain brain areas have developed to give rise to people's groupishness. He wrote: "In fact, it seems clear that so deeply ingrained are the evolutionary products of group-selected behaviors, so completely a part of the contemporary human condition are they, that we are prone to regard them as fixtures of nature, like air and water" (E. O. Wilson, 2014, p. 30).

Theorists who advocate this view assume that natural selection works at multiple levels, including the group level, and this can explain why traits that benefit groups, individuals, and genes can all be naturally selected. It is important to note that group selection is different to kin selection, which operates at the level of genes and not at the group level (Dawkins, 1979). Nonetheless, other have argued that there is no fine line between the two when it comes to human evolution because for much of human evolution groups consisted of closely biologically related individuals (Gat, 2010).

A critique of theories invoking biology and evolution

There are important problems with biological and evolutionary explanations. First, twin research does not control well for many non-genetic factors in human prenatal and postnatal development (Joseph, 2004, 2015; Suhay, Kalmoe, & McDermott, 2007). Even if genes do have an effect on ethnocentrism, that effect is often complex because genes often interact with other genes and the environment, which includes other individuals and social groups, in producing psychological and behavioural outcomes (Cikara & Van Bavel, 2014; Manuck & McCaffery, 2014). Organisms, including human organisms, tend to be different from others within the species not only because of genes, but also because of variable biological processes and those relating to the organism's reactions to the environment (Bateson, 2015).

The work on the role of oxytocin in human social behaviour has also been criticised because effects of oxytocin found in studies tend to be generally weak (Bartz, Zaki, Bolger, & Ochsner, 2011), and often non-existent (Lane, Luminet, Nave, & Mikolajczak, 2016), indicating a more complex interplay of oxytocin with dispositional and situational factors (Bartz et al., 2011). In addition, research into the role of oxytocin on ethnocentrism is based on external administration of oxytocin, and it is unclear whether endogenous oxytocin has the same causal effects on ethnocentrism. Further, research linking different brain regions appears mainly descriptive and is not conclusive about whether brain regions may shape ethnocentrism, or whether ethnocentrism, caused by socialisation, has shaped these brain regions in a particular way.

Critics of evolutionary theory have claimed that mechanisms that enable the extension of kin selection to ethnic groups have not been elucidated (A. D. Smith, 2001). They also argued that it is difficult to separate the role of genes and culture in ethnocentrism – especially in large contemporary groups (Dawson, 1996). Other critics claimed that central elements of sociobiological explanations are often not testable (Ross, 1991), that rigorous scientific investigation in this area is challenging (McEvoy, 2002), and that alternative explanations of the data are often equally plausible, with some data (e.g., hostility, non-cooperation, and destruction within kin groups) even contradicting the theory (Ross, 1991). Finally, the theory of group selection is controversial, with most contemporary evolutionary theorists rejecting it (Barash, 2007). Nevertheless, M. B. Smith (1992) acknowledged that "ethnocentrism ... may well have biological roots in human evolution, although not necessarily of the sort assumed by the biodeterministic pessimists" (p. 84).

It is, however, important to note that many evolutionary theorists are not biodeterministic pessimists. For example, van den Berghe (1999) asserted that ethnicity although rooted in genes can be easily manipulated. E. O. Wilson (1978) claimed that although our behaviour is strongly influenced by genes, it does not fully determine our actions. Similarly, Dawkins (1989) wrote that even though we are "gene machines", we do not have to behave in line with our genes and can resist them. Our understanding of this genetic influence on our behaviour can enable us to behave in a way that may be opposite to what our genes predispose us to do. Nonetheless, Singer (2000), who advocated a form of Darwinism, still argued that phenomena concerned with ethnicity and ethnocentrism are only somewhat variable across cultures, and although ethnic tolerance can be widespread in a society, it is not difficult for demagogues to make ethnic issues salient.

It is important to point out that there is a group of theories that propose different versions of cultural evolution, which is distinct from biological evolution. What they all have in common is the view that culture is inherited because people acquire beliefs, values, norms, and practices through social learning, and then pass their culture to their descendants (Boyd & Richerson, 1985, 1987). Accordingly, cultural evolution is ultimately about selection of practices and norms, but not genes (Dawson, 1996) – although many theorists assume also that culture and genes interact, and that it is not impossible that cultural evolution may shape genes when the pressures of cultural selection do not change over many years (Haidt, 2007).

For example, cultural evolution can explain the phenomenon of disease avoidance. People may have learned over millennia that ethnocentrism has been useful to prevent diseases, and people incorporated ethnocentrism in norms and values to prevent diseases, but this worked entirely at the cultural, and not biological, level. Navarrete et al. (2007) maintained that an interaction is also possible, and that the association of cultural/ethnic groups with disease threat may be an interaction of biology, social learning, and historical experiences of cultural groups.

Discussion

Ethnocentrism is found across almost all human groups – both modern and pre-industrial – and it is improbable that it is coincidental. It is, however, not found in every person, and in certain situations, especially in oppressed and lower-status ethnic groups, ethnocentrism is less likely to exist – and this is why certain theorists contested and questioned its universality (Hagendoorn, 1995; Tajfel, Jahoda, Nemeth, Campbell, & Johnson, 1970; Tajfel, Jahoda, Nemeth, Rim, & Johnson, 1972). Nevertheless, no one has contested that it is extraordinarily widespread. Thus, it is difficult to say whether ethnocentrism emerged just because of social factors, such as socialisation and social norms, having similar effects across many ethnic groups and across many time periods, possibly due to its cultural evolution resulting from ethnic groups facing similar environmental problems. It is also difficult to say whether ethnocentrism emerged because evolution has affected our biological makeup, and has wired ethnocentrism into our genes. It is most likely that over the long evolution of our species both cultural and genetic evolution interacted in creating a species prone to ethnocentrism and its six dimensions.

The power of ethnocentrism has waxed and waned over time, but it has not gone away. Around 30 years ago, Hamburg (1986) wrote: "The world is now, as it has been for a long time, awash in a sea of ethnocentrism, prejudice, and violent conflict" (p. 533). Few observers of the world today would disagree with what Hamburg wrote in 1986. For example, at the time that I write this chapter, Donald Trump is US president, following a successful campaign for US presidency, which rested on pandering to the ethnocentric views of Anglo/White-Americans. Similarly, the 2016 Brexit vote in the UK appears to be driven by ethnocentric sentiments. Accordingly, although ethnocentrism, prejudice, and violent conflict are possibly less pervasive today than 100 or 1000 years ago (Pinker, 2011), we certainly do not live in a world free from ethnocentrism, and it is questionable that we ever will live in such a world.

Given this pervasiveness and possible inevitability of ethnocentrism, research reviewed in this chapter tells us that humans, although pre-wired for ethnocentrism, are not necessarily likely to be extremely ethnocentric unless social factors exert a strong influence upon them. As was observed, "culture does have an influence in sharpening or softening even those tendencies that are most deeply rooted in our human nature" (Singer, 2000, p. 37). This is the most likely solution for the problem of ethnocentrism. Ethnocentrism, as long as it is controlled by individual and social factors, may be subdued. This is not the best solution to the problem of ethnocentrism, but it is the most likely one.

Summary and conclusions

This chapter first reviewed a number of theoretical approaches linking social factors to the development of ethnocentrism. There is empirical support for the view that social factors could increase or decrease people's levels of ethnocentrism. This is not surprising given that ethnocentrism is an attitude, and there is a lot of research showing that attitudes can be affected by external influences. Given its universality across cultures and time periods, it is highly unlikely that ethnocentrism is entirely a social construction shaped by the social environment. Biological and evolutionary explanations reviewed in this chapter make a strong argument that ethnocentrism is ultimately shaped by biological and evolutionary factors over millions of years. None of the evolutionary theorists have assumed that ethnocentrism cannot be modified by social environment. Theory and research coming from the biological and evolutionary approaches, as well as cross-cultural and historical evidence of the universality of ethnocentrism, appear convincing in the argument that ethnocentrism is not entirely shaped by social factors. It is most likely that the interaction between cultural and biological evolution is responsible for the observed almost near universality of ethnocentrism across the world and time periods.

5

THE CONSEQUENCES OF ETHNOCENTRISM

Ethnocentrism is an attitudinal construct. More precisely, ethnocentrism is a configuration of the six latent variables representing the six internal ethnocentric attitudes that operate in a six-dimensional space. Ethnocentrism is, therefore, a phenomenon existing within a person's head – and it predisposes the person to a variety of consequences, such as individual attitudes and behaviours. Ethnocentric attitudes can be shared within a group – and a group consisting of many individuals with high levels of ethnocentrism would most often, though not always, be an ethnocentric group. In this chapter, I will discuss possible consequences of ethnocentrism. As mentioned before, ethnocentrism has been a permanent feature of ethnic groups, even though there have always been individuals who are low on ethnocentrism, ethnically tolerant, or anti-ethnocentric. It is important to note that being ethnocentric does not automatically mean that the individual will automatically engage in all the consequences.

Racism and nationalism as consequences of ethnocentrism

Both racism and nationalism are in part consequences of ethnocentrism. For example, D. E. Brown (2004) wrote: "The virulent nationalisms and racisms of modern times may well be 'hypertrophies' of an ethnocentrism that for many millennia played itself out on a much smaller scale" (p. 54). Both racial groups and national groups have often been implicated in ethnocentrism. Racial groups could be seen as a particular case of ethnic groups (Williams, 1994), in which certain supposed genetic phenotypical characteristics (e.g., skin colour, facial features) indicate group membership (Green & Seher, 2003). Racism, however, although similar, is usually not perceived to be equivalent to ethnocentrism. Racism, like ethnocentrism, involves the ideas of group superiority and purity, but it also involves sentiments of hostility towards other races and the belief that biological racial traits are associated with cultural, psychological, and moral traits (Rattansi, 2007). Accordingly, racism and ethnocentrism overlap to a certain extent, but are also distinct. Ethnocentrism appears to have existed since the time of early humans (Mihalyi, 1984), whereas racism is a relatively recent phenomenon, which has been prominent only in the last several centuries (Rattansi, 2007), and which has never been, and probably never will be, universal (van den Berghe, 1999). Moreover, many ethnocentric people do not necessarily tend to be racists, because for ethnocentric people racial groups may not be of central importance and their main concern is with ethnicity and not race (cf. van den Berghe, 1967).

Ethnocentrism, however, could predispose and lead people to racism, given the ethnocentric emphasis on superiority, purity, and exploitativeness. The belief in races, which is central to racism, may be fuelled by ethnocentric attitudes as racial categories have been frequently promulgated to include ethnic ingroup (e.g., White Anglos, White Germans) at the top of the hierarchy of racial categories. Accordingly, one possible consequence of ethnocentrism has been racism, but only in societies where the concept of race has existed.

Nationalism is another closely related and widely studied consequence of nationalism (Bizumic & Iino, 2017; Kellas, 1991; Rosenblatt, 1964; Worchel & Coutant, 1997). Nationalism is a modern consequence of ancient ethnocentrism in the world of nations. Patriotism may also be included as a possible consequence of ethnocentrism, but it appears to be more similar to the concept of ethnic identification or mere ingroup positivity than to the concept of ethnocentrism. Patriotism can be defined as mere positivity towards and attachment to the national group (see also Kosterman & Feshbach, 1989), and therefore is distinct from nationalism – both factorially – as items measuring nationalism and those measuring patriotism load on distinct factors and predict external variables differently (Blank & Schmidt, 2003; Karasawa, 2002; Kosterman & Feshbach, 1989). For example, nationalism in Germany predicted stronger anti-Jewish and anti-foreigner attitudes, whereas patriotism predicted stronger pro-Jewish and pro-foreigner attitudes. Accordingly, patriotism is also distinct from ethnocentrism – in a similar way that ethnocentrism is distinct from ethnic identity. Nevertheless, the concept of blind patriotism (Schatz & Staub, 1997; Schatz et al., 1999; Staub, 1997) comes close to the devotion facet of ethnocentrism; however, the focus of blind patriotism is on one's own national group, and the focus of devotion is on one's own ethnic group.

Ethnocentrism, therefore, appears to have much more in common with nationalism than with patriotism. Ethnocentrism is indeed similar to nationalism, and all the expressions of ethnocentrism could be easily attributed to nationalism – but at the level of a national group. Although nationalism has been defined in many ways, the main theme in most definitions is a paramount and central concern with a nation (A. D. Smith, 2010). Similarly, when it comes to the measurement of nationalism in social and political psychology, nationalism has often been seen as a sense of national superiority and dominance (Kosterman & Feshbach, 1989) or as blind and uncritical devotion to one's nation (Blank & Schmidt, 2003; Mummendey,

Klink, & Brown, 2001; Roccas, Klar, & Liviatan, 2006), and this has clear parallels with how ethnocentrism has often been defined and how I define it in this book.

Nevertheless, it is important to note that the relationship between ethnocentrism and nationalism is complex. First of all, as a modern-day phenomenon, nationalism also assumes certain factors that are not necessary for ethnocentrism. Whereas national groups are defined by the belonging to a group that inhabits or at least desires to form a national state, has a shared public culture, and historical territory, ethnic groups do not require states to be called ethnic groups, and often they may lack a shared public culture or even territory (A. D. Smith, 2010). Nationalism assumes the world of nations, which in turn assumes clear physical boundaries between nations (Billig, 1995; A. D. Smith, 2010). In addition, national boundaries change, and people may leave their nations to become citizens of other nations, but this rarely, if ever, happens in ethnic groups (Worchel & Coutant, 1997). Nationalism requires nations to be acknowledged by the international community (Billig, 1995) – nations, in fact, crave to be acknowledged by others. Ethnic groups do not crave to be acknowledged by any other ethnic groups, given that ethnocentrism is concerned with isolation (Allport, 1954) and may lead people to completely reject all other ethnic groups as unimportant. Moreover, it was not rare for ethnic groups to consider people from other groups as invisible ghosts – lacking any importance and essence (Levi-Strauss, 1976).

Thus, the relationship between ethnocentrism and nationalism is far from being unambiguous, and it can vary according to different conditions. For example, the relationship between the two would be much stronger among ethnic majority members in societies that possess ethnic as opposed to civic forms of nationalism. The large literature on nationalism suggests that there are two general kinds of nationalism: ethnic nationalism and civic nationalism (D. Brown, 1999; Miscevic, 2010; A. D. Smith, 2010). Ethnic nationalism involves ethnocentric dimensions of superiority, purity, and subordination of the individuals to the group (D. Brown, 1999), whereas the civic kind attempts to transcend ethnocentrism of the ethnic groups that constitute the national state. People who are opposed to ethnocentrism, such as people who promote multiculturalism, may be nationalistic in the sense that they may believe that their national state, including all the ethnic groups in it, is better than others and should exploit and dominate other nations. For example, a Swiss nationalist may believe in the superiority of all Swiss citizens who identify with their country – regardless of their ethnicity.

And when it comes to the territory, the relationship between ethnic and national groups, and with it, between ethnocentrism and nationalism can be very complex. Worchel and Coutant (1997) listed five common relationships between ethnic groups and national groups: (a) complete overlap between the two so that an ethnic group is completely within a nation (e.g., Japan is an approximation for this); (b) an ethnic group lives within one nation, but it also lives in one or more other nations (e.g., Koreans in South and North Korea); (c) a nation has several ethnic groups, some of which live only in that nation (e.g., New Zealand has a multi-ethnic population, with Maori living only in New Zealand); (d) an ethnic group does not have a nation, but lives in several nations (e.g., Kurds living in Iraq, Turkey and Iran, but without their own national state); and (e) a nation composed of several ethnic groups that also exist in other nations (e.g., Switzerland consists of several ethnic groups, the main being Italians, Germans, and French, who also inhabit other nations). Given these complex relationships, the link between nationalism and ethnocentrism should vary according to different circumstances. Consequently, despite the certain overlap between nations and ethnic groups, the two are distinct.

It is also important to note that nationalism, in contrast to ethnocentrism, is a recent historic phenomenon, probably not older than the eighteenth century (Kohn, 1944; Ozkirimli, 2000). Ethnocentric feelings and attitudes, such as preference for a familiar culture and group superiority, have been exploited by nationalism:

> These feelings have always existed. They do not form nationalism; they correspond to certain facts – territory, language, common descent – which we also find in nationalism … but nationalism is not a natural phenomenon … it is a product of the growth of social and intellectual factors at a certain stage of history.
>
> *Kohn, 1944, p. 6*

Accordingly, ethnocentrism can be seen as a more basic and fundamental, as well as much older, construct than its more recent historical manifestation and modification, nationalism. It is probable that given their unique and recent development, nations and national states will disappear at some point, but it is highly improbable that ethnic groups will disappear. For example, in many independent national states (e.g., in Asia and Africa) that were developed following the withdrawal of European colonialists, national states do not mean much to people and ethnic groups are more important sources of group attachment.

Nationalism, defined as an attitude, may mediate many of the effects of ethnocentrism on outcome variables dealing with national states. For example, nation-building and irredentism (which includes a nation "recovering" a territory with a large ethnic ingroup population from another nation) are largely driven by ethnocentric sentiments, but they require nationalism. In short, ethnocentrism may predispose people to nationalism, which in turn may predispose them to nation-building, irredentism, or national dominance over other nations. Nevertheless, at the core of nationalism is ethnocentrism and it is not a historic accident that national states have been constructed around an ethnic core, that is, around one ethnic group (Staerklé, Sidanius, Green, & Molina, 2010), and not around another social grouping. As pointed out above, nations that have been artificially created from many ethnic groups, and these were usually invented by external agents (principally colonial powers or world powers) or were created as a result of conquest, have rarely been cohesive. For example, in many African nations, it is ethnicity and not nationality that is of central importance. Such nations are also likely to disintegrate in times of conflict, threat, economic decline, and uncertainty.

In summary, one important consequence of ethnocentrism is nationalism. Ethnocentric sentiments cause nationalistic sentiments, but ethnocentrism is primary and nationalism is secondary. Nationalism requires the world of nations, and without such a world nationalism would disappear, whereas ethnocentrism would not. In fact, ethnocentrism does not require contact and interaction with ethnic outgroups. Accordingly, ethnic groups have been with humans since time immemorial and will no doubt continue into the future, and with them ethnocentrism will continue even when nationalism becomes a historical phenomenon. Ethnocentrism, and not nationalism, is "the end of the road" (Mihalyi, 1984, p. 107).

Behavioural consequences of ethnocentrism

Ethnocentrism is an attitude. Many researchers, mainly social psychologists, have asked whether attitudes translate into behaviours. The answer was confusing for a long time. Wicker (1969), in an influential review of the literature on the attitude-behaviour relationship, claimed that attitudes often do not lead to behaviour and that the relationship is often weak and non-significant. He concluded that an "implication of the weak attitude-behaviour relationship is that it may be desirable to abandon the attitude concept" (Wicker, 1969, p. 29). Later research, however, showed that attitudes often do translate into behaviours (Fazio & Roskos-Ewoldsen, 2005). Although general attitudes may not correlate strongly with instances of single behaviours, they may correlate strongly with a behavioural pattern. For example, a Likert-type measure of attitudes towards religiosity correlated on average only .14 with single instances of 100 religious behaviours, whereas it correlated .68 with the religious pattern, that is, with the aggregate behaviours, that is, the overall number of religious behaviours (Fishbein & Ajzen, 1974). Although the relationship between intergroup attitudes and discrimination tends to be generally weaker than for many other attitude-behaviour relationships, it is consistently statistically significant, and much stronger at the aggregate level than at the level of a single behaviour (Dovidio, Schellhaas, & Pearson, In Press).

Ethnocentrism is a broad and general attitude that gives a lot of importance to one's own ethnic group. An ethnocentric person sees their ethnic group as the centre around which everything, including the life of the person, revolves. Accordingly, ethnocentrism can be expected to relate to many behaviours that give more importance to the person's ethnic group over other groups and over individual ingroup members. As attitudes most often lead to behaviours, the main, and most widely studied, behavioural outcome of ethnocentrism is discrimination in favour of members of one's own group and against people from other ethnic groups. Although ethnocentrism, as a broad attitudinal construct, may lead to a variety of behaviours and may explain a broad behavioural pattern, every specific dimension of ethnocentrism can lead to a specific pattern of behaviours.

When it comes to intragroup ethnocentrism, both devotion and group cohesion would result in distinct behaviours. Devotion would result in performing many sacrifices for one's own ethnic group, including the ultimate sacrifice of dying for the group. Group cohesion, however, would lead people to engage in various kinds of political intolerance, such as censoring the speech of those who disagree with the views of most ethnic group members, as well as punishing, hurting, and even liquidating defectors, deviants, and ingroup traitors.

All four expressions of intergroup ethnocentrism would also have distinct behavioural consequences. First, ethnocentric preference may predispose people to discriminate in favour of the ethnic ingroup across many domains. For example, when confronted with a choice of politicians for whom to vote or romantic partners to date, or simply deciding to sit next to a person, ethnic preference would make people choose ethnic ingroup as opposed to outgroup members. Superiority may predispose people to celebrate one's own ethnic group and important events in its history, to openly glorify achievements of the ethnic group, to engage in actions that would improve the status and power of one's ethnic group, and to behave arrogantly and haughtily in relation to ethnic outgroup members. For example, many people participated in Donald Trump's rallies because he allowed them "to feel superior to those they considered 'other' or beneath them" (Hochschild, 2016, p. 163). Next, purity may predispose people to engage in various forms of social distance in relation to ethnic outgroups, such as living only in neighbourhoods that are not ethnically diverse, and marrying and having children only with ethnic ingroup members – in order to keep the blood of one's ethnic group "pure" (Sumner et al., 1928). Similarly, purity, and not hatred and hostility towards immigrants, may predispose many people to vote for political candidates and parties that promote anti-immigration policies. Finally, exploitativeness may predispose people to actively manipulate, lie to, harm, hurt, injure, and even kill ethnic outgroup members, when people perceive these actions to be in the interest of their ethnic group. All these behaviours may be caused by prejudice, hatred, and hostility, but the underlying motivation is different.

It is, therefore, important to note that many behaviours that are consequences of intergroup ethnocentrism can also be consequences of prejudice, hatred, disdain, and hostility towards ethnic outgroups. People who hate ethnic outgroups are motivated by hatred to harm and destroy the objects of hate, whereas people who are ethnocentric hurt and harm ethnic outgroups most often because they prefer their ethnic ingroups and perceive ethnic outgroups to stand in the way of ingroup interests. These outgroups may in fact even be liked, as was often the case in slave-owning societies, where paternalistic attitudes were frequent (McGary, 1998). Although outgroup hatred and ethnocentrism are intertwined, and may result in similar behaviours towards outgroups, they are theoretically and conceptually distinct, and their underlying motivations are distinct.

Ethnocentrism, as conceptualised in this book, has numerous specific behavioural consequences for political life. Ethnocentrism, but not other related constructs, such as hostility, disdain, and dislike of ethnic outgroups, may predispose people to vote for political candidates and parties that favour ethnic ingroups across diverse policies. Ethnic group membership often drives voting behaviours, with people more likely to vote for their ethnic ingroups than outgroups (e.g., Graves & Lee, 2000; Parenti, 1967). The most comprehensive investigation of consequences of ethnocentrism, conceptualised as affective and cognitive preference for one's ethnic group over other ethnic groups, on political opinion has been conducted by Kinder and Kam (2009). Studying implications of ethnocentrism for public opinion, they demonstrated empirically that:

> Across a diverse and wide-ranging set of policy domains, ethnocentrism emerges time and again as an important force in American public opinion. Protecting the homeland; dealing harshly with enemies abroad; withholding help to foreign lands; stemming the tide of immigration; pushing back against gay rights; cutting welfare while expanding social insurance; putting an end to affirmative action: in all these cases, ethnocentrism plays a significant and sizeable role.
>
> *Kinder & Kam, 2009, pp. 219–220*

Given these findings, it is not surprising that in democratic societies, where political power is, at least in part, attained through voting, many politicians strongly tap into the constituents' ethnocentrism and promote ethnocentric policies. Even though group identities tend to be fluid, and other group identities (e.g., related to religion, ideology, and class) may underlie preferences across different contexts, it can still be expected that individuals who are chronically ethnocentric may, given that they believe that their ingroup is immensely important, also chronically vote for political candidates and parties that favour the ethnic ingroup.

Prejudice and xenophobia as consequences of ethnocentrism

As pointed out earlier in the book, ethnocentrism and ethnic prejudice (or outgroup hostility, outgroup negativity, or negative outgroup attitudes) are commonly lumped together as one concept. Usually, it is not negativity towards a single ethnic outgroup that is lumped together with ethnocentrism (but see Chang & Ritter, 1976, who conceptualised ethnocentrism among Black Americans as a pro-Black and anti-White attitude), but generalised negativity towards many, most, or even all ethnic outgroups. For many scholars, outgroup hatred is the main consequence of ethnocentrism and, therefore, it is often merged with ethnocentrism, perceived as one dimension (Adorno et al., 1950; Altemeyer, 1998; Chang & Ritter, 1976). I argue here that outgroup hatred is a possible consequence of ethnocentrism given its emphasis on superiority, exploitativeness, and purity, but that ethnocentrism is conceptually distinct from outgroup hatred as shown in Chapter 2, and that at times ethnocentrism can even be associated with outgroup positivity, liking for other groups, and not prejudice. Nevertheless, under certain conditions, ethnocentrism may predispose people to outgroup hatred. It should be noted that prejudice, including ethnic prejudice, is defined in many ways, and recently, in line with other movements in psychology to broaden the meanings of negative concepts (Haslam, 2016), there has been an attempt to extend the meaning of prejudice across many more domains (Dovidio, Hewstone, Glick, & Esses, 2010; Dovidio et al., in press). Nevertheless, I define ethnic prejudice in line with work in social psychology as a negative attitude towards a particular ethnic outgroup (Stephan & Stephan, 2000) and, as such, it involves negative evaluations, including hatred, disdain, dislike, and hostility towards that group.

Xenophobia is usually defined as fear and dislike of foreigners, and it is certainly a close concept to ethnocentrism. At times, the two terms are used interchangeably (e.g., R. Brown, 1995), but they are distinct. They are similar in the sense that both xenophobia and ethnocentrism involve rejecting those who are different. Xenophobia, however, involves an amalgam of outgroup fear and hatred (Watts, 1996), and neither of these two is necessary in ethnocentrism. As mentioned, outgroup negativity, including hatred, is distinct from ethnocentrism, and, although ethnocentrism may sometimes predispose individuals to fear outgroups, it may under certain circumstances predispose them to a range of attitudes and emotions, including contempt, neutrality, pity, or even liking (cf. Duckitt, 1992; Fiske et al., 2002; Jackman, 1994; van den Berghe, 1967).

There are influential social psychological theories (e.g., Cottrell & Neuberg, 2005; Mackie, Devos, & Smith, 2000) that have claimed that, given that prejudice is a very broad construct, in order to better understand intergroup relations and attitudes, psychologists need to focus on people's distinct emotional reactions to outgroups. For example, intergroup emotions theory (Mackie et al., 2000; Mackie, Maitner, & Smith, 2016; Mackie & Smith, 2003; E. R. Smith & Mackie, 2016) claims that people can experience specific emotions towards specific groups (both outgroups and ingroups) and that these tend to be the product of people's categorisation into groups and people's appraisal of the specific nature of intergroup relations. For certain individuals, that is, high group identifiers, ingroup membership is particularly important, and they, even though individually unaffected, may strongly feel specific emotions on behalf of the group. This theory is situationist because it focuses on specific emotions felt within specific situations, and constructionist because it considers people's subjective perceptions of the events eliciting specific emotions. According to this approach, outgroups that are perceived as both strong and threatening may invoke fear. Yet, outgroups that are perceived as threatening, but not strong, may elicit anger. The important point here is that emotions are felt on behalf of the group because people self-categorise as group members and identify with others in the group. These theorists also acknowledge that people's views of the ingroup may affect the kind of emotion felt on behalf of the group.

It could be expected that individuals with chronic and specific beliefs about the importance of their ethnic group may hold specific, but chronic, negative emotions towards particular outgroups. Accordingly, although ethnocentrism may relate to prejudice, a more intricate relationship may exist between particular dimensions of ethnocentrism and specific emotions towards specific ethnic outgroups, such as ethnic minorities. For example, superiority may predispose people to feel contempt towards ethnic minorities, purity may predispose them to feel fear, and exploitativeness may predispose them to feel less sympathy.

It should be mentioned that hostility, including specific emotional reactions, may not only relate to ethnic outgroups, but can be expressed against people within one's own ethnic group. Individual ingroup members who may weaken or create disunity within the ingroup, such as those who violate and attempt to change the fundamental values, beliefs, and norms of the ethnic group, or those who are perceived to threaten the superiority and strength of the ingroup, such as the mentally ill or intellectually handicapped, may also be targets of hostility of ethnocentric individuals. Ethnocentrism may also predispose people to hostility towards ethnic deviants, such as drug addicts, gays, and lesbians. These groups may not only threaten the traditions of one's own ethnic group, but may be perceived to weaken the group. Ethnocentric individuals can also strongly dislike xenophiles, xenocentrics, and anti-ethnocentrics within one's own group. Accordingly, ethnocentric people may often dislike many ingroup members and, as mentioned in Chapter 2, they may at times derogate the whole ingroup, asserting that it has lost its true way.

Dehumanisation, delegitimisation, and moral exclusion as consequences of ethnocentrism

Ethnocentrism may also result in and extend into various perceptions of outgroups as being less than human or even non-human. This process is evident in ethnocentrism in many non-industrial societies, which often see other ethnic groups as non-human (Sumner, 1906). Gumplowicz (1883, 1887) explicitly related ethnocentrism to the view that people's current ethnic group is the best representative of the whole of humanity, and that other groups are therefore lacking at least some humanness. Erikson (1966, 1968) coined the term pseudospeciation to describe the phenomenon whereby humans categorise different ethnic human groups as different species. An example of pseudospeciation can be found in Hitler's book *Mein Kampf*, where he wrote that in the same way that it is unnatural for cats and dogs to interbreed, it is unnatural for people from different ethnic groups to interbreed (Hitler, 1925/1941). According to Levi-Strauss (1976), for many traditional ethnic groups, "Mankind stops at the frontiers of the tribe, of the linguistic group, and sometimes even of the village" (p. 329), and many outgroups are perceived to lack humanity, being called "land monkeys" or "lice eggs", or are even perceived to lack life and any substance, being called "ghosts" or "apparitions".

The process of placing human outgroups into categories with less humanity appears to be deeply ingrained in the human mind, and social psychological research shows that people in modern societies often assume that outgroups are less human than ingroups. There are numerous studies (Castano & Giner-Sorolla, 2006; Leyens et al., 2000, 2001, 2003; Perez, Rodriguez, Rodriguez, Leyens, & Vaes, 2011; Vaes, Paladino, Castelli, Leyens, & Giovanazzi, 2003) that found that people select more uniquely human emotions, including positive and negative ones (e.g., compassion, resentment, pride), when describing ingroup members than when describing outgroup members. This effect does not occur for the attribution of non-uniquely human emotions (e.g., pleasure, anger, irritation). This phenomenon is called infrahumanisation and is described as a normal social-cognitive process whereby human outgroups are perceived as less human than ingroups, but not necessarily lacking humanity. Research into infrahumanisation suggests that the perception that ingroups tend to better represent humans than outgroups do is ever-present, even in everyday situations, and appears to be part of normal social cognition.

Building on the infrahumanisation work, a related theoretical and empirical development was proposed by Haslam (2006; see also Haslam & Loughnan, 2014). It provided an integrated approach to dehumanisation by covering both weaker and subtler instances of dehumanisation, such as those covered by infrahumanisation, and the more extreme kinds, which completely strip ethnic outgroups of humanity (e.g., those used to justify genocide). Haslam's dual model of dehumanisation assumes that people engage in two forms of dehumanisation: animalistic dehumanisation and mechanistic dehumanisation. The first form of dehumanisation relates to likening other people implicitly or explicitly to animals, and perceiving them to be unrefined, unintelligent, irrational, and uncivil. The second form relates to likening other people to inanimate objects, and perceiving them to be cold, unemotional, and lifeless. Both forms of dehumanisation are closely related to ethnocentrism and research suggests that participants may engage in both kinds of dehumanisation when perceiving ethnic outgroups – although both will not always emerge at the same time. For example, a study showed that Anglo-Australians were more likely to perceive ethnic outgroups, that is, East Asians, as being closer to machines than the ethnic ingroup, that is, Anglo-Australians; however, they tended to perceive the same ethnic outgroups as less animal-like than the ethnic ingroup (Bain, Park, Kwok, & Haslam, 2009).

Another process that also covers extreme forms of dehumanisation is delegitimisation, introduced by Bar-Tal (1989, 1990, 2007, 2013) to explain the process whereby certain social groups are perceived in an exceptionally negative way. Bar-Tal explicitly linked ethnocentrism to delegitimisation. He argued that people characterise delegitimatised groups as completely separate from other social groups that behave in accordance with appropriate human norms and values. Delegitimisation is more extreme than prejudice because people can be prejudiced against social groups, but still perceive them to behave in accordance with human norms and values. It is characterised by extreme negativity, the rejection of humanity, the intense emotions of hatred, contempt, disgust, and fear, the view that the delegitimised social group is capable of extreme negative actions against the ingroup, and the belief that, given that it does not behave in accordance with human norms and values, the outgroup does not deserve to be treated as a human group.

According to Bar-Tal, people tend to delegitimise other social groups because they want to enhance their own groups, see their own groups as superior, differentiate their own groups from other groups, exploit other groups (and justify this exploitation), and increase group unity. To use the terminology of ethnocentrism from this book, one can say that delegitimisation, therefore, can be caused by ethnocentric superiority, purity, exploitativeness, and group cohesion. Bar-Tal argued that at times of conflict with another group, delegitimisation may be used to justify prejudice and harmful actions against outgroups. So, one consequence of ethnocentrism – in particular, during conflicts – is the delegitimisation of ethnic outgroups.

A related process, called moral exclusion (Opotow, 1990; Opotow, Gerson, & Woodside, 2005; Opotow & Weiss, 2000), is also a potential consequence of ethnocentrism. The concept was introduced to label the phenomenon of placing the other "outside the boundary in which moral values, rules, and considerations of fairness apply" (Opotow, 1990, p. 1). When others are morally excluded, they are perceived as psychologically highly distant from the self and undeserving. Therefore, inflicting any kind of suffering on them seems acceptable. Ethnocentrism, which gives extreme importance to one's own ethnic group, may easily lead people to morally exclude other groups which highly ethnocentric people perceive to be psychologically very distant from the self. Moral exclusion has been typically studied in relation to human groups, such as ethnic groups, but other species may also be morally excluded. In fact, people may morally exclude certain human outgroups, but not certain animal species (e.g., highly ethnocentric Hindus may morally exclude Muslims, but not animals, such as cows).

In summary, theory and research support the view that ethnocentrism underlies a variety of phenomena whereby members of other ethnic groups are infrahumanised, dehumanised, delegitimised, and morally excluded. Researchers, in fact, explicitly placed ethnocentrism as a central concept that is responsible for these phenomena (Bar-Tal, 1990; Vaes, Bain, & Leyens, 2014). Although these phenomena may relate to a variety of other social groups or even individuals, the most frequent and possibly the most extreme instances of these phenomena appear to be linked to ethnicity and ethnocentrism. This, again, suggests that ethnicity and ethnocentrism play a special role in human psychology.

Ethnic war, cleansing, and genocide as consequences of ethnocentrism

Ingroup-outgroup differentiation, with categorising certain humans as ethnic ingroup members and everyone else as ethnic outgroup members, may predispose people to ethnocentrism. Ethnocentrism may give rise to ethnic outgroup prejudice, and both may lead to discrimination, exploitation, dehumanisation, delegitimisation, and moral exclusion. All of them may facilitate the emergence of many ethnic conflicts, such as ethnic war, cleansing, violence, and ultimately genocide, which includes the complete destruction of an ethnic group. Here I will focus on three highly detrimental consequences of ethnocentrism: ethnic war, ethnic cleansing, and ethnic genocide.

Most large-scale conflicts in the world appear to be between ethnic groups and not between national states (Williams, 1994). Ethnic conflict can be defined as "confrontation between members of two or more ethnic groups" (Green & Seher, 2003, p. 511) and it, in general, involves public actions, including various warlike activities. There are many explanations of ethnic conflicts and wars (Cashman, 2013), but there is no doubt that ethnocentrism may play a role in predisposing people to warlike attitudes. This is not surprising given its focus on exploitativeness and superiority. Sumner (1911) saw close links between ethnocentrism and wars, and he discussed ethnocentrism at length in one chapter on war. Although he argued that "brotherhood within, warlikeness without … grow together, common products of the same situation" (Sumner, 1906, p. 13), empirical studies suggest (Cashdan, 2001; Ross, 1983) "warlikeness within" may often go together with "warlikeness without", that is, those ethnic groups that tend to have more intragroup conflict tend also to have more intergroup conflict. So, a more reasonable postulate is that only certain dimensions of ethnocentrism may predispose people to warlikeness.

Research with the Ethnocentrism Scale 1 has consistently found that ethnocentric individuals, and primarily those who are high on intergroup dimensions, tend to have warlike attitudes (Bizumic et al., 2009). Why is ethnocentrism related to warlikeness? The self-aggrandising attitudes in ethnocentrism may give rise to the exploitation of other ethnic groups, and when these are not achieved peacefully, then ethnic groups may engage in warfare. Second, in contemporary societies, one path from ethnocentrism to warlikeness is through nationalism. Ethnocentrism may give rise to nationalism, and nationalism may predispose people to nation-building and irredentism. These may be, at times, achieved peacefully, but often if peaceful solutions are not possible, ethnic groups may use military tactics to achieve their aims. Further, a sense of danger and fear may predispose ethnocentric people, such as leaders, to favourable attitudes towards military tactics to defend against threats.

Ethnocentrism can also result in ethnic cleansing. Bell-Fialkoff (1992) argues that it is difficult to precisely define the phenomenon of ethnic cleansing because it includes forcing people to emigrate, and also genocide. Nevertheless, he writes: "At the most general level, however, ethnic cleansing can be understood as the expulsion of an 'undesirable' population from a given territory due to religious or ethnic discrimination, political, strategic or ideological considerations, or a combination of these" (Bell-Fialkoff, 1992, p. 110). Given the preceding definition of ethnic cleansing, for example, Americans were ethnically cleansing much of the US of Indians over several centuries, but their importing of Africans into the US is not an instance of cleansing.

Ethnic cleansers may use numerous methods to create an ethnically homogeneous territory, and genocide is one such method. The other methods of ethnic cleansing are: non-violent (e.g., administrative discriminatory measures that show that certain ethnic groups are undesirable, dismissing ethnic outgroups from work, harassing ethnic outgroups), terrorising performed by civilians (e.g., shooting ethnic outgroup members, blowing up the homes of ethnic outgroup members, deporting ethnic outgroups), and military measures (e.g., executing ethnic outgroups, torturing ethnic outgroups, holding the towns of ethnic outgroups under siege) (Petrovic, 1994). Although ethnic cleansing has a long history – with the first recorded instances in Assyria – it became widespread in the nineteenth and twentieth centuries when many national states wanted to "ethnically purify" nations (Bell-Fialkoff, 1992). For example, Preece (1998) offers a long list of instances of ethnic cleansing in the twentieth century, with the most gruesome being the physical elimination of 6,000,000 Jews by Germans during the Second World War, and possibly the largest being the expulsion of 14,000,000 Germans from Eastern European countries after the war.

Although there are many reasons behind ethnic cleansing and genocide, there is no doubt that both ethnocentrism, with its insistence on ethnic superiority, purity, and exploitativeness, and ethnic prejudice, with its insistence on hatred, dislike, and disdain for ethnic outgroups, would contribute to and facilitate them. Although all six dimensions of ethnocentrism might, under certain conditions, predispose people to ethnic cleansing and genocide, the intergroup dimensions of superiority, purity, and exploitativeness appear most relevant. In fact, ethnocentric purity is closely related to ethnic cleansing because both are related to "purifying" an ethnic group with regard to ethnic outgroups. Accordingly, ethnic purity may cause ethnic cleansing, including its most negative form, genocide. Ethnic superiority may also give rise to ethnic cleansing – especially when ethnic outgroups are perceived to undermine the superiority of the ethnic ingroup. Exploitativeness, with its ruthless ignorance of other people's suffering, is also an attitude that may predispose people to ethnic cleansing and facilitate its execution.

Specific forms and consequences of ethnocentrism

Finally, ethnocentrism is a broad and general phenomenon. It can, however, predispose people to specific forms and consequences. Researchers have, for example, investigated and used the term ethnocentrism in relation to a variety of specific constructs, which represent specific forms and consequences of general ethnocentrism. For example, researchers have discussed and studied religiocentrism (Ray & Doratis, 1972) or religious ethnocentrism (Altemeyer, 2003, 2006), where ethnocentric preferences and rejection are related to religious social groups. Probably, the term religiocentrism is more suitable here than the term religious ethnocentrism because ethnicity is not central in this phenomenon. Although in most cases there is a lot of overlap between ethnocentrism and religiocentrism, this does not have to be the case. For example, in Northern Ireland, religion trumps ethnicity. Nonetheless, the process of ethnification may transform a religious group into an ethnic group, as was the case with Muslims in Bosnia. Another specific form of ethnocentrism is musical ethnocentrism (Boer et al., 2013; Elliott, 1984), related to ethnocentrism within a specific domain, music. It relates to individuals preferring to engage with the music of their own ethnic group rather than with the music of other ethnic groups. Probably, the most studied specific form of ethnocentrism is consumer ethnocentrism.

Consumer ethnocentrism

Consumer ethnocentrism has been widely studied in the marketing literature (Balabanis, Diamantopoulos, Mueller, & Melewar, 2001; Shimp & Sharma, 1987; Siamagka & Balabanis, 2015; Zeugner-Roth, Žabkar, & Diamantopoulos, 2015), and a measure of consumer ethnocentrism, the CETSCALE (Shimp & Sharma, 1987), has been described as one of the most frequently used scales in the area of marketing research (Jiménez-Guerrero, Gázquez-Abad, & Linares-Agüera, 2014). The phenomenon of consumer ethnocentrism has become particularly popular in the last several years as many countries around the world face economic difficulties and many political leaders and companies have promoted the idea that, to help their country's economy, consumers should buy local domestic products and not foreign products (Siamagka & Balabanis, 2015). Shimp and Sharma (1987) introduced the concept (including the CETSCALE), describing it as "the beliefs held by American consumers about the appropriateness, indeed morality, of purchasing foreign-made products. From the perspective of ethnocentric consumers, purchasing imported products is wrong because, in their minds, it hurts the domestic economy, causes loss of jobs, and is plainly unpatriotic" (p. 280). Although the original concept and the items were developed for US purposes, later researchers have broadened the concept to relate to any country, and later usages used the name of the relevant national state in the items, such as Korea, China, Germany, Slovenia, Austria, Turkey, and Czech Republic (Balabanis et al., 2001; Ishii, 2009; Jiménez-Guerrero et al., 2014; Sharma, Shimp, & Shin, 1995; Zeugner-Roth et al., 2015).

Consumer ethnocentrism is defined as a distinct form of ethnocentrism, which relates only to consumer and economic matters (Balabanis et al., 2001). Although consumer ethnocentrism may be used as a general concept regarding people's views about buying products from other countries or one's own country, it can also be more specific where the focus is on a particular product. For example, researchers have used a measure of consumer ethnocentrism where the target was vegetables produced by one's own or other countries (Jiménez-Guerrero et al., 2014).

Sharma et al. (1995) assumed that ethnocentrism exists to help groups and their cultures survive and enforce commitment, effectivity, and solidarity. Specifically, they assumed that consumer ethnocentrism is caused by loving one's own country and perceiving threats to the individual's and country's economic interests as a result of consuming foreign products. People's individual levels of consumer ethnocentrism are assumed to be caused by a constellation of social psychological and demographic factors (Sharma et al., 1995).

There has been much research showing that consumer ethnocentrism is a valid construct which is related to expected causes and consequences. For example, the original research in the US showed that people who score higher on the CETSCALE tend to have less positive attitudes to foreign-made products, are less likely to want to purchase foreign-made products, and are less likely to own foreign-made products than participants who score lower on the scale (Shimp & Sharma, 1987). A subsequent study in Korea by the developers of the scale (Sharma et al., 1995) showed that the social psychological factors of patriotism, conservatism, collectivism, and low cultural openness, as well as the demographic factors of gender (being female) and lower education and lower income, all tended to be positively associated with consumer ethnocentrism. In addition, this study showed that when people higher in consumer ethnocentrism believed that they or their countries were endangered by importing products, they were more likely to reject imports of 10 different products. Other studies in different countries, such as Turkey and Czech Republic (Balabanis et al., 2001), China (Ishii, 2009), and Serbia (Marinkovic, Stanisic, & Kostic, 2011), have tended to relate consumer ethnocentrism to a variety of predictors, such as gender, patriotism, nationalism, and low internationalism.

Researchers in the area have also studied a number of related constructs, such as consumer animosity, which includes dislike of foreign products (Klein & Ettenson, 1999), consumer xenocentrism, which includes attraction to foreign products (Balabanis & Diamantopoulos, 2016), and consumer cosmopolitanism, which includes openness to other countries, appreciation of the diversity caused by having available products from various countries, and positive attitude towards consuming foreign products (Riefler & Diamantopoulos, 2009; Riefler, Diamantopoulos, & Siguaw, 2012). These constructs are related to consumer ethnocentrism, with consumer animosity positively related to it, and consumer xenocentrism and consumer cosmopolitanism negatively related to it, but appear to be constructs conceptually and empirically distinct from consumer ethnocentrism. None of these constructs have, however, received as much attention as consumer ethnocentrism.

There are several problems with the concept and measurement. For example, the dimensionality of the original scale has not been demonstrated well, with different studies demonstrating different factor solutions (see Jiménez-Guerrero et al., 2014; Siamagka & Balabanis, 2015). This led researchers to propose a new multidimensional measure of ethnocentrism, the Consumer Ethnocentrism Extended Scale (CEESCALE), which appears to be a promising measure of the construct (Siamagka & Balabanis, 2015).

Nevertheless, the central conceptual problem is that the focus of consumer ethnocentrism is on national states, and not on ethnic groups. Although most countries are formed around an ethnic core (Staerklé et al., 2010), and certain countries are almost entirely ethnically homogeneous, consumer ethnocentrism appears closer to nationalism and patriotism than to ethnocentrism. The items of the original measure tap both preference for domestic products, devotion to buying domestic products, rejection of imported products, and the belief that people in one's own country should put the country's economic interests as primary.

Nonetheless, consumer ethnocentrism does appear relevant to ethnocentrism as defined in this book and should be seen as a relevant outcome of ethnocentrism, at least among ethnic majority groups. It is, however, most likely that ethnocentrism may predispose people to nationalism, which in turn may predispose them to consumer ethnocentrism. Accordingly, although consumer ethnocentrism is an outcome of ethnocentrism, at least among ethnic majority participants, its effect appears to be indirect and expressed through both intragroup and intergroup kinds of nationalism.

Summary and conclusions

This chapter discussed possibly the most important consequences of ethnocentrism. Ethnocentrism appears to give rise to racism, with its emphasis on preference, superiority, purity, and exploitativeness, and to nationalism, which is a modern consequence of ancient ethnocentrism in the world of nations. Ethnocentrism, as an attitude, tends to lead to specific behaviours, such as discriminatory behaviours in favour of one's own ethnic group. It also has an important role in political life and may predispose people to support and vote for political candidates who promote social policies that favour the ethnic ingroup and its interests. Moreover, ethnocentrism, although distinct from outgroup hatred or prejudice, may under certain conditions lead to it. It can also lead to specific intergroup emotions, such as fear and contempt. Ethnocentrism can also predispose people to the dehumanisation, delegitimisation, and moral exclusion of ethnic outgroups. Possibly the most frequent and gruesome forms and instances of dehumanisation, delegitimisation, and moral exclusion are related to ethnicity. Ethnocentrism could also fuel ethnic wars, ethnic cleansing, and even the genocide of ethnic outgroups. Finally, ethnocentrism can be expressed in specific forms and consequences, such as consumer ethnocentrism.

Ethnocentrism, therefore, appears to be a fundamental driver of different kinds of attitudes, emotions, and behaviours. Ethnocentrism, as an ancient phenomenon, still has a powerful grasp on the human mind in contemporary societies, and is driving many phenomena. It is, therefore, not surprising that many politicians tap into ethnocentrism to garner support, popularity, and influence. The presented conceptualisation of ethnocentrism, which sees it as a complex multidimensional construct, offers a fruitful approach for the study of its consequences, given that different dimensions of ethnocentrism may lead to specific outcomes.

6

INTEGRATING THE CAUSES AND CONSEQUENCES

I showed in the previous three chapters that theorists and researchers have proposed numerous causes of ethnocentrism and linked ethnocentrism to numerous possible consequences. I also presented a critique of the literature. In this section I will integrate the causes and consequences to explain the concept of ethnocentrism as defined in this book. The theoretical approaches discussed before had a variety of views of what ethnocentrism involves, and they did not see ethnocentrism in the same way as I defined it in this book.

An important implication of the current perspective is that ethnocentrism is not just a simple unidimensional phenomenon of ingroup positivity motivating outgroup hatred. It is also not just ingroup bias. It is a more complex phenomenon comprising six distinct facets and two major higher-order factors or expressions. In the first section, I will present the results of previously unpublished empirical studies, which have related different versions of the Ethnocentrism Scale 1 and 2 to numerous causes and consequences. I will then explain how a person becomes ethnocentric, and how ethnocentrism predisposes people to numerous consequences. I will, finally, argue that ethnocentrism is largely based on the need to strengthen one's own ethnic group.

Empirical studies of the causes and consequences of reconceptualised ethnocentrism

The previous chapters included many causes and consequences of ethnocentrism. Here I will be focusing on empirical research where different, mainly the 36-item and 12-item, versions of the Ethnocentrism Scale 1 and 2 were used in surveys with relatively large samples. This research has studied ethnocentrism in many thousands of participants from different, primarily English-speaking, countries, and used survey methods. Most participants were internet-based community samples, and the two main samples were from two websites, YourMorals.Org and CrowdFlower. There were also several samples from Australia, including both community and student samples.

It should be noted that there are a number of causes and consequences that I have not studied or could not study empirically, and whether these do relate to ethnocentrism will be discussed later in the chapter. For example, the role of elites, genes, or biology has not been studied here – although some of these could be inferred from the findings. For example, if there are significant effects of personality traits on ethnocentrism, it is most likely that biology plays a role given ample evidence that personality traits have biological origins. Likewise, how exactly reconceptualised ethnocentrism results in ethnic wars, ethnic cleansing, or genocide is difficult, if not impossible, to study, but this can be inferred from the relationships of the six dimensions of ethnocentrism with certain attitudes and support for specific policies. For example, if ethnocentric people are favourable to wars and opposed to peace, and if they favour policies that aim to reduce the number of ethnic minority people in their countries, then one can say that ethnocentrism may contribute to ethnic wars, ethnic cleansing, and possibly under certain circumstances to ethnic genocide.

I will first focus on causes and then on consequences of ethnocentrism. It is not, however, easy to differentiate causes from consequences. For example, there may be feedback loops whereby causes may also become consequences: for example, people who have little contact with ethnic outgroups may end up being ethnocentric, and ethnocentrism in turn may predispose them to behaviours that prevent them having contact with ethnic outgroups. Nevertheless, if a phenomenon is mainly seen as a cause of ethnocentrism, and may only secondarily also become a consequence of ethnocentrism, I will include it among causes. In contrast, those phenomena that are mainly seen as consequences of ethnocentrism, but may further reinforce ethnocentrism, will be included in consequences.

Table 6.1 shows, first, that in line with both the social identity and identity fusion approaches, ethnic identification and identity fusion predisposed people to ethnocentrism – and most strongly to devotion. Still, the effects of identity fusion appeared somewhat weaker than the effects of ethnic identification. Accordingly, evidence shows that ethnic identification and the overlap between personal and ethnic identity generate all the dimensions of ethnocentrism, and most strongly devotion.

In line with the theoretical approaches that assume that realistic and symbolic threats predispose people to ethnocentrism, this table shows that perceived realistic threat from ethnic minorities (i.e., the perception that ethnic minorities are taking power from White ethnic majorities, are taking jobs, and increasing crime) and symbolic threat from ethnic minorities (i.e., the perception that ethnic minorities have very different values and ways of life to White ethnic majorities) appeared to strongly drive ethnocentrism. Effects appeared to be generally strong across all the dimensions of ethnocentrism, with realistic threats most strongly underlying exploitativeness, making people less considerate of ethnic outgroups and making

TABLE 6.1 Origins of ethnocentrism: ethnic attachment and threat

Variable	Sample	N	Devotion	Group cohesion	Preference	Superiority	Purity	Exploitativeness
Ethnic group attachment								
Identity fusion (ethnicity)	Australia	256	**.45*****	.18**	.35***	.30***	.21***	.18**
Ethnic identification	YourMorals.Org	4187	**.62*****	.37***	.54***	.43***	.35***	.35***
Threat								
Realistic (ethnic minorities)	CrowdFlower (Whites)	424	.43***	.50***	.56***	.64***	.62***	**.65*****
Symbolic (ethnic minorities)	CrowdFlower (Whites)	424	.44***	.53***	.54***	**.68*****	.61***	.62***

Note: Ethnic identification was measured with the two-item scale from Bizumic et al. (2009). Identity fusion was measured with the one-item fusion scale (Swann et al., 2009). Realistic threat was measured with a slightly modified existing three-item measure and symbolic threat with a slightly modified existing two-item measure (Schmid, Ramiah, & Hewstone, 2014). The samples from YourMorals.Org and Australia were administered the 36-item version of the Ethnocentrism Scale 1, and the sample from CrowdFlower was administered the 12-item version of the Ethnocentrism Scale 2. The values in bold represent the largest correlation of the variable with a dimension of ethnocentrism.

them care only for their own ethnic group interests, and with symbolic threats most strongly underlying ethnocentric superiority, which can be seen as defensive because it reasserts the threatened value of one's own symbolic universe over those of other groups. Accordingly, the results strongly confirm that ethnocentrism has its origins in fears, threats, and insecurities, with all dimensions of ethnocentrism relatively strongly affected – and in particular several dimensions of intergroup ethnocentrism – by realistic and symbolic fears.

As seen in Table 6.2, personality traits did not appear to exert very strong influences upon ethnocentrism, but despite their somewhat distal effects they had a relatively consistent influence – especially, as expected, openness to experience and agreeableness. This gives certain support to biological approaches by showing that personality traits, which are theorised to be strongly influenced by biological factors, predispose people to ethnocentrism. First, people who were low on openness to experience tended to be higher on all six dimensions of ethnocentrism, and this effect appeared to be strongest for purity. Similarly, people who were low on agreeableness were likely to value five dimensions of ethnocentrism, and the effect appeared strongest for exploitativeness. These two traits appear particularly important for ethnocentrism, whereas the effects of the other three traits appear much weaker and inconsistent. Still, conscientious people may be somewhat higher on devotion and group cohesion because they perhaps care about group norms, rules, and unity, and dislike the possible disorganisation that may happen when people are allowed to do whatever they want. Extraverted people, possibly because they are focused on other people, appear to become slightly more attracted to devotion and group cohesion, but also less likely to reject other people, scoring somewhat lower on the purity dimension of ethnocentrism than introverted people.

A number of self-aggrandisement approaches assume that self-esteem may be related to ethnocentrism. Here we find that no dimension of ethnocentrism was related to either higher or lower personal self-esteem. Nonetheless, and in line with Bizumic and Duckitt (2008), it was narcissistic self-esteem that appeared to predispose people to ethnocentrism. People who are grandiose narcissists (these are more self-assured, exhibitionistic narcissists) tended to value five dimensions of ethnocentrism, and most strongly superiority, but not significantly group cohesion. This suggests that personal narcissism, with its grandiose self-esteem, does appear to underlie ethnocentrism, and primarily its grandiose expression of superiority. This is probably because narcissistic people want to see other individuals and groups to which they are connected as superior and important (Bizumic & Duckitt, 2008). Vulnerable narcissists (the more insecure and hypersensitive narcissists), however, tended to value preference, superiority, and most strongly purity, but they rejected group cohesion – suggesting that they do not value group unity over individual freedoms.

Overall, these findings show that self-aggrandisement at the personal level underlies ethnocentric attitudes, and mainly intergroup expressions of ethnocentrism, and may be unrelated, or even opposed, to intragroup expressions. The findings also show that the dimensions of ethnocentrism have different personality

TABLE 6.2 Origins of ethnocentrism: personality traits, self-esteem, and narcissism

Variable	Sample	N	Devotion	Group cohesion	Preference	Superiority	Purity	Exploitativeness
The Big-Five personality traits								
Extraversion	YourMorals.Org	1198	.06*	.07*	-.03	.02	**-.10*****	-.01
Agreeableness	YourMorals.Org	1198	-.07*	-.03	-.16***	-.22***	-.25**	**-.34*****
Conscientiousness	YourMorals.Org	1198	.09**	**.11*****	.05	.03	.02	.02
Neuroticism	YourMorals.Org	1198	.002	.01	-.01	-.06	.03	**-.08****
Openness to experience	YourMorals.Org	1198	-.14***	-.13***	-.19***	-.10***	**-.21*****	-.20***
Self-esteem and narcissism								
Self-esteem (personal)	Australia	228	.07	.07	.12	.03	-.03	-.07
Narcissism (grandiose)	Australia	494	**.18*****	.07	.12**	**.28****	.11*	.22***
Narcissism (vulnerable)	Australia	494	-.05	-.11*	.10*	.14**	**.19*****	.09

Note: The Big-Five personality traits were measured with the 44-item Big Five Inventory (John et al., 2008). Self-esteem (personal) was measured with the 10-item Rosenberg's Self-Esteem Scale (Rosenberg, 1965). Grandiose narcissism was measured with the 40-item Narcissistic Personality Inventory (Raskin & Terry, 1988), and vulnerable narcissism with the 10-item Hypersensitive Narcissism Scale (Hendin & Cheek, 1997). Ethnocentrism was measured with the 36-item version of the Ethnocentrism Scale 1. The values in bold represent the largest correlation of the variable with a dimension of ethnocentrism.

causes, showing that ethnocentrism is a complex group of attitudes, where certain causes may at the same time increase certain dimensions, but decrease others. This gives a very strong rationale for treating ethnocentrism as a multidimensional phenomenon, and not a single unidimensional phenomenon.

When it comes to people's personal values (Schwartz, 1992), Table 6.3 shows that the values of conservation, consisting of conformity, tradition, and security, tended to promote ethnocentrism, with conformity and tradition primarily predisposing people to positively evaluate devotion and group cohesion, and security primarily predisposing people to positively evaluate purity and exploitativeness. The values of openness to change, consisting of self-direction, stimulation, and hedonism, tended to oppose ethnocentrism, with self-direction and stimulation primarily predisposing people to reject group cohesion, and stimulation to primarily reject purity. In line with self-aggrandisement approaches, two values of self-enhancement, consisting of power and achievement, tended to promote ethnocentrism, with achievement predisposing people to one intragroup and four intergroup dimensions of ethnocentrism, but most strongly to exploitativeness, and power predisposing people to all dimensions of ethnocentrism, and also most strongly to exploitativeness. Finally, the values of self-transcendence, consisting of benevolence and universalism, tended to oppose ethnocentrism, with benevolence predisposing people to reject five dimensions of ethnocentrism, and most strongly exploitativeness, and universalism to reject all six dimensions, and again most strongly exploitativeness. These largely followed the expectations from Chapter 3 about how personal values may shape ethnocentric attitudes.

The moral values from Haidt's (2012) theory somewhat overlap with Schwartz's values (1992). They are, however, focused on morality, whereas Schwartz's model has values, such as hedonism and stimulation, which are not necessarily related to morality. The five moral values tended to have particularly strong and consistent effects on ethnocentrism. People who strongly value (avoiding) harm and those who value fairness tended to reject all dimensions of ethnocentrism, and most strongly exploitativeness, whereas those who strongly value ingroup loyalty, authority, and purity tended to evaluate positively all dimensions of ethnocentrism, and most strongly devotion.

These findings overall show that people's personal and moral values are highly relevant to ethnocentrism, with all values being associated with at least several dimensions of ethnocentrism, and most being associated with all six dimensions. Further, in line with theories discussed before, fear and self-aggrandisement appear to underlie various values and these in turn have significant effects on all dimensions of ethnocentrism. Accordingly, what people value across various contexts appears to have significant implications for their positive or negative evaluations of the six expressions of ethnocentrism. The findings show that ethnocentrism has a very intricate basis in values, especially moral values, and it is not surprising that ethnocentrism, rooted in people's main guiding life principles, may be difficult to change.

Table 6.4 describes a number of principally social causes of ethnocentrism. Their effects do not appear to be very strong, which is not surprising given that they are

TABLE 6.3 Origins of ethnocentrism: values

Variable	Sample	N	Devotion	Group cohesion	Preference	Superiority	Purity	Exploitativeness
Personal values (Schwartz)								
Conformity	YourMorals.Org	1548	**.36*****	.35***	.21***	.21***	.23***	.20***
Security	YourMorals.Org	1548	.38***	.29***	.34***	.38***	**.39*****	**.39*****
Tradition	YourMorals.Org	1548	.31***	**.31*****	.13***	.15***	.15**	.11***
Self-direction	YourMorals.Org	1548	-.23***	-**.34*****	-.07**	-.04	-.04	.04
Stimulation	YourMorals.Org	1548	-.09***	-.12***	-.15***	-.08**	-**.18*****	-.01
Hedonism	YourMorals.Org	1548	-.19***	-**.24*****	-.05*	-.05*	-.06*	-.01
Achievement	YourMorals.Org	1548	.07**	-.02	.06	.18***	.11***	**.25*****
Power	YourMorals.Org	1548	.28***	.19***	.28***	.35***	.31***	**.44*****
Benevolence	YourMorals.Org	1548	-.08**	.00	-.12***	-.15***	-.17***	-**.28*****
Universalism	YourMorals.Org	1548	-.45***	-.22***	-.41***	-.53***	-.47***	-**.62*****
Moral values (Haidt)								
Harm	YourMorals.Org	2286	-.18***	-.05*	-.30***	-.41***	-.42***	-**.52*****
Fairness	YourMorals.Org	2286	-.25***	-.15***	-.31***	-.39***	-.41***	-**.46*****
Ingroup loyalty	YourMorals.Org	2286	**.55*****	.45***	.34***	.37***	.32***	.38***
Authority	YourMorals.Org	2286	**.52*****	.48***	.39***	.39***	.37***	.40***
Purity	YourMorals.Org	2286	**.52*****	.47***	.33***	.37***	.36***	.33***

Note: The 10 personal values were measured with the 57-item Schwartz's Values Scale (Sagiv & Schwartz, 1995; Schwartz, 1992). The five moral values/foundations were measured with the 30-item Moral Foundations Questionnaire (Graham et al., 2011). Ethnocentrism was measured with the 36-item version of the Ethnocentrism Scale 1. The values in bold represent the largest correlation of the variable with a dimension of ethnocentrism.

TABLE 6.4 Origins of ethnocentrism: demographics and contact

Variable	Sample	N	Devotion	Group cohesion	Preference	Superiority	Purity	Exploitativeness
Demographics								
Socioeconomic status	YourMorals.Org	3830	.01	-.04*	.07***	.10***	.01	.03
Year of birth	YourMorals.Org	4173	.03	-.02	-.06***	.03	.03	.07***
Education	YourMorals.Org	3999	-.06***	-.07***	.0002	-.02	-.09***	-.07***
Religious attendance	YourMorals.Org	3710	.25***	.19***	.14***	.12***	.11***	.05**
Gender (men)	YourMorals.Org	4173	.05**	-.03*	.11***	.25***	.20***	.24***
Frequency of contact with:								
Ethnic outgroups	CrowdFlower (US)	375	-.12*	-.03	-.30***	-.24***	-.33***	-.23***
National outgroups	CrowdFlower (US)	375	-.03	.05	-.22***	-.04	-.14**	-.08

Note: Socioeconomic status was measured with a 10-point scale: the MacArthur Scale of Subjective Social Status (Adler, Epel, Castellazzo, & Ickovics, 2000). Education was measured with a 9-point scale (from 1 = *some high school* to 9 = *completed graduate/professional school*). Religious attendance was measured with a 7-point scale regarding the frequency of religious attendance (from 1 – *Never* to 7 – *One or more times each week*). The frequency of contact included two items asking participants how often (from 1 – *Never* to 7 – *Daily*) they interact with someone from another ethnic group or with a citizen of another country. Ethnocentrism was measured with the 36-item version of the Ethnocentrism Scale 1 (YourMorals.Org) and the 12-item version of the Ethnocentrism Scale 2 (CrowdFlower). The values in bold represent the largest correlation of the variable with a dimension of ethnocentrism.

somewhat distal influences. Nevertheless, all these causes had effects on at least two dimensions of ethnocentrism, and several on all the dimensions. In certain cases, such as with effects of socioeconomic status and the year of birth on ethnocentrism, there were opposite effects in that these variables increased certain dimensions of ethnocentrism and decreased others. Having a higher socioeconomic status predisposed people to ethnocentric preference and superiority, but having a lower socioeconomic status predisposed them to group cohesion. People who were born more recently tended to positively value exploitativeness, whereas people who were born earlier tended to positively value preference. Education had generally negative effects on ethnocentrism: people with lower education tended to be ethnocentric, and the effect, though weak, was strongest for purity. Religious attendance seemed to increase ethnocentrism – including all its aspects, but primarily devotion, which in fact has the most religious undertones of the six dimensions.

Further, men tended to be generally more ethnocentric than women – and the effect was strongest for superiority. Women, however, were very slightly higher than men in their positive evaluation of group cohesion. Still, as mentioned in Chapter 3, it is unclear whether the overall effects may be due to socialisation or biology – or possibly the interaction between the two. Finally, confirming the theories that propose that ignorance of outgroups leads to ethnocentrism, people who are rarely in contact with outgroups tended to be more ethnocentric than those who are more frequently in contact with outgroups. Those with little contact with ethnic outgroups tended to positively evaluate five dimensions of ethnocentrism, and most strongly purity. Yet, people who have little contact with national outgroups tended to positively evaluate only preference and purity, with the effect being somewhat stronger for preference. The overall findings generally support the view that social factors influence the six dimensions of ethnocentrism. These factors most likely have indirect effects, predisposing people to particular values and ideologies, which in turn predispose them to ethnocentrism.

Table 6.5 shows that political ideologies, which do overlap a lot with values (e.g., Cohrs et al., 2005; Federico et al., 2013), are a major influence on ethnocentrism. General conservatism in a CrowdFlower sample was generally weakly to moderately related to all dimensions of ethnocentrism, and most strongly to exploitativeness. Both social and economic conservatism in the YourMorals. Org sample predisposed people to all dimensions of ethnocentrism. Social conservatism primarily related to purity, whereas economic conservatism primarily related to exploitativeness. Figure 6.1, however, shows a somewhat more complex relationship between specific political ideologies and ethnocentrism. In general, conservatives tended to be most ethnocentric, followed by libertarians, moderates, and then liberals. Libertarians appeared to be similar to, but somewhat lower than, conservatives when it comes to all intergroup dimensions of ethnocentrism, but they appeared to be lower than moderates on devotion, and even lower than liberals on group cohesion. No political group completely rejected ethnocentrism, and no group was exceptionally high on ethnocentrism.

TABLE 6.5 Origins of ethnocentrism: political ideology

Variable	Sample	N	Devotion	Group cohesion	Preference	Superiority	Purity	Exploitativeness
Conservatism	CrowdFlower	524	.19***	.13**	.20***	.17***	.18***	**.22***
Social conservatism	YourMorals.Org	2898	.52***	.42***	.40***	.48***	**.58***	.51***
Economic conservatism	YourMorals.Org	2821	.29***	.08***	.31***	.41***	.35***	**.47***
Right-wing authoritarianism	CrowdFlower	654	**.51***	.45***	.35***	.40***	.37***	.41***
ACT (authoritarianism)	CrowdFlower	654	**.30***	.21***	.23***	.23***	.22***	.24***
ACT (conservatism)	CrowdFlower	654	**.48***	.46***	.30***	.36***	.33***	.39***
ACT (traditionalism)	CrowdFlower	654	**.49***	.43***	.33***	.39***	.36***	.38***
SDO	CrowdFlower	654	.47***	.44***	.53***	.70***	**.77***	.76***
SDO (egalitarianism)	CrowdFlower	654	.36***	.32***	.46***	.59***	**.68***	.66***
SDO (dominance)	CrowdFlower	654	.52***	.51***	.54***	.73***	.76***	**.77***

Note: Conservatism was measured with one item on a 7-point scale (from 1 – *strongly liberal* to 7 – *strongly conservative*). Social and economic conservatism were each measured with one item on a 7-point scale (from 1 – *very liberal* to 7 – *very conservative*). Right-wing authoritarianism was measured with the 18-item version of the Authoritarianism–Conservatism–Traditionalism (ACT) Scale, with six items measuring each dimension (Duckitt et al., 2010). SDO was measured with the 16-item balanced measure, with eight items measuring each of the two dimensions (Ho et al., 2015). Ethnocentrism was measured with the 36-item version of the Ethnocentrism Scale 1 (YourMorals.Org), the 12-item version of the Ethnocentrism Scale (CrowdFlower, *N* = 524), and the 36-item version of the Ethnocentrism Scale 2 (CrowdFlower, *N* = 654). The values in bold represent the largest correlation of the variable with a dimension of ethnocentrism.

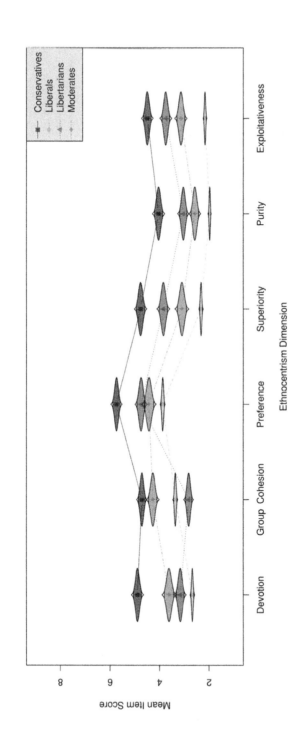

FIGURE 6.1 Means and 95% confidence intervals for the six dimensions of ethnocentrism across four political groups ($N = 3716$)

Note: Ethnocentrism was measured with the 36–item version of the Ethnocentrism Scale 1, using a 9–point rating scale. There were 598 conservatives, 2192 liberals, 571 libertarians, and 355 moderates in the sample.

Table 6.5 also shows that right-wing authoritarianism, including all its three dimensions from Duckitt et al. (2010), tended to predispose people to endorse all six dimensions of ethnocentrism, and particularly devotion. This confirms the often reported finding that authoritarianism leads to ethnocentrism – possibly due to its sense of societal insecurity and socialisation. SDO tended to also predispose people to all dimensions of ethnocentrism, and the effects were particularly strong for purity and exploitativeness. The SDO-Egalitarianism dimension had the strongest effect on purity, and the SDO-Dominance dimension on exploitativeness; nonetheless, the effects of the two dimensions of SDO on the two dimensions of ethnocentrism were almost equivalent. This also confirms the often reported findings about the links between SDO and ethnocentrism, and indicates that group self-aggrandisement makes people highly ethnocentric. The effects of SDO were very strong – suggesting that it is a very similar concept to ethnocentrism, especially to its purity and exploitativeness dimensions, and may in many people's minds be difficult to distinguish from ethnocentrism (cf. Schmitt et al., 2003). Still, SDO relates to social groups in general, whereas ethnocentrism relates to ethnic groups in particular.

Table 6.6 shows that when it comes attitudinal consequences of ethnocentrism, ethnocentrism predisposed people to many kinds of prejudices, but also to increased liking of certain groups. Table 6.6 shows that each dimension of ethnocentrism tended to predispose people to dislike numerous groups, such as ethnic outgroups, feminists, homosexuals, illegal immigrants, atheists, and people with mental illness. The most consistent effect was that of purity, which particularly strongly influenced negativity towards Muslims, homosexuals, illegal immigrants, atheists, people with depression, Arabs, and Chinese. The effects of other dimensions were more selective: group cohesion predisposed participants most strongly to dislike prostitutes; preference predisposed participants most strongly to dislike people with schizophrenia; exploitativeness predisposed participants most strongly to dislike feminists; and both purity and exploitativeness predisposed people equally strongly to dislike illegal immigrants.

In addition, almost all the dimensions of ethnocentrism predisposed people to positive attitudes towards various groups which in a way were ingroups for ethnocentric people, with particularly strong effects of intragroup expressions: devotion most strongly predisposed people to like soldiers, virgins, and priests; group cohesion predisposed people to particularly strongly like police officers and elderly people; and the only intergroup aspect of ethnocentrism that emerged as the strongest predictor of positive attitudes was exploitativeness for predicting positivity towards conservatives.

These findings show that the dimensions of ethnocentrism do influence people's attitudes towards a variety of groups. Ethnocentric people like those who could strengthen the group, and these are police officers, soldiers, and possibly conservatives (given that they in general tend to be more ethnocentric themselves), and like those who care about or promote its traditional moral and religious strength, such as virgins, priests, and the elderly. Ethnocentric people, however, dislike those

TABLE 6.6 Consequences of ethnocentrism: negative and positive attitudes towards social groups

Variable	Sample	N	Devotion	Group cohesion	Preference	Superiority	Purity	Exploitativeness
Negative attitudes (prejudice) towards								
Muslims	YourMorals.Org	1042	.27***	.14***	.39***	.44***	**.48*****	.42***
Feminists	YourMorals.Org	1038	.39***	.24***	.38***	.51***	.55***	**.58*****
Prostitutes	YourMorals.Org	1038	.23***	**.25*****	.19***	.18***	.25***	.15***
Homosexuals	YourMorals.Org	1042	.39***	.31***	.37***	.45***	**.51*****	.47***
Illegal immigrants	YourMorals.Org	1042	.44***	.33***	.44***	.49***	**.54*****	**.54*****
Atheists	YourMorals.Org	1039	**.36*****	.28***	.25***	.28***	.31***	.30***
People with schizophrenia	CrowdFlower	654	.16***	.09*	**.29*****	.24***	.28***	.27***
People with depression	CrowdFlower	654	.19***	.20***	.27***	.35***	**.36*****	.35***
Arabs	CrowdFlower	654	.22***	.08*	.42***	.40***	**.48*****	.41***
Chinese	CrowdFlower	654	.16***	.15***	.33***	.33***	**.41*****	.33***
Positive attitudes towards								
Soldiers	YourMorals.Org	1040	**.30*****	.19***	.14***	.21***	.10**	.22***
Police officers	YourMorals.Org	1040	.14***	**.17*****	.10**	.07*	.03	.05
Elderly	YourMorals.Org	1043	.10***	**.11*****	-.01	-.04	-.08*	-.04
Conservatives	YourMorals.Org	1042	.44***	.28***	.34***	.46***	.41***	**.49*****
Virgins	YourMorals.Org	1038	**.28*****	.23***	.17***	.22***	.24***	.22***
Priests	YourMorals.Org	1039	**.29*****	.23***	.17***	.17***	.15***	.17***

Note: Attitudes towards social groups were measured using Graham et al.'s (2013) 7-point measure (YourMorals.Org) and a 101-point feeling thermometer measure (CrowdFlower). Ethnocentrism was measured with the 36-item version of the Ethnocentrism Scale 1 (YourMorals.Org) and the 36-item version of the Ethnocentrism Scale 2 (CrowdFlower). The values in bold represent the largest correlation of the variable with a dimension of ethnocentrism.

whom they perceive could weaken the ethnic group, including the group's symbolic aspects: immigrants, ethnic and religious outgroups, ingroup deviants, such as prostitutes, homosexuals, feminists, and people with mental illness. These are all groups that are often the targets of negativity for members of highly ethnocentric groups, such as fascists, and these groups are frequent targets of hate crimes.

Table 6.7 shows that ethnocentrism predisposed Whites, that is, the members of ethnic majority groups, to a variety of specific negative emotions, as well as to the absence of positive emotions, towards ethnic outgroups (i.e., ethnic minorities within one's country). As can be seen, almost all dimensions of ethnocentrism predisposed people to feel increased anger, contempt, fear, disgust, pity, envy, resentment, as well decreased admiration and sympathy towards ethnic minorities. Ethnocentric purity appeared as a particularly strong driver of most of these emotions: anger, fear, disgust, pity, envy, resentment, and lack of sympathy towards people from ethnic minority groups. Superiority tended to primarily make people feel contempt, fear, and envy towards ethnic minorities. Exploitativeness tended to make people feel resentment, and less admiration and sympathy. Finally, five dimensions of ethnocentrism weakly predisposed people to feel pity for ethnic minorities, and group cohesion, purity, and exploitativeness appeared to be equally strong predictors of pity.

These findings indicate that ethnocentrism, as a broad attitude, may make people experience, in addition to prejudice towards particular groups, many specific negative emotional reactions – as well as decreased positive emotional reactions. These emotions appear to be held over many contexts when ethnic majority members interact with people from ethnic minority groups, and may contribute to many negative outcomes of these interactions. These findings also show that being ethnocentric, with its negative emotional profile, may have consequences for people's well-being.

The same table shows that ethnocentrism translates into a variety of, principally discriminatory, behavioural consequences. People higher in ethnocentrism were less likely than those lower in ethnocentrism to report that they were making friends with ethnic outgroups, but more likely to report that they purposely ignored ethnic outgroups on one or more occasions. Purity appeared to have the strongest effects on these behaviours. People higher in ethnocentrism were less likely than those lower in ethnocentrism to reveal that they visited another country – with group cohesion most strongly driving this behaviour. Those who scored higher on intragroup ethnocentrism, and primarily devotion, were likely to report that they were giving money to charities that support their ethnic ingroup members. People who scored higher on all the dimensions of ethnocentrism, and primarily on superiority, were likely to report that they were participating in demonstrations that supported the causes of people from their ethnic group and rejected sitting next to someone who was of a visibly different ethnicity to them. Finally, people who scored higher on ethnocentric preference were less likely than those who scored lower to report that they dated people from a different ethnic group. These overall findings show that ethnocentrism as an attitude may translate into a variety

TABLE 6.7 Consequences of ethnocentrism: emotions and behaviours

Variable	Sample	N	Devotion	Group cohesion	Preference	Superiority	Purity	Exploitativeness
Emotions (to ethnic minorities in one's country)								
Anger	CrowdFlower (Whites)	424	.22***	.22***	.38***	.42***	.46***	.44***
Contempt	CrowdFlower (Whites)	424	.25***	.41***	.26***	.43***	.42***	.39***
Fear	CrowdFlower (Whites)	424	.19***	.22***	.29***	.33***	.33***	.31***
Disgust	CrowdFlower (Whites)	424	.23***	.27***	.35***	.42***	.49***	.45***
Pity	CrowdFlower (Whites)	424	.07	.13**	.12*	.10*	.13**	.13**
Envy	CrowdFlower (Whites)	424	.16***	.28***	.15**	.29***	.29***	.25***
Resentment	CrowdFlower (Whites)	424	.25***	.26***	.38***	.45***	.47***	.47***
Admiration	CrowdFlower (Whites)	424	-.04	.00	-.27***	-.19***	-.26***	-.29***
Sympathy	CrowdFlower (Whites)	424	-.09	-.04	-.22***	-.23***	-.28***	-.28***
Behaviours								
Made a friend of someone who is from a different ethnic group	CrowdFlower	524	-.11*	-.25***	-.25***	-.35***	-.41***	-.34***
Purposely ignored someone from a different ethnic group	CrowdFlower	524	.20***	.24***	.34***	.37***	.43***	.32***
Visited a foreign country	CrowdFlower	524	-.08	-.11**	-.07	-.09*	-.09*	-.10*
Gave money to charities that support members of my ethnic group	CrowdFlower	524	.13**	.09*	.05	.07	-.01	.03

Participated in demonstrations that support the causes of people from my ethnic group	CrowdFlower	524	.22***	.28***	.15***	**.31*****	.21***	.25***
Rejected sitting next to someone who is of a visibly different ethnicity to mine	CrowdFlower	524	.14***	.25***	.23***	**.42*****	.40***	.37***
Dated a person from a different ethnic group	CrowdFlower	524	.00	.04	**−.11****	.05	−.05	.02

Note: Participants indicated how much (1 – *Not at all* to 7 – *Extremely*) they experienced specific emotions in relation to ethnic minorities in their country. Participants indicated how often (0 – *Never* to 3 – *Three or more times*) they have engaged in these behaviours, using a modified existing measure (Rey & Gibson, 1998). Ethnocentrism was measured with the 12-item version of the Ethnocentrism Scale 2. The values in bold represent the largest correlation of the variable with a dimension of ethnocentrism.

of behaviours, both in support of one's own ethnic group and discriminatory behaviours against other ethnic groups.

Table 6.8 shows that ethnocentrism led people to endorse various socio-political attitudes. All dimensions of ethnocentrism appeared to predispose people to evaluate war positively and peace negatively, with exploitativeness being the strongest driver of these attitudes. All the dimensions of ethnocentrism, and in particular ethnocentric purity, led people to advocate consumer ethnocentrism. Among ethnic minorities, that is, Sri Lankans in Australia, ethnocentric preference, and somewhat less strongly, superiority predisposed people to identify less with the national state in which they lived, that is, Australia. Five dimensions of ethnocentrism, and most strongly preference, led participants from this ethnic minority group to prefer to maintain their culture in Australia. Finally, five dimensions of ethnocentrism, and most strongly superiority, led members of this ethnic minority group in Australia to have less preference for contact with the ethnic majority group.

During the year leading to the 2016 US presidential election, ethnocentrism appeared to drive US citizens' support for Donald Trump. Although all the dimensions were relevant, purity had the strongest influence on support for Donald Trump, whose election campaign stirred the ethnocentric sentiments of White/Anglo Americans. In fact, it was argued that ethnocentrism differentiated Donald Trump supporters from the supporters of the other Republican candidates (Kalkan, 2016). Three dimensions of ethnocentrism, and equally strongly purity and exploitativeness, led people to oppose Hillary Clinton. Further, five dimensions of ethnocentrism, and again most strongly purity and exploitativeness, predisposed people to oppose Bernie Sanders. These findings show that ethnocentric attitudes significantly underlie support for and opposition to political candidates, and it is not surprising that political candidates often tap into the ethnocentric sentiments of potential voters.

Finally, ethnocentrism had little influence upon people's levels of identification with their country and community, with devotion influencing more, and purity influencing less, these kinds of identification. Yet, all four intergroup expressions of ethnocentrism, and principally purity, predisposed people to reject identification with humanity. These effects were not, however, particularly strong, suggesting that identification with all humanity is not the opposite of ethnocentrism, and that there may be ethnocentric people who identify with all humanity, and people who reject both ethnocentrism and identification with all humanity. Still, ethnocentrism, with its narrow focus on one's own ethnic group, does in part predispose people to reject identification with all humanity.

The final table, Table 6.9, shows that ethnocentrism makes people support a variety of policy issues. First, all dimensions of ethnocentrism, and most strongly devotion, led people to support more funding for the military of their country. All dimensions of ethnocentrism, and primarily preference and purity, influenced people to support military action against North Korea. Likewise, all dimensions of ethnocentrism, and most strongly preference and superiority, led people to support spending more money on war on terror. Among US participants, ethnocentric

TABLE 6.8 Consequences of ethnocentrism: socio–political attitudes, political support, and identification with all humanity

Variable	Sample	N	Devotion	Group cohesion	Preference	Superiority	Purity	Exploitativeness
Socio-political attitudes								
Pro-war attitudes	YourMorals.Org	211	.44***	.15*	.47***	.53***	.49***	**.63***
Anti-peace attitudes	YourMorals.Org	211	.43***	.18*	.40***	.52***	.42***	**.55**
Consumer ethnocentrism	CrowdFlower (US)	304	.27***	.17**	.28***	.33***	**.40***	.37***
Nationalism	CrowdFlower (US)	304	.53***	.49***	.48***	.54***	.49***	**.56***
National (Australian) identification	Sri Lankans (Australia)	177	–.13	–.05	**–.20**	–.17*	–.14	–.06
Cultural maintenance	Sri Lankans (Australia)	177	.42***	.18*	**.44***	.32***	.32***	.09
Preference for contact with the ethnic majority	Sri Lankans (Australia)	177	–.28***	–.13	–.23**	**–.34***	–.29***	–.25***
Political support for								
Donald Trump	CrowdFlower (US)	375	.29***	.17***	.28***	.34***	**.43***	.39***
Hillary Clinton	CrowdFlower (US)	375	–.06	.05	–.12*	–.09	**–.16**	**–.16**
Bernie Sanders	CrowdFlower (US)	375	–.18***	–.07	–.21***	–.24***	**–.25***	**–.25***
Identification with All Humanity Scale								
Identification with one's country	CrowdFlower	524	**.18***	.14**	.00	.03	–.12**	.00
Identification with one's community	CrowdFlower	524	**.17***	.16***	.01	.05	–.09*	–.04
Identification with all humanity	CrowdFlower	524	.02	.04	–.25***	–.18***	**–.29***	–.22***

Note: Pro-war and anti-peace attitudes were measured with the Attitudes Towards Peace and War Scale (Bizumic et al., 2013). Consumer ethnocentrism was measure with the 10-item version of the Consumer Ethnocentrism Scale (Shimp & Sharma, 1987). Nationalism was measured with the eight-item Nationalism Scale (Kosterman & Feshbach, 1989). National identification was measured with two modified items previously used to measure ethnic identification (Bizumic et al., 2009). Cultural maintenance and preference for contact with the ethnic majority in Australia were measured with three items each (Zagefka & Brown, 2002). Political support (1 – *completely oppose* to 7 – *completely support*) was measured for the three presidential candidates before the 2016 US presidential election. Identification with one's country, community and all humanity was measured using the nine three-part items from the Identification with All Humanity Scale (McFarland et al., 2012). Ethnocentrism was measured with the 36-item version of the Ethnocentrism Scale 1 (YourMorals.Org and Sri Lankans in Australia), the 36-item version of the Ethnocentrism Scale 2 (CrowdFlower, *N* = 304) and the 12-item version of the Ethnocentrism Scale 2 (CrowdFlower, *N* = 375 and 524). The values in bold represent the largest correlation of the variable with a dimension of ethnocentrism.

TABLE 6.9 Consequences of ethnocentrism: support for policy issues

Variable	Sample	N	Devotion	Group cohesion	Preference	Superiority	Purity	Exploitativeness
More funding for our country's military	CrowdFlower	524	**.29*****	.18***	.18***	.23***	.16***	.22***
Military action against North Korea	CrowdFlower	524	.16***	.09*	**.22*****	.19***	**.22*****	.20***
Spending more on war on terror	CrowdFlower	524	.19***	.09*	**.23*****	**.23*****	.20***	.18***
More funding for museums that commemorate slavery and acknowledge its injustices in the US	CrowdFlower (US)	402	-.09	.04	**-.14****	-.05	-.10*	-.13**
Decreasing immigration from the Middle East into my country	CrowdFlower	524	.29***	.22***	**.36*****	.35***	.34***	**.36*****
Cutting foreign aid	CrowdFlower	524	.22***	.20***	.28***	.25***	**.32*****	.29***
Decreasing the number of ethnic minority people in my country	CrowdFlower (Whites)	424	.35***	.38***	.46***	**.56*****	**.56*****	.53***
Building a wall along the US-Mexico border	CrowdFlower (US)	402	.29***	.24***	.31***	.35***	.41***	**.44*****
Tougher immigration policies in my country	CrowdFlower	524	.26***	.15***	.25***	.25***	.24***	**.28*****
Legalising same-sex marriage in my country	CrowdFlower	524	-.26***	-.28***	-.27***	-.31***	-.34***	**-.38*****

Note: Support for policy issues was rated on an 11-point scale (from 1 – *Totally oppose* to 11 – *Totally support*). Ethnocentrism was measured with the 12-item version of the Ethnocentrism Scale 2. The values in bold represent the largest correlation of the variable with a dimension of ethnocentrism.

purity, exploitativeness, and most strongly preference predisposed them to oppose funding for museums that commemorate slavery. All dimensions of ethnocentrism, and most strongly preference and exploitativeness, predisposed participants to favour decreased immigration from the Middle East. Likewise, all dimensions of ethnocentrism, with purity most strongly, predisposed people to support cutting foreign aid. In addition, there was a relatively strong effect of all dimensions of ethnocentrism, and strongest for superiority and purity, on support for what can be described as ethnic cleansing within one's national state: "Decreasing the number of ethnic minority people in my country". Finally, all the dimensions of ethnocentrism, but particularly exploitativeness, led participants to support tougher immigration policies, to oppose legalising same-sex marriage, and among US participants to support building a wall along the US-Mexico border.

These findings show that ethnocentrism plays a huge role in public opinion when it comes to important policy issues. It is not, therefore, surprising that ethnocentrism plays a huge role in politics. These findings in general show that ethnocentric participants want policies that favour the ethnic ingroup, and, further, those that strengthen the ethnic ingroup (e.g., more funding for the military), potentially weaken other ethnic groups (e.g., cutting foreign aid), and increase the unity and purity of their own ethnic group (e.g., tougher immigration, fewer ethnic minorities). The findings support Kinder and Kam's (2009) conclusion regarding the importance of ethnocentrism in politics: "ethnocentrism is a foundational element of public opinion" (p. 220). However, the findings reported in this book relate ethnocentrism to a different conceptualisation of ethnocentrism than that of Kinder and Kam (2009), and show that all six dimensions of ethnocentrism play a foundational role in public opinion.

Integrating the causes and consequences of reconceptualised ethnocentrism

The presented data show important influences on and consequences of ethnocentrism. Participants in these studies were adults from different backgrounds, and they tended to vary a lot in ethnocentrism. For example, as seen in Figure 6.2, most of the 4187 participants from YourMorals.Org scored relatively low on the Ethnocentrism Scale, but there was a sizeable number of those who scored high and some who scored exceptionally high. On the other hand, there were not many participants who very strongly rejected ethnocentrism.

Thus, there is a large diversity of individual differences in ethnocentrism. But how exactly does a person get their particular standing on the dimension from low to high ethnocentrism? That is, how exactly does one become ethnocentric? The presented theories and data suggest that ethnocentrism has diverse causes, both distal and proximal. First, it is highly likely that the distal cause of ethnocentrism is in evolution and biology, and that humans are pre-wired for ethnocentrism. Cross-cultural evidence shows that ethnocentrism exists under most conditions in all ethnic groups, and it shows that there are important individual differences

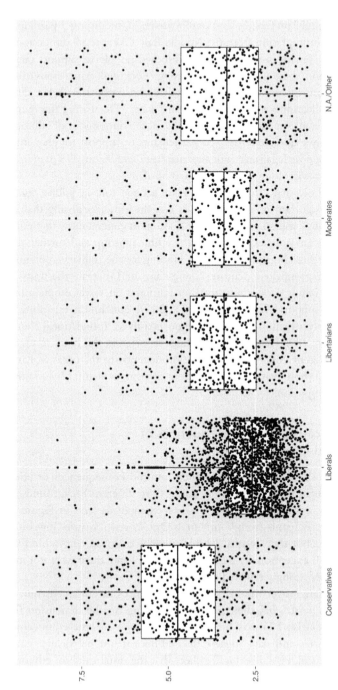

FIGURE 6.2 Boxplots for overall ethnocentrism across political groups ($N = 4187$)

Note: Ethnocentrism was measured with the 36-item version of the Ethnocentrism Scale 1, using a 9-point rating scale. There were 598 conservatives, 2192 liberals, 571 libertarians, 355 moderates, and 471 participants in the sample who were apolitical or had other political orientations. One dot represents one or more individual cases.

in ethnocentrism across societies. In fact, as shown in Figure 6.2, there are large differences in ethnocentrism even within the same ideological group, so that there are ethnically tolerant conservatives, and highly ethnocentric liberals. Given its cross-cultural universality, ethnocentrism is most likely an evolutionary adaptation and has evolved over millions of years with the evolution of our species. It is also highly probable that cultural and genetic evolution have interacted with each other in producing this universal phenomenon of ethnocentrism.

It is also possible that individual differences in genetic predispositions can affect people's proneness to becoming ethnocentric. Genetic differences, which always interact with environmental influences, even before birth, predispose people to have specific temperaments at birth, which further shape personality traits. The two central personality traits that contribute to ethnocentrism are openness to experience and agreeableness: more precisely, closed-minded and disagreeable people appear likely to become ethnocentric. Related personality constructs that affect ethnocentrism deal with personal self-centredness, that is, narcissism; however, the effect of narcissism, including both grandiose and vulnerable narcissism, is not much stronger than the effect of other personality constructs. Unfortunately, at this stage of scientific development we do not know which genes affect the development of ethnocentrism and precisely how they do so. How exactly specific genes and groups of genes that underlie ethnocentrism express themselves, and how they interact with the myriad environmental influences in creating expressions of ethnocentrism, is still beyond our knowledge and may be many years in the future. Nevertheless, a lot of theoretical and empirical work shows that evolutionary and biological causes do predispose people to have particular personalities and social and political attitudes, including ethnocentrism.

The above explanation is speculative, but appears supported by existing data. Nevertheless, much more data are needed, and data need to be related to each of the six dimensions of ethnocentrism. We can, however, be certain based on data from this and other research that ethnocentrism is shaped by socialisation and broader social factors. People need to be socialised into groups that emphasise ethnicity as an important category. People also need to categorise themselves as ethnic group members and identify with, or become fused with, their own ethnicity. Both of these processes appear relevant to each of the six dimensions of ethnocentrism, and in particular to the intragroup expressions. There is also little doubt that an ethnic group's elites, most often for self-aggrandising purposes, are instrumental in affecting a variety of social factors, such as the media, education system, and political system, which all emphasise the importance of ethnicity for self-categorisation and may also emphasise each of the dimensions of ethnocentrism.

The reported data show that various social factors, such as socioeconomic status, education, religious attendance, frequency of contact with ethnic and national outgroups, and also those associated with age and gender, appear to predispose people to ethnocentrism. Most of the effects of these variables, however, are not very strong and some of these variables do not directly affect each dimension of ethnocentrism. Nevertheless, the data do support the view that relatively more distal social factors predispose people to ethnocentrism.

Nonetheless, the strongest effects appear to be proximal, including values, political ideologies, and realistic and symbolic fears. As a result of biological, personality, and social development, people develop particular values, including moral values, and particular ideologies. Values and ideologies do overlap significantly, and are difficult to distinguish, and can be broadly seen as one general level of influences that guide people's attitudes. Ethnocentrism is, therefore, broadly based on people's fundamental guiding principles, including their sense of right and wrong, and their ideas about how the social world should be organised. These values and ideologies can either promote or inhibit ethnocentrism. Research suggests that ethnocentrism is promoted as a result of possessing the values of conformity, security, tradition, achievement, power, loyalty, authority, and purity, but inhibited as a result of possessing the values of self-direction, stimulation, hedonism, benevolence, and universalism. Further, it is promoted as a result of possessing conservative, libertarian, authoritarian, and socially dominant political ideologies, but inhibited as a result of possessing liberal, non-authoritarian, and socially egalitarian political ideologies. Similarly, the more proximal influences, such as the perception of realistic and symbolic threats to one's own ethnic group, also generate the attitude of ethnocentrism.

It is, nevertheless, evident that many of these variables do overlap significantly in producing a particular ethnocentric profile. Because most of the variables, especially personality traits, values, and political ideologies, are generally stable and highly resistant to change, ethnocentrism also has a relatively stable profile (cf. Lewis & Bates, 2017). It is, therefore, not surprising that most attempts to reduce ethnocentrism often require fundamental changes in socialisation and social norms. Nevertheless, even when ethnocentrism becomes subdued as a result of social factors, elites have shown on countless occasions that it is not too difficult to stir it. This often requires manipulation and propaganda – often tapping into realistic and symbolic fears in ethnic ingroups, as well as into people's and their ethnic group's self-interest.

Once a relatively stable profile of individual ethnocentrism is formed, it gives rise to numerous consequences. People who are highly ethnocentric tend to dislike a variety of groups, such as ethnic outgroups and ingroup deviants. However, they like the ingroup members who may apparently increase their ethnic group's strength, including moral strength. Further, ethnocentrism predisposes people to particular, mainly negative, emotional reactions towards ethnic outgroups, and towards a variety of behaviours on behalf of the ethnic ingroup and against ethnic outgroups. Moreover, ethnocentrism may also predispose people to hold numerous socio-political attitudes relevant to ethnocentrism, such as nationalism, favourability to wars, consumer ethnocentrism, and cultural maintenance. Finally, ethnocentrism appears to play an important role in people's support for political leaders and specific policies that enhance principally the strength and well-being of their own ethnic group, and which may disadvantage other ethnic groups.

The presented results and theory also suggest that most causes and consequences of ethnocentrism appear to be common across the dimensions of ethnocentrism. Nevertheless, there also appear to be specific and more relevant causes and consequences at the level of each dimension of ethnocentrism. Devotion appears to be a remarkably strong consequence of ethnic identification and to a lesser extent of ethnic identity fusion. It also appears to be particularly strongly based on the values of conformity, tradition, ingroup loyalty, authority, and purity, and the ideology of right-wing authoritarianism. Devotion predisposes people to positive attitudes towards particular ingroup members who appear to uphold the strength and morality of the ingroup; to identification with their country and with their community – at least among the ethnic majority members; to behaviours that help members of their own ethnic group; and to support for policies that promote their country's military. Devotion, as an intragroup ethnocentric attitude, appears to have its main causes in the variables that are also concerned principally with ingroup processes. In this research, group cohesion appeared to have much fewer unique causes and consequences than devotion. It nevertheless appeared to be in general related more strongly than other dimensions of ethnocentrism to the causes in the personality traits of conscientiousness, to the value of tradition, to lower values of self-direction and hedonism, and to disliking those who violate ingroup norms, but liking those who enforce them.

When it comes to intergroup dimensions, preference appeared not to be more strongly related to most causes than other dimensions of ethnocentrism, apart from less contact with national outgroups, but it was related more strongly to numerous consequences, such as prejudice, less identification with the nation in ethnic minority group members, preference for cultural maintenance, less likelihood to date a person from a different ethnic group, and less support for certain policies, such as funding for museums that commemorate slavery. Superiority was caused more strongly than other dimensions by the perception of symbolic threats, grandiose narcissism, higher socioeconomic status, and being male. It also appeared to result in preferences for less contact with the ethnic majority among ethnic minorities, in behaviours that support the causes of one's ethnic group, and rejection of other ethnic groups. It also gave rise to specific emotions, such as contempt, and support for certain policies.

Both purity and exploitativeness, however, were each related to numerous causes and consequences more strongly than the other dimensions of ethnocentrism. Purity was related to lower extraversion and openness to experience, higher vulnerable narcissism, the value of security, but rejection of the value of stimulation, higher social conservatism, higher SDO, primarily SDO-Egalitarianism, lower education level, and less contact with ethnic outgroups. Purity had many consequences, such as prejudice against ethnic and religious outgroups, consumer ethnocentrism, support for political leaders such as Donald Trump among US participants, less identification with all humanity; more negative emotions, such as anger, disgust, and envy; more discriminatory behaviours, such as making friends with ethnic outgroups, and support for policies that disadvantage other ethnic groups, such as cutting foreign aid. Finally, exploitativeness appeared to be related more strongly than other dimensions to low agreeableness and neuroticism, the perception of realistic threats, the values of power and achievement, but low benevolence, universalism, harm, and fairness, overall conservatism, economic conservatism, and

SDO-Dominance. It also resulted in prejudice against feminists, but positive evaluation of conservatives; pro-war and anti-peace attitudes, nationalism; more pity, but less sympathy and admiration for ethnic minorities; support for building a wall along the US-Mexico border among US participants, tougher immigration polices, and opposition to legalising same-sex marriage in one's country.

These results suggest that, as expected, ethnocentrism is a complex attitude and different dimensions appear to have somewhat different causes and consequences. Although most of the causes and consequences were significantly related to all the dimensions of ethnocentrism, certain causes appeared to be more likely to influence specific dimensions, and specific dimensions of ethnocentrism were more likely to lead to specific consequences.

The group strength model of ethnocentrism

If there is one overwhelming theme that emerges in the causes, consequences, and dimensions of ethnocentrism, it seems to be a strong concern with ethnic group strength and resilience. Self-aggrandising explanations clearly indicate that an important cause of ethnocentrism is in making one's own ethnic group big and powerful. The explanations dealing with fears also show that ethnocentrism is a kind of group defence mechanism (Mihalyi, 1984) which gives ethnic groups strength. Moreover, evolutionary explanations suggest that ethnocentrism was most likely an evolutionary adaptation that helped groups and their members become resilient in order to survive and prosper. Many of the consequences of ethnocentrism suggest that ethnocentrism leads people to dislike and reject ingroup members who may interfere with maintaining or achieving group strength. Many of the consequences of ethnocentrism suggest that ethnocentrism leads people to dislike, reject, discriminate against, and even harm ethnic outgroup members who might at present or in the future weaken their own ethnic group.

Ethnocentrism as an individual attitude, although it has multiple causes and consequences, is largely concerned with enforcing ethnic strength and resilience. Ethnocentric people give extreme importance to their groups, even more than to their individuality and their individual lives, because they want and need their ethnic groups to be strong, resilient, and resistant to weakness, powerlessness, decay, and disintegration. Strong ethnic groups are a guarantee that the individuals and more importantly their offspring, kin, and by extension the whole ethnic group will survive and thrive.

Ethnic groups have highly benefited from individuals with ethnocentric attitudes, and would weaken and even disintegrate with a large number of people who strongly rejected ethnocentrism. Individuals who pursue their own individual goals and who reject sacrifice for their ethnic ingroup would not usually benefit their ethnic groups much. And when in competition with another ethnic group, an ethnic ingroup would lose and may even disintegrate if it consisted of numerous individuals who did not prefer the ingroup over outgroups, who did not think it was particularly special, who were equally accepting of ethnic ingroups and outgroups, and who were highly considerate of ethnic outgroups.

To test whether ethnic strength in fact relates to the dimensions of ethnocentrism, for this study I have built a brief measure of people's need for their ethnic group to be strong and powerful as I have not been able to find such a measure in the literature. It included the following items: "I want my ethnic group to be strong", "I want my ethnic group to resist anyone who may undermine it", "In my view, it is extremely important for my ethnic group to be powerful", "I don't mind if my ethnic group is weaker than other ethnic groups" (reverse-scored), "I dislike people who can weaken my ethnic group", and "I want my ethnic group to be able to survive all difficulties". Its reliability among 524 participants from CrowdFlower was excellent (Cronbach's alpha = .80). As seen in Figure 6.3, participants' scores on the variable were normally distributed, and most people agreed with these items. The variable as expected related positively to ethnocentrism and each of its dimensions. More precisely, there were generally strong correlations with overall ethnocentrism ($r = .55, p < .001$), including almost all its dimensions: devotion ($r = .55, p < .001$), group cohesion ($r = .42, p < .001$), preference ($r = .42, p < .001$), superiority ($r = .44, p < .001$), purity ($r = .23, p < .001$), and exploitativeness ($r = .41, p < .001$). Each of these dimensions consisted of only two items, potentially decreasing the magnitude of correlations. Nevertheless, ethnic strength features prominently in the mind of ethnocentric individuals. Ethnic groups benefit from ethnocentric individuals because these individuals give the groups their strength and resilience.

Each of the dimensions of ethnocentrism appears to reinforce ethnic groups' strength. Both intragroup dimensions give strength to ingroups by giving more importance to the ingroup than to individuals within the group. Devotion makes groups stronger because of an almost blind and emotional attitude in favour of the ethnic ingroup over one's own individuality, which includes sacrificing a lot, even one's own life, in support of one's own ethnic ingroup. Group cohesion is an attitude in favour of group unity at the expense of individualism and disagreements that may weaken and threaten the group from within. It is not surprising that the symbol of Italian fascism is "fasces", which represents a bundle of rods. Such a bundle is stronger than separate individual rods, which could be easily broken on their own. Likewise, a united group would be stronger than a group consisting of diverse, disunited, and separate individuals. Group cohesion is about what an individual favours that all ethnic group members, including oneself, should think (i.e., that everyone should think the same) and do (i.e., that everyone should behave the same) in order to enforce a strong ethnic group. Devotion, on the other hand, is about what an individual favours that he or she should think (i.e., uncritically support one's ethnic group), feel (i.e., be passionately attached to one's ethnic group), and do (sacrifice oneself for the group) in order to enforce a strong ethnic group. Group strength through these two dimensions is achievable because people perceive themselves as interchangeable with other ethnic group members and lose individual differences for the sake of their group. In the words of Ibn Khaldun, they have high *asabiyyah* or group feeling, or, in the words of Gumplowicz, a high sense of syngenism, or, in the words of self-categorisation theory, a high sense of depersonalisation.

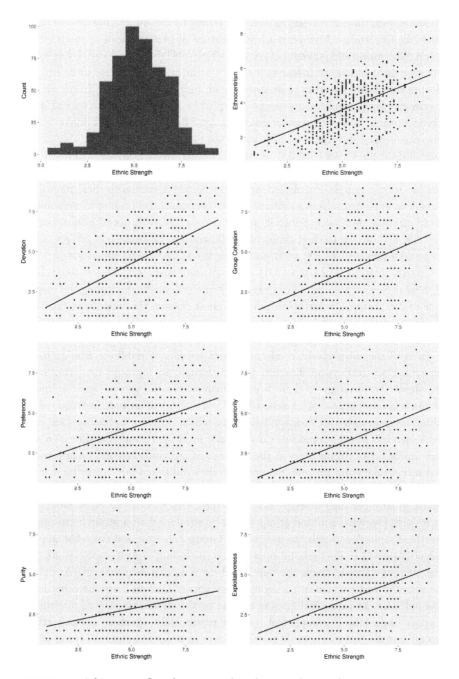

FIGURE 6.3 A histogram for ethnic strength and scatterplots, with regression lines, presenting the relationships of ethnic strength with ethnocentrism and its six dimensions ($N = 524$)

Note: Ethnocentrism was measured with the 12-item version of the Ethnocentrism Scale 2. All items used a 9-point rating scale.

Intergroup expressions fuel strength by giving more importance to people's own ethnic group than to other ethnic groups. Preference fuels strength through the preferential attraction to ethnic ingroups over outgroups. It is the basic element of differentiating one's own ethnic group from others. Ethnic groups may become stronger – especially in competition with other groups – when ingroup members share more positive and trusting sentiments with each other than with those outside the group. Superiority includes the attitude regarding the exaggerated belief in the objective supremacy and eminence of one's own ethnic group over others. This sense of superiority may make people feel elated because they feel that they are, not only socially, but biologically, part of an ethnic group that is better than any other, and it gives them the certainty that their values, beliefs, and practices are the only right ones. This "delusion" may give groups more strength than the belief that the group is nothing special or even inferior in relation to other groups. Purity is an attitude in favour of keeping the group ethnically pure, and may give the ethnic groups strength through a sense of enhanced biological, but also cultural, homogeneity. Further, purity may strengthen ethnic groups through valuing segregation from and subordination of other ethnic groups. Finally, exploitativeness is an attitude in favour of valuing ethnic group interests over the interests of any other ethnic group. It is the most aggressive of the six attitudes, and is explicitly concerned with strengthening the ethnic group and its interests through selfishly pursuing them against any other ethnic group and their interests.

Ethnic group strength can relate to both more and less tangible aspects of ethnic groups. When it comes to more tangible aspects, strength can be reflected in economic well-being (e.g., a strong economy and existence of jobs in modern societies), strong military, healthy group members, freedom from being dominated by ethnic outgroups, access to valuable resources, and so forth. When it comes to less tangible aspects, ethnic group strength relates to symbolic aspects, such as strong values, norms, beliefs, and practices – and these usually relate to traditional ethnic values, norms, beliefs, and practices. These, in the mind of ethnocentric individuals, have stood the test of time, and therefore tend to show the best and most meaningful way to live life within the ethnic group. These should be, therefore, upheld and defended against any ingroup deviants, innovators, and ethnic outgroups, who may have very different values. Given the overwhelming focus on ethnic strength, it is not surprising that ethnocentric people may dislike many subgroups that they perceive could weaken the ethnic ingroup from within and many ethnic outgroups that they perceive could weaken the ethnic ingroup from outside. It is also not surprising that they may like those who they perceive could strengthen the ethnic group, including its physical and moral attributes.

Given the overwhelming focus on ethnic strength, it is also possible that once people feel that their ethnic group is exceptionally strong, resilient, and under no threat, their ethnocentrism may somewhat reduce, but not disappear. Under these circumstances, many people in ethnic groups can allow themselves to be tolerant of ethnic outgroups, and ethnically tolerant social norms may emerge. This has often been the case with very powerful ethnic groups, and is the case with wealthy

Western societies today, which, however, are becoming less ethnically tolerant as threats from ingroup innovators and deviants and many outside ethnic groups become stronger and more salient. In addition, ethnocentrism can be reduced and even disappear when ethnic groups are perceived to be extremely weak, vulnerable, and under overwhelming threats from another ethnic group. Under these circumstances, ethnic group members may reject their ethnic group and may begin the slow process of being assimilated into another ethnic group.

Summary and conclusions

In this chapter, I attempted to integrate the material presented in the previous chapters on origins and consequences of ethnocentrism. To do so, I first presented the results of previously unpublished studies with relatively large samples and that used versions of the Ethnocentrism Scale 1 and 2. These studies related ethnocentrism to its causes and consequences in mainly Western samples. Ethnocentrism, conceptualised as ethnic group self-centredness, appears to have multiple origins. Ethnocentrism, also, has multiple and very diverse consequences. It is most likely that the distal cause of ethnocentrism is in evolution and biology, and that humans are pre-wired for ethnocentrism, but it is also evident that ethnocentrism, like other attitudes, is also shaped by social influences, such as social norms and learning. I also argued that a dominant theme that appears in the causes, consequences, and structure of ethnocentrism is related to the need to strengthen one's own ethnic group.

It is important to point out that more research into ethnocentrism, conceptualised as in this book, is needed. The presented findings, and other findings reported in the book and which also used different versions of the Ethnocentrism Scale 1 and 2, appear to primarily relate to ethnocentrism in several mainly English-speaking countries. Several studies that were conducted in different ethnic groups, such as among Serbs, Sri Lankans, and the Chinese, do appear to support the existence of ethnocentrism as conceptualised in this book, and also support the relevance of the proposed causes and consequences.

Nonetheless, it should be acknowledged that this empirical research was affected in part by different kinds of Western cultural "ethnocentrism", which pervade the study of ethnocentrism in psychology. This kind of ethnocentrism deeply affects psychology in general (Teo & Febbraro, 2003). The problem of how ethnocentrism affects psychology will be discussed in more detail in the final chapter of the book.

7

ETHNOCENTRISM IN PSYCHOLOGY

Ludwig Gumplowicz, who introduced the concept of ethnocentrism in the 1870s, argued that a successful social science must get rid of ethnocentrism (Gumplowicz, 1895). He was optimistic about this possibility, saying in the 1890s that ethnocentrism was beginning to decline as a result of progress in the social sciences: "Well, the modern sociology has shone into the face of the ghost of Ethnocentrism – and it begins to wane" (Gumplowicz, 1895, p. 2). Nevertheless, although ethnocentrism had appeared to wane at one point, it has not disappeared, and writing over 120 years later in the *American Psychologist*, Hall, Yip, and Zarate (2016) lamented: "those studies that include ethnocultural diversity as a primary aim are often marginalized and directed to specialized journals. From our perspectives as clinical, developmental, and social psychologists, and as journal editors, ethnocentric research approaches that do not make explicit attempts to include diverse samples have dominated the field" (p. 41). These authors also mentioned that topics such as race, ethnicity, and diversity are rarely studied or even ignored in psychology, being mentioned in even less than 4% of the journal articles in top journals, such as *Journal of Consulting and Clinical Psychology*, *Developmental Psychology*, and *Journal of Personality and Social Psychology*, during the last 15 years.

Thus, the influence of ethnocentrism is pervasive, and ethnocentrism affects not only those whom psychology studies, but also the study of psychology itself. Possibly the only discipline that has taken a strong stand against ethnocentrism is anthropology – although whether it has freed itself, or could ever free itself, of ethnocentrism is debatable (Brodkin, 1997; Embree, 1950; van der Geest, 2005). As shown in this book, psychologists have invested a lot of energy in studying ethnocentrism, but there has been little study into how psychology suffers from ethnocentrism.

International psychology suffers considerably from ethnocentrism – primarily, from Western-centrism or Eurocentrism. This kind of ethnocentrism can be seen as a rough aggregation of different ethnocentrisms from various Western ethnic groups. If one wants to be more specific, one can say that probably the strongest influence on international psychology has US Anglo/White ethnocentrism (and not Hispanic-American, Asian-American, African-American, or Native-American ethnocentrism). Next, there is also an influence of ethnocentrism of English-speaking countries, that is, of their dominant ethnic groups, such as White English and Anglo-Canadians. Next, Western European ethnocentrism is also involved – though several Western European ethnic groups dominate – such as Germans and the Dutch. Nonetheless, this kind of ethnocentrism is just an aspect of the historically dominant Eurocentrism – which is an amalgam of different kinds of European ethnocentrisms. At present, other kinds of ethnocentrism have marginal effects on international psychology.

To understand international psychology, it is very useful to look at Moghaddam's (1987) distinction regarding different worlds in psychology, which is still relevant today. He claimed that there are three main worlds of psychology: (1) the First World, which includes only the US; (2) the Second World, which includes countries such as the UK and Canada; and (3) the Third World, which includes all other countries where psychology is studied, such as India and Nigeria. There is a huge disparity of influences on international psychology, given the disparities in resources and infrastructure between these three worlds, and the influence is overwhelmingly from the First World on the other two worlds, and somewhat from the Second World on the Third World. There is not much, if any, influence from the Third World on the First and Second Worlds, and only a slight influence from the Second World on the First World.

On the following pages I will show that ethnocentrism deeply affects psychology across many levels. When it comes to the six dimensions of ethnocentrism, it is predominantly the preference and superiority dimensions that affect the study of psychology, though it is possible that other dimensions may have certain influences. It is, however, important to point out that it is improbable that ethnic prejudice (i.e., hatred, dislike, or disdain of ethnic outgroups) considerably affects the study of psychology.

Influences of ethnocentrism on psychology

1. Topics of study

The first level at which ethnocentrism affects psychology is in the choice of topics of study. Hot topics are usually those that are at a particular time most relevant to the researchers' culture, and one is often less likely to find topics that are relevant to other cultures, such as pre-industrial societies. This is evident in the area of social psychology, where researchers usually take the most salient societal problems as topics of study (Moscovici, 1972); for example, the topic of conformity was central to US social psychologists because it is an immigrant society, which has valued assimilation of ethnic groups into the dominant Anglo/White American culture. This kind of focus may be less important to researchers in other ethnic groups and countries, which may have different preoccupations and histories. Nonetheless, topics and issues that may matter to people in other ethnic groups, such as social shaming or emotions specific to certain cultures, may be of little interest to psychologists from Western countries (Wang, 2017).

Even when it comes to the study of prejudice, much of the literature on prejudice in psychology "focuses to an extraordinary degree on the narrow politics of the United States, often from the even narrower perspective of college undergraduates" (Green & Seher, 2003, p. 525). For example, a typical article in a mainstream psychology journal that studies prejudice is most likely to study prejudice of Anglo/ White-Americans against African-Americans despite this being just one out of probably tens of thousands of different kinds of ethnic prejudice in the world. Further, when focusing on specific aspects of prejudice, researchers have usually focused on the most salient societal issues related to prejudice at the time of the study (Duckitt, 2010). For example, psychologists in the 1960s typically focused on the study of sociocultural aspects of prejudice, such as prejudiced norms and culture, most likely because of the salience of civil rights campaigns concerning the status of African-Americans in the US.

2. Theoretical frameworks

In contrast to certain disciplines, such as anthropology, psychology is open to the idea that there are human universals (D. E. Brown, 2004). Nevertheless, theoretical frameworks in psychology are often based on local assumptions and findings, which are presented as universal. Often theorists in psychology assume that their theory should apply to humans everywhere, and that theories developed based on a local group usually require no, or at times minor, modifications when applied to different contexts (Hall et al., 2016).

Furthermore, ethnocentrism is often hidden because "non-Euro-American views are not taken into account and only Euro-American perspectives of an object, event or story are discussed" (Teo & Febbraro, 2003, p. 678). For example, at least since Allport's (1954) seminal book on prejudice, the phenomenon of prejudice is usually considered by psychologists to be bad, irrational, abhorrent, and unjustified. This idea is contested theoretically and conceptually (Dixon & Levine, 2012), and is possibly not represented in many, or perhaps, most ethnic groups' views of prejudice, which may include the views that prejudice against certain groups, including ethnic groups, could be good, rational, acceptable, and justified.

Greeson (1994) declared that ethnocentrism may create academic cultural imperialism because the perspectives of dominant groups can be enforced upon other groups. Writing about how psychological theories historically represented non-White, mostly Black, ethnic groups, Naidoo (1996), for example, claimed that these theories often assumed the superiority of Whites and a variety of deficiencies of other ethnic groups. For example, Naidoo wrote that three broad theoretical models have been prominent in representing "them", that is, ethnic outgroups: (a) the inferiority model, which assumed that "they" are primitive and inferior; (b) the genetic deficiency model, which assumed that "they" have genetic deficiencies and, therefore, have inadequate outcomes; and (c) the culturally deprived or deficient model, which assumed that "their" deprived environments create inadequate outcomes and that "their" culture should emulate Western culture to become "normal" and not "deprived". At times, these descriptions have gone as far as is seen in the following description:

> Studying Africans "in health and disease," Carothers (1953) concluded from a small sample of patients in a Kenyan psychiatric hospital that Africans were akin to "lobotomized Europeans" or at least to neurotic Europeans. Other researchers measured IQ pegged to their culture and affirmed that Africans and their descendants show lower intelligence in comparison to Europeans (e.g., Croizet, 2008; Croizet & Dutrévis, 2004; Kamin, 1974).
>
> *as quoted in Bulhan, 2015, p. 249*

As a result of these broad influences on psychology, psychology often represents existing social structures and relations as normative and studies them as they are, without challenging them in any way (Moghaddam, 1990). In such a way, psychological theories often validate and justify the existing social structures within the theorist's own society, which is most often dominated by one ethnic group. They also validate the existing intergroup relations within a society as normal, and, as a result, psychologists rarely challenge the status quo (Billig, 1976). Psychological descriptions have often, possibly unintentionally, described those from other ethnic groups as deviant, deficient, and requiring instruction or even control. It is not, therefore, surprising that when other ethnic groups learn Western psychology, they may experience their identities as problematic and feel that their concepts are irrelevant and outdated (Marsella, 1998, p. 1285). For example, one of the most eminent psychologists from Europe, Serge Moscovici (1972), mentioned that he found many ideas in American social psychology foreign as they did not speak to his experiences and understanding of the social world. Only after spending time in the US, talking to American social psychologists, and understanding their viewpoint, was he able to understand more fully these ideas. It is interesting that many people in developing countries even find cross-cultural psychological research largely irrelevant (Berry, Poortinga, Segall, & Dasen, 1992).

3. Methods

The choice of methods that psychologists use may also reflect the ethnocentrism of the researchers. For example, psychologists have tended to use empirical, and primarily experimental, methods to study humans, and for a long time the dominant approach was profoundly empiricist, as was the case with behaviourism (Watson, 1925). Empiricism has been, in fact, the dominant method in psychology – at least since behaviourism. Empiricism itself is a philosophical approach that has been most influenced by British empiricist philosophers, such as John Locke, David

Hume, and Jeremy Bentham. Experimentation itself has a particular emphasis on control and prediction – which are seen as hallmarks of the behaviourist theoretical approach. Even cross-cultural psychology usually uses Western methods to empirically study non-Western populations. Accordingly, a broad methodological approach in psychology would usually reflect a particular ethnocentric viewpoint.

Whom do psychologists usually study? One would like to think that psychologists randomly sample from the full population of humans as they make inferences about the whole of humanity. Nonetheless, there has not been a single psychological study that has actually done this. Psychologists most often sample participants from their own nations, primarily the dominant ethnic groups, which are most likely privileged and go to university to study psychology, and then assume that inferences made about these participants hold for the whole of humanity. In fact, almost all psychological knowledge is based on participants from countries where most psychological work is done: Western, Educated, Industrialised, Rich, and Democratic (WEIRD) societies (Henrich, Heine, & Norenzayan, 2010). Not only that participants in these countries are not representative of humans, they actually resemble typical humans much less than most other human groups do (Henrich et al., 2010). For example, Atran and Medin (2008) wrote that psychological research is almost completely focused on students at major research universities doing an introductory psychology course: "Only with considerable effort could one come up with a more select, narrow population to study" (Atran & Medin, 2008, p. 5). That this is rarely acknowledged as a fundamental limitation of psychological methods is evidence of ethnocentrism, whereby people, on the basis of their ethnic group, infer what humans are alike (Gumplowicz, 1883, 1887; Wenzel et al., 2007). Even when research includes people from other ethnic groups and nations, participants are usually students, who are different in many ways (e.g., socioeconomic status, age, cognitive ability) to most people from their ethnic groups and nations (Goodwin, 1996).

Similarly, materials and procedures used in psychological research are almost exclusively developed by Western psychologists, who have the power to judge what materials and procedures are appropriate or not (e.g., through editorial and review processes for major international journals). The materials and procedures are commonly exported to other parts of the world to study phenomena originally identified, conceptualised, measured, and investigated in Western countries. It is rare that materials and procedures are developed by non-Western researchers, and if at times they are developed, these tend to be ignored and not widely used. In general, when it comes to cross-cultural research, it has often been done by Western researchers, interpreted by Western researchers, reviewed and edited by Western researchers, and shared with other Western researchers. As a consequence, when it comes to the study of humans, Europeans are the subjects who actively do the studies, and the others, if involved in studies at all, are most often quiet and passive objects of these studies: Europeans are in the foreground and non-Europeans in the background (Alatas, 2014). Consequently, it was argued that "until alternative approaches, focusing on other research topics and theories, and rooted in other cultures, have been formulated and extensively tested, psychology will unfortunately remain a Western, ethnocentric, and incomplete science" (Berry et al., 1992, p. 10).

4. Representations of the history of psychology

It has been recognised for a long time that ethnocentrism affects how scientists represent the history of science. In general, when it comes to broad developments in the history of ideas, Europeans credit themselves and ignore the multicultural origins of many ideas (Alatas, 2014). Nevertheless, even within the European tradition, there is a lot of competition between different ethnic groups and nations. For example, an editorial from a 1948 Russian scientific journal stated: "The Russian people has the richest history. In the course of this history, it has created the richest culture, and all the other countries of the world have drawn upon it and continue to draw upon it to this day" (as quoted in Merton, 1973, p. 296). Merton (1973) discussed the problem of ethnocentrism in the sociology of science, and wrote about ethnocentric competition and ethnocentric glorification that comes with discoveries and development of science. He observed that:

> In a world made up of national states, each with its own share of ethnocentrism, the new discovery rebounds to the credit of the discoverer not as an individual only, but also as a national. From at least the seventeenth century, Britons, Frenchmen, Germans, Dutchmen, and Italians have urged their country's claims to priority; a little later, Americans and Russians entered the lists to make it clear that they had primacy.
>
> *Merton, 1973, p. 296*

This is often implicit or explicit in psychology as well. For example, Allport's (1968) history of social psychology implied that the first social psychological experiment was done by an American, Triplett (1898). As a result, these days American textbooks, and even books about the history of psychology, see Triplett as the originator of experimental social psychology – even though there had been other social psychological experiments before Triplett's work (see Haines & Vaughan, 1979, for a discussion). For example, Binet and Henri (1894), French researchers, studied suggestibility in children using the technique that many years later Asch (1955) would largely reuse in his studies of conformity. Asch, however, never acknowledged the previous work by Binet and Henri (Nicolas, Collins, Gounden, & Roediger, 2011) and Asch's work is usually seen as a pioneering work on conformity in social psychology. In fact, as discussed before, it is ironic that Sumner, a US social scientist who wrote in English, has been celebrated as the inventor of the term ethnocentrism despite Gumplowicz using it before Sumner in numerous non-English-language publications. Finally, it is often the case that representations of the history of psychology are hidden in that non-Western psychological sources are not mentioned at all when teaching or covering the history of psychology (Teo & Febbraro, 2003).

5. Psychological institutions

Psychological institutions, such as associations and societies, which tend to administer flagship journals and organise conferences, often reflect Western ethnocentrism, and they declare what is valued and what is not. Although psychological conferences are important, psychological journals represent the state of psychology as a science. For example, Arnett (2008) has conducted a careful analysis of publishing in the American Psychological Association's top journals in the period 2003–2007. His analyses showed that overall 73% of journal authors were based at US universities, a minority were from other English-speaking countries and Europe, with only 2% of the first authors being from outside English-speaking countries and Europe (with 1% from Israel and 1% from Asia, and none from South America, Africa, and the rest of the Middle East). When it comes to the other authors (second, third, and others), 74% of them were American-based, the minority from other English-speaking countries and Europe, and only 2% from the remaining parts of the world (1% Israel and 1% Asia). Similarly, there were 68% US, largely European/White American, samples, a minority of samples were from English-speaking countries and Europe, and again only 3% of the sample from the rest of the world (Asia, South America, Israel, and less than 1% from Africa and the Middle East). Furthermore, all editors were American, 82% of associated editors and 82% of editorial board members/consulting editors were from the US, with almost all others from other English-speaking countries or Europe.

Arnett went on to say: "If the goal of APA journals is to promote psychology as a human science and not just a science of Americans, their content and their editorial leadership should reflect this" (Arnett, 2008, p. 604). He claimed that strong ethnocentric assumptions underlie the world of academic research and publishing, and that these biases stem from US wealth, which enables a lot of research and publishing, but also from the already discussed view that any human participant is a good representative of all humans. A more recent analysis (Cheek, 2017) of articles from five journals published by the Association for Psychological Science (APS), such as *Perspectives on Psychological Science* and *Psychological Science*, which "is, according to its website, the most prominent empirical psychology journal" (Cheek, 2017, p. 1136), shows similar findings, where the percentage of the first authors is overwhelmingly in favour of US psychologists.

Finally, Teo and Febbraro (2003) pointed out that those familiar with academic institutions are likely to know what needs to be done to succeed in psychology as they are knowledgeable about the system and how to game it. Accordingly, outsiders, although they may be exceptionally knowledgeable about psychology in their own cultural context, but with little or no understanding of how the system works, may make little or no contribution to the field of international psychology. In the words of Teo and Febbraro (2003): "Euro-American psychology comes with a whole apparatus of power (money, infrastructure, technologies, cultural support) that does not provide other ideas the same footing for their distribution" (p. 679).

6. Scientific social networks

Related to the above point is the role of ethnocentrism in scientific social networks. These are usually formed within one's country, most likely within one ethnic group, and this may have implications for conforming psychologists' assumptions and views. For example, US psychologists are more likely to be exposed to or collaborate with other US psychologists, or Chinese psychologists with other Chinese psychologists. In fact, even within nations, social networks appear to be formed around ethnicity. A recent study showed that out of 2.57 million scientific papers in the Thomson-Reuters Web of Science database, American scientists, even controlling for other variables, were more likely to collaborate and publish with other scientists from their own ethnic group than with those from another ethnic group (Freeman & Huang, 2015). These scientific social networks also influence the reputation of scientists, and, given the somewhat vague subject matter in the social sciences, reputations there have much more impact on the definition of success than in disciplines such as physics, further reinforcing ethnocentrism (Gareau, 1983; Melanson, 1972).

It is not surprising that recently Diener, Oishi, and Park (2014) found that on their list of eminent modern-era psychologists only nine out of the top 100 most eminent psychologists spent most or all of their careers outside the US. In addition, only five out of 348 most eminent psychologists on this list were ethnic minorities in the US. Commenting on these results, the authors state: "It is shocking that only slightly more than 1% of our eminent list was made up of three major ethnic minorities in a society in which these groups comprise 34% of the population" (Diener et al., 2014, p. 31). Social networks are extremely important here because people who are already eminent most often appoint other people from their social networks to eminent academic positions (Zarate, Hall, & Plaut, 2017) or to those that could lead to eminence.

7. Citation patterns

Closely related to the role of scientific social networks is citation patterns. In an ideal world, scholars should be fair and should be obliged to cite only those authors "who have contributed to the current state of the understanding, rather than favor oneself or one's group" (Chugh, Bazerman, & Banaji, 2005, p. 87). There is, however, a game in science that helps authors increase their own reputation. This game is of the nature "I cite you, you cite me", whereby academics are encouraged to cite researchers who cite them (Taleb, 2010; Webster, Jonason, & Schember, 2009). Accordingly, as a result of the clusters of mutual citations, there are various cliques of authors who cite each other. Given the nature of scientific networks, these cliques may often consist of people of the same ethnic group.

Research in general supports the role of ethnocentrism in citations. Research found evidence for ethnic biases among social scientists: Jewish social scientists were particularly likely to cite other Jewish social scientists, whereas non-Jewish social scientists were particularly likely to cite other non-Jewish social scientists (Greenwald & Schuh, 1994). It is interesting the same finding was replicated in this research even when analysing the citations of social scientists who study prejudice.

Further, these days it is rare to cite non-English-language sources in mainstream psychology. Greeson (1991) analysed ethnocentrism in citations, comparing American and Scandinavian journals, and found that American journals prefer to cite American authors and largely ignore psychological work from other countries. Yet, Scandinavian journals tend to primarily cite articles from American journals, but also often cite articles from psychological journals from Europe and other parts of the world. Similarly, White (1990) showed that American, and to a certain extent British, journals report a tiny amount of citations of educational psychology publications from the rest of the world. A recent analysis of citations in the journals published by the APS (Cheek, 2017) showed that articles by US first authors appeared to received more citations than articles by authors from outside the US, although the effects were not statistically significant for all APS journals.

When it comes to the sheer volume of research in psychology, much is done in the US because it has a sophisticated and supportive infrastructure (Moghaddam, 1987). In consequence, it is not surprising that reference lists these days are populated with English-language sources, and one hardly finds a reference to articles or books written in other languages. Unfortunately, psychology researchers and theorists writing in languages other than English are, unless translated into English, condemned to international obscurity. Ethnocentrism is therefore visible when one examines the reference section in journal articles or books. It is highly improbable that the author of an article or a book has thoroughly read everything that has been published on the topic in many languages, and across different time periods. Nevertheless, due to the sheer power of influence of the English language (which has historically been due to the influence of the British Empire and, more recently, due to the influence of the US), citations in the English language are dominant.

Barriers to non-ethnocentric psychology

It is widely agreed on in psychology that it should be the study of all humans everywhere, and its theories and explanations should be ultimately relevant to all humans. Psychology is fundamentally a generalising science, which attempts to reach conclusions about humans in general, and not only about specific humans within a specific culture or time period. For example, Sherif and Sherif warned us a long time ago: "The use of scientific methods and techniques does not guard against the danger that finding will be applicable only to a particular set of people at a particular time and place" (1969, p. 5). More recently, another group of psychologists wrote: "Psychologists who choose not to do cross-cultural psychology may have chosen to be ethnographers instead" (Nisbett, Peng, Choi, & Norenzayan, 2001, p. 307). Many psychologists are aware of these problems, but we still do not have non-ethnocentric psychology, and in this section I will discuss why.

For psychologists not to be ethnographers, but scholars interested in the psychology of all humans, we need to understand, analyse, and transcend barriers. The first group of barriers relates to societal and institutional barriers, and the second to individual barriers. The two groups of barriers could affect each other.

National governments usually represent the interests of dominant ethnic groups and often their elites. Psychology is focused on dominant social problems within a society, and funding for research is often given to researchers who conduct research that is beneficial to national governments and the elites. Advanced and powerful countries benefit from ethnocentrism, and tend to promote national interests and those of the dominant ethnic groups. For example, the US Army funded cross-cultural research, called Project Camelot, in developing countries because it wanted to better understand the potential for insurgency in these countries in order to contain and fight it (Warwick, 1980). Psychological institutions have also played a role even in appalling practices, such as torture (see Eidelson, 2015). It appears that societies and institutions are not ready to expend a lot of the resources needed for non-ethnocentric psychology. In line with these points, it has been recently argued that:

> Contrary to the rhetoric of scientific inquiry, scientific institutions and practices are not a transcendent or neutral enterprise disembedded from culture, politics, and power. Instead, science is a positioned form of knowledge that reflects the understandings and interests of people in positions of dominance (e.g., what is worthy of study, what counts as basic theory or narrow application, etc.). The production and reproduction of some understandings (and simultaneous silencing of others) is not a simple triumph of truth over ignorance, but often reflects the agenda of funding agencies and demands of various consumers of the scientific product.
>
> *Adams, Dobles, Gómez, Kurtiş, & Molina, 2015, p. 217*

Individuals have their own barriers, and often they conform to or react to the societal barriers. For example, individual psychologists do not have much to gain from challenging the society and institutions. When it comes to academic institutions, modern academia is conducive not to slow scholarship, but to fast publishing. To do non-ethnocentric psychology, one needs to gain a sufficient understanding of other cultures, of other languages, of historical writings in different disciplines, and so forth. One therefore needs to be devoted to slow scholarship – to learning and reading a lot rather than to quickly publishing a lot. One needs to be prepared for very expensive, elaborate, and sophisticated cross-cultural studies, which require a lot of time. Nevertheless, in the words of Billig (2013): "By and large, academics today are not writing in answer to a higher calling or because they have dedicated themselves to the pursuit of truth. We are, to put it bluntly, hacks who write for a living" (p. 14).

In consequence, psychologists are not rewarded for doing non-ethnocentric psychology. In fact, doing conventional research concerned with ethnicity and culture appears to be disadvantageous to researchers. For example, a recent analysis has shown that "researchers whose publications are on cognitive issues have at least six-fold more opportunities to be cited than researchers whose publications are on race, ethnicity, or diversity" (Zarate et al., 2017, pp. 1177–1178). Given that citations are indicators of success in academia these days, doing non-ethnocentric psychology that is explicitly focused on ethnic and cultural issues is not much rewarded by institutions. Although many commentators on ethnocentrism in psychology appear to think that doing non-ethnocentric psychology is a choice, there are substantial risks associated with it and careers may suffer (e.g., those who want to do non-ethnocentric psychology may be less likely to get jobs in academia, less likely to secure tenure, less likely to be promoted, less likely to become eminent). Nonetheless, ignoring the problem is not a solution either. Teo and Febbraro (2003) claimed that psychologists "who are not willing to inquire about alternative constructions in other cultures or subcultures must either admit from the beginning that their knowledge is particular, Western-focused and eurocentric, or they must accept the assessment that they are part of the hidden ethnocentrism of Euro-American psychology." (p. 684)

The way forward

Although many suggestions about how to transcend ethnocentrism in psychology tend to be casual and mundane (e.g., articles often finish with a statement that a study should be done in a different context or culture), certain suggestions tend to carry more weight, and they require internal and institutional changes of the discipline of psychology. As mentioned above, psychology is currently dominated by ethnocentrism from America and people from English-speaking countries (and several Western European countries). Psychology could transform through institutional changes, but also through individual changes. For example, Arnett's (2008) suggestions about how to transcend US dominance in psychology call for institutional changes. These include appointing non-American editors and associate editors, having special issues by non-American authors, helping non-American authors with publishing, making it compulsory for undergraduate psychology students to study cultural psychology and anthropology, and having major funding bodies fund cross-cultural research, international collaborations, and non-US graduate students. These are mainly specific suggestions for US psychologists.

More broadly, researchers should acknowledge, study, and understand their own ethnocentrism and be confronted by it. Although this may appear easy, and researchers may believe they are tolerant of people from other ethnicities and possibly free of ethnocentrism, ethnocentric biases do appear deeply ingrained within individuals and institutions. Nevertheless, psychologists need to work on themselves if they want to transcend ethnocentrism. They should also study topics and develop theoretical models that may not be of immediate interest to people in their ethnic group, but that may be of interest to people from very distant ethnic groups. Psychologists should do cultural psychology because it "is succeeding in divesting academic psychology of implicit and ingrained ethnocentric biases" (Atran & Medin, 2008, p. 145).

Psychologists should also learn different languages and attempt to write and publish in journals in different languages. Moreover, learning a different, preferably non-European, language may need to be required of psychologists. In fact, the best solution would be to use or construct an artificial language for all scientific communication (cf. Gordin, 2015). Today in science, there is a particular kind of ethnocentrism whereby non-English-speakers may perceive themselves to be outsiders, who struggle with learning and writing a foreign language, whereas English-speaking scientists do not have any incentives to learn foreign languages, perceiving them as irrelevant (Gordin, 2015). Non-ethnocentric psychology would be easier to develop when there is no obvious preference for a language associated with one ethnic group.

Further, psychologists should attempt to develop theories that would be universal, but that would attempt to integrate a variety of cultural perspectives on the topics they try to explain. They should attempt to design studies which could be fully replicated in non-Western countries. A lot has been written on failures to replicate studies even in the same culture, but even the most ambitious attempts to replicate in psychology (such as Open Science Collaboration, 2015) rarely or never try to replicate findings in extremely different cultures. Further, psychologists in Western countries should be more open to theories and methods coming from non-Western countries – as well as to those coming from ethnic minority groups within Western countries. Psychologists would need to be more open to hearing the perspectives of people from other ethnic groups about their interpretations of psychological phenomena, without imposing ethnocentric interpretations while judging psychological phenomena in other cultural groups (see Wang, 2017).

Psychologists should also influence their societies, such as psychology institutions, universities, and governments, to focus on and fund research that truly promotes universal and non-ethnocentric psychology. This would also need to involve transcending the publish-or-perish world of modern academia. To gain a sufficient understanding of other cultures, languages, or historical writings in different disciplines, one needs to be devoted to reading and learning a lot rather than quickly publishing a lot. The current practices value researchers who read journal articles in top journals, mainly those published in the US and a few Western European countries, conduct research on hot topics, and then publish that research in these same journals. Psychologists are not rewarded for the painstaking work that non-ethnocentric psychology requires. In fact, doing this kind of work may have detrimental consequences for one's career.

Additionally, psychologists should devote more time and energy to learning and knowing the history of their own discipline. As mentioned earlier, psychology suffers from disciplinary amnesia (Nisbett, 1990; Oishi, Kesebir, & Snyder, 2009), perhaps even more than sociology, which was also accused of the same condition (Agger, 2007; Steinmetz, 2013). There might be various reasons apart from ethnocentrism for this (e.g., psychology is seen as a cumulative discipline, where newer theories and studies are superior to older theories and studies), but understanding historical perspectives on psychological theories and concepts could help psychologists see that many important psychological ideas have been developed across many cultures and time periods. This can help psychologists transcend both ethnocentrism and acrochronism (cf. Gumplowicz, 1895).

Summary and conclusions

In this chapter I showed that ethnocentrism still affects the study of psychology at many levels: the topics of study, theoretical frameworks, the choice of methods, such as participants, materials, and procedures, the representations of the history of psychology, psychological institutions, scientific social networks, and the citation patterns in psychology. Additionally, there appear to be both institutional and individual barriers that prevent us from developing and practising non-ethnocentric psychology. Ethnocentrism is, therefore, not just something that affects people whom psychologists study, but something that deeply affects the study of psychology and sciences more broadly. In fact, it probably affects all areas of human endeavour.

In this chapter, I also presented several suggestions that could help psychologists along the path towards reducing ethnocentrism in psychology and creating non-ethnocentric psychology. There are certainly many others. For example, Marsella and Pedersen (2004) proposed 50 specific suggestions for how to internationalise psychology, and many of these could well help us create a non-ethnocentric discipline. It is likely that psychologists cannot fully escape ethnocentrism (Berry et al., 1992; Brislin, 1983), but they could undoubtedly do more to lessen its impact across many domains and move us much further towards a truly universal science of the human mind.

REFERENCES

Abercrombie, N., Hill, S., & Turner, B. S. (1994). *The Penguin dictionary of sociology* (3rd ed.). London: Penguin.

Aberson, C. L., Healy, M., & Romero, V. (2000). Ingroup bias and self-esteem: A meta-analysis. *Personality and Social Psychology Review*, 4, 157–173. https://doi.org/10.1207/S15327957PSPR0402_04

Aboud, F. E. (1988). *Children and prejudice*. Oxford: Basil Blackwell.

Abrams, D., & Hogg, M. A. (1988). Comments on the motivational status of self-esteem in social identity and intergroup discrimination. *European Journal of Social Psychology*, 18, 317–334. https://doi.org/10.1002/ejsp.2420180403

Abrams, D., & Hogg, M. A. (2004). Metatheory: Lessons from social identity research. *Personality and Social Psychology Review*, 8, 98–106. https://doi.org/10.1207/s15327957pspr0802_2

Adams, G., Dobles, I., Gómez, L. H., Kurtiş, T., & Molina, L. E. (2015). Decolonizing psychological science: Introduction to the special thematic section. *Journal of Social and Political Psychology*, 3, 213–238. https://doi.org/10.5964/jspp.v3i1.564

Adler, N. E., Epel, E. S., Castellazzo, G., & Ickovics, J. R. (2000). Relationship of subjective and objective social status with psychological and physiological functioning: Preliminary data in healthy white women. *Health Psychology*, 19, 586–592.

Adorno, T. W., Frenkel-Brunswik, E., Levinson, D. J., & Sanford, R. N. (1950). *The authoritarian personality*. New York, NY: Harper.

Agger, B. (2007). *Public sociology: From social facts to literary acts* (2nd ed.). Lanham, MD: Rowman & Littlefield.

Akrami, N., & Ekehammar, B. (2006). Right-wing authoritarianism and social dominance orientation: Their roots in Big-Five personality factors and facets. *Journal of Individual Differences*, 27, 117–126. https://doi.org/10.1027/1614-0001.27.3.117

Alatas, S. F. (2014). *Applying Ibn Khaldūn: The recovery of a lost tradition in sociology*. Abingdon: Routledge.

Allport, G. W. (1937). *Personality: A psychological interpretation*. New York, NY: Henry Holt.

Allport, G. W. (1954). *The nature of prejudice*. Reading, MA: Addison-Wesley.

Allport, G. W. (1960). *Personality and social encounter: Selected essays*. Boston, MA: Beacon.

Allport, G. W. (1968). The historical background of modern social psychology. In G. Lindzey & E. Aronson (Eds.), *Handbook of social psychology* (2nd ed., Vol. 1, pp. 3–56). Reading, MA: Addison Wesley.

Allport, G. W., & Odbert, H. S. (1936). Trait-names: A psycho-lexical study. *Psychological Monographs: General and Applied, 47*, i-171. https://doi.org/10.1037/h0093360

Altemeyer, B. (1981). *Right-wing authoritarianism.* Winnipeg: University of Manitoba Press.

Altemeyer, B. (1996). *The authoritarian specter.* Cambridge, MA: Harvard University Press.

Altemeyer, B. (1998). The other "authoritarian personality". *Advances in Experimental Social Psychology, 30*, 47–92. https://doi.org/10.1016/S0065-2601(08)60382-2

Altemeyer, B. (2003). Why do religious fundamentalists tend to be prejudiced? *The International Journal for the Psychology of Religion, 13*, 17–28. https://doi.org/10.1207/S15327582IJPR1301_03

Altemeyer, B. (2006). *The authoritarians.* Winnipeg: Author. Retrieved from http://theauthoritarians.org/Downloads/TheAuthoritarians.pdf

Aly, G. (2016). *Hitler's beneficiaries: Plunder, racial war, and the Nazi welfare state* (J. Chase, Trans.). London: Verso. (Original work published 2005)

American Psychological Association. (2001). *Thesaurus of psychological index terms* (9th ed.). Washington DC: Author.

Andreski, S. (1972). *Social sciences as sorcery.* London: Deutsch.

Aristotle. (1881). *The Nicomachean Ethics of Aristotle* (F. H. Peters, Trans.). London: C. Kegan Paul.

Arndt, J., Greenberg, J., & Cook, A. (2002). Mortality salience and the spreading activation of worldview-relevant constructs: Exploring the cognitive architecture of terror management. *Journal of Experimental Psychology: General, 131*, 307–324. https://doi.org/10.1037/0096-3445.131.3.307

Arndt, J., Greenberg, J., Pyszczynski, T., & Solomon, S. (1997). Subliminal exposure to death-related stimuli increases defense of the cultural worldview. *Psychological Science, 8*, 379–385. https://doi.org/10.1111/j.1467-9280.1997.tb00429.x

Arnett, J. (2008). The neglected 95%: Why American psychology needs to become less American. *American Psychologist, 63*, 602–614. https://doi.org/10.1037/0003-066X.63.7.602

Asch, S. E. (1955). Opinions and social pressure. *Scientific American, 193*, 31–35. https://doi.org/10.1038/scientificamerican1155-31

Ashmore, R. D. (1970). The problem of intergroup prejudice. In B. E. Collins (Ed.), *Social psychology: Social influence, attitude change, group processes, and prejudice* (pp. 243–296). Reading, MA: Addison-Wesley.

Atran, S., & Medin, D. L. (2008). *The native mind and the cultural construction of nature.* Cambridge, MA: A Bradford Book.

Bain, P. G., Park, J., Kwok, C., & Haslam, N. (2009). Attributing human uniqueness and human nature to cultural groups: Distinct forms of subtle dehumanization. *Group Processes & Intergroup Relations, 12*, 789–805. https://doi.org/10.1177/1368430209340415

Balabanis, G., & Diamantopoulos, A. (2016). Consumer xenocentrism as determinant of foreign product preference: A system justification perspective. *Journal of International Marketing.* https://doi.org/10.1509/JIM.15.0138

Balabanis, G., Diamantopoulos, A., Mueller, R. D., & Melewar, T. C. (2001). The impact of nationalism, patriotism and internationalism on consumer ethnocentric tendencies. *Journal of International Business Studies, 32*, 157–175. https://doi.org/10.1057/palgrave.jibs.8490943

Balliet, D., Wu, J., & De Dreu, C. K. W. (2014). Ingroup favoritism in cooperation: A meta-analysis. *Psychological Bulletin, 140*, 1556–1581. https://doi.org/10.1037/a0037737

Bandura, A. (1999). Social cognitive theory of personality. In L. A. Pervin & O. P. John (Eds.), *Handbook of personality* (2nd ed., pp. 185–241). New York, NY: Guilford.

Bannister, R. C. (1991). *Sociology and scientism: The American quest for objectivity, 1880–1940.* Chapel Hill, NC: UNC Press.

Banton, M. P. (1967). *Race relations.* London: Tavistock.

Banton, M. P. (1998). *Racial theories* (2nd ed). Cambridge: Cambridge University Press.

Barash, D. P. (2007). Evolution and group selection. *Science*, 317, 596–597.

Bar-Tal, D. (1989). Delegitimization: The extreme case of stereotyping and prejudice. In D. Bar-Tal, A. W. Kruglanski, & W. Stroebe (Eds.), *Stereotyping and prejudice: Changing conceptions* (pp. 169–182). New York, NY: Springer.

Bar-Tal, D. (1990). Causes and consequences of delegitimization: Models of conflict and ethnocentrism. *Journal of Social Issues*, 46, 65–81. https://doi.org/10.1111/j.1540-4560.1990.tb00272.x

Bar-Tal, D. (2007). Sociopsychological foundations of intractable conflicts. *American Behavioral Scientist*, 50, 1430–1453. https://doi.org/10.1177/0002764207302462

Bar-Tal, D. (2013). *Intractable conflicts: Socio-psychological foundations and dynamics.* New York, NY: Cambridge University Press.

Bartz, J. A., Zaki, J., Bolger, N., & Ochsner, K. N. (2011). Social effects of oxytocin in humans: Context and person matter. *Trends in Cognitive Sciences*, 15, 301–309. https://doi.org/10.1016/j.tics.2011.05.002

Bateson, P. (2015). Why are individuals so different from each other? *Heredity*, 115, 285–292. https://doi.org/10.1038/hdy.2014.103

Baumgartner, T., Nash, K., Hill, C., & Knoch, D. (2015). Neuroanatomy of intergroup bias: A white matter microstructure study of individual differences. *NeuroImage*, 122, 345–354. https://doi.org/10.1016/j.neuroimage.2015.08.011

Baumgartner, T., Schiller, B., Rieskamp, J., Gianotti, L. R. R., & Knoch, D. (2014). Diminishing parochialism in intergroup conflict by disrupting the right temporo-parietal junction. *Social Cognitive and Affective Neuroscience*, 9, 653–660. https://doi.org/10.1093/scan/nst023

Bausch, A. W. (2015). The geography of ethnocentrism. *Journal of Conflict Resolution*, 59, 510–527. https://doi.org/10.1177/0022002713515401

Bayar, M. (2009). Reconsidering primordialism: An alternative approach to the study of ethnicity. *Ethnic and Racial Studies*, 32, 1639–1657. https://doi.org/10.1080/01419870902763878

Becker, E. (1962). *The birth and death of meaning.* New York, NY: Free Press.

Becker, E. (1973). *The denial of death.* New York, NY: Free Press.

Becker, E. (1975). *Escape from evil.* New York, NY: Free Press.

Bell-Fialkoff, A. (1992). A brief history of ethnic cleansing. *Foreign Affairs*, 72, 110–121. https://doi.org/10.2307/20045626

Bennet, C. (1995). *Yugoslavia's bloody collapse: Cause, course and consequences.* New York, NY: New York University Press.

Berger, P. L., & Luckmann, T. (1966). *The social construction of reality: A treatise in the sociology of knowledge.* Garden City, NY: Doubleday.

Berry, J. W., & Kalin, R. (1995). Multicultural and ethnic attitudes in Canada: An overview of the 1991 national survey. *Canadian Journal of Behavioural Science*, 27, 301–320. https://doi.org/10.1037/0008-400X.27.3.301

Berry, J. W., Poortinga, Y. H., Segall, M. H., & Dasen, P. R. (1992). *Cross-cultural psychology: Research and applications.* Cambridge: Cambridge University Press.

Beswick, D. G., & Hills, M. D. (1969). An Australian Ethnocentrism Scale. *Australian Journal of Psychology*, 21, 211–225. https://doi.org/10.1080/00049536908257791

Bethlehem, R. A. I., Baron-Cohen, S., van Honk, J., Auyeung, B., & Bos, P. A. (2014). The oxytocin paradox. *Frontiers in Behavioral Neuroscience*, 8. https://doi.org/10.3389/fnbeh.2014.00048

Bettelheim, B. (1947). Individual and mass behavior in extreme situations. In M. Newcomb, E. L. Hartley, & others (Eds.), *Readings in social psychology* (pp. 628–638). New York, NY: Henry Holt.

Bettencourt, B. A., Dorr, N., Charlton, K., & Hume, D. L. (2001). Status differences and in-group bias: A meta-analytic examination of the effects of status stability, legitimacy, and group permeability. *Psychological Bulletin*, 127, 520–542. https://doi.org/10.1037/0033-2909.127.4.520

Billiet, J., Maddens, B., & Beerten, R. (2003). National identity and attitude toward foreigners in a multinational state: A replication. *Political Psychology*, 24, 241–257. https://doi.org/10.1111/0162-895X.00327

Billig, M. (1976). *Social psychology and intergroup relations*. London: Academic Press.

Billig, M. (1995). *Banal nationalism*. London: Sage.

Billig, M. (2013). *Learn to write badly: How to succeed in the social sciences*. Cambridge: Cambridge University Press.

Binet, A., & Henri, V. (1894). De la suggestibilité naturelle chez les enfants [Natural suggestibility in children]. *Revue Philosophique de La France et de l'Étranger*, 38, 337–347.

Bizumic, B. (2012). Theories of ethnocentrism and their implications for peacebuilding. In O. Simic, Z. Volcic, & C. R. Philpot (Eds.), *Peace psychology in the Balkans: Dealing with a violent past while building peace* (pp. 35–56). New York, NY: Springer.

Bizumic, B. (2014). Who coined the concept of ethnocentrism? A brief report. *Journal of Social and Political Psychology*, 2, 3–10. https://doi.org/10.5964/jspp.v2i1.264

Bizumic, B., & Duckitt, J. (2007). Varieties of group self-centeredness and dislike of the specific other. *Basic and Applied Social Psychology*, 29, 195–202. https://doi.org/10.1080/01973530701332252

Bizumic, B., & Duckitt, J. (2008). 'My group is not worthy of me': Narcissism and ethnocentrism. *Political Psychology*, 29, 437–453. https://doi.org/10.1111/j.1467-9221.2008.00638.x

Bizumic, B., & Duckitt, J. (2009). Narcissism and ethnocentrism: A review. *Directions in Psychiatry*, 29, 99–109.

Bizumic, B., & Duckitt, J. (2012). What is and is not ethnocentrism? A conceptual analysis and political implications. *Political Psychology*, 33, 887–909. https://doi.org/10.1111/j.1467-9221.2012.00907.x

Bizumic, B., Duckitt, J., Popadic, D., Dru, V., & Krauss, S. (2009). A cross-cultural investigation into a reconceptualization of ethnocentrism. *European Journal of Social Psychology*, 39, 871–899. https://doi.org/10.1002/ejsp.589

Bizumic, B., & Iino, N. (2017). *Applying the ethnocentrism framework to nationalism*. Unpublished manuscript, The Australian National University, Australia.

Bizumic, B., Smithson, M., & van Rooy, D. (2010, July). *Reconceptualized ethnocentrism and its consequences*. Paper presented at the Thirty-Third Annual Scientific Meeting of the International Society of Political Psychology, San Francisco, CA, USA.

Bizumic, B., Stubager, R., Mellon, S., Van der Linden, N., Iyer, R., & Jones, B. M. (2013). On the (in)compatibility of attitudes toward peace and war. *Political Psychology*, 34, 673–693. https://doi.org/10.1111/pops.12032

Blalock, H. M., Jr. (1982). *Race and ethnic relations*. Englewood Cliffs, NJ: Prentice Hall.

Blank, T., & Schmidt, P. (2003). National identity in a united Germany: Nationalism or patriotism? An empirical test with representative data. *Political Psychology*, 24, 289–312. https://doi.org/10.1111/0162-895X.00329

Blanton, H., & Jaccard, J. (2006). Arbitrary metrics in psychology. *American Psychologist*, 61, 27–41. https://doi.org/10.1037/0003-066X.61.1.27

Block, J. (1996). Some jangly remarks on Baumeister and Heatherton. *Psychological Inquiry*, 7, 28–32. https://doi.org/10.1207/s15327965pli0701_5

Blumer, H. (1958). Race prejudice as a sense of group position. *Pacific Sociological Review*, 1, 3–7. https://doi.org/10.2307/1388607

Boas, F. (1931). Race and progress. *Science*, 74, 1–8. https://doi.org/10.2307/1657119

Boas, F. (1934). *Aryans and non-Aryans.* New York, NY: Information and Service Associates.

Boas, F. (1940). *Race, language and culture.* New York, NY: Macmillan.

Boas, F. (1962). *Anthropology and modern life.* New York, NY: Norton. (Original work published 1928)

Bobo, L. (1988). Group conflict, prejudice, and the paradox of contemporary racial attitudes. In P. A. Katz & D. A. Taylor (Eds.), *Eliminating racism* (pp. 85–114). New York, NY: Springer US. https://doi.org/10.1007/978-1-4899-0818-6_5

Bobo, L. (1999). Prejudice as group position: Microfoundations of a sociological approach to race relations. *Journal of Social Issues*, 55, 445–472. https://doi.org/10.1111/0022-4537.00127

Bobo, L., & Zubrinsky, C. L. (1996). Attitudes on residential integration: Perceived status differences, mere in-group preference, or racial prejudice? *Social Forces*, 74, 883–909. https://doi.org/10.1093/sf/74.3.883

Boer, D., Fischer, R., González Atilano, M. L., de Garay Hernández, J., Moreno García, L. I., Mendoza, S., … Lo, E. (2013). Music, identity, and musical ethnocentrism of young people in six Asian, Latin American, and Western cultures. *Journal of Applied Social Psychology*, 43, 2360–2376. https://doi.org/10.1111/jasp.12185

Bogardus, E. S. (1922). *A history of social thought.* Los Angeles, CA: University of Southern California Press.

Bohannan, P. (1993). Preliminary notes on ethnocentrism and xenophobia. In M. T. McGuire (Ed.), *Human nature and the new Europe* (pp. 75–82). Boulder, CO: Westview Press.

Boodin, J. E. (1918). Social systems. *American Journal of Sociology*, 23, 705–734. https://doi.org/10.1086/212819

Booth, K. (2014). *Strategy and ethnocentrism.* Abingdon: Routledge. (Original work published 1979)

Bouchard, T. J., & Loehlin, J. C. (2001). Genes, evolution, and personality. *Behavior Genetics*, 31, 243–273. https://doi.org/10.1023/A:1012294324713

Boyd, R., & Richerson, P. J. (1985). *Culture and the evolutionary process.* Chicago, IL: University of Chicago Press.

Boyd, R., & Richerson, P. J. (1987). The evolution of ethnic markers. *Cultural Anthropology*, 2, 65–79. https://doi.org/10.1525/can.1987.2.1.02a00070

Bracq, J. C. (1902). A stronger sense of international justice needed. In W. R. Rose (Ed.), *Report of the Eighth Annual Lake Mohonk Conference on International Arbitration* (pp. 18–22). Mohonk Lake, NY: The Lake Mohonk Arbitration Conference.

Bredo, E. (2006). Conceptual confusion and educational psychology. In P. A. Alexander & P. H. Winne (Eds.), *Handbook of educational psychology* (2nd ed., pp. 43–57). Mahwah, NJ: Lawrence Erlbaum Associates.

Brewer, M. B. (1979). In-group bias in the minimal intergroup situation: A cognitive-motivational analysis. *Psychological Bulletin*, 86, 307–324. https://doi.org/10.1037/0033-2909.86.2.307

Brewer, M. B. (1981). Ethnocentrism and its role in interpersonal trust. In M. B. Brewer & B. C. Collins (Eds.), *Scientific inquiry and the social sciences* (pp. 345–360). San Francisco, CA: Jossey-Bass.

Brewer, M. B. (1997). The social psychology of intergroup relations: Can research inform practice. *Journal of Social Issues*, 53, 197–211. https://doi.org/10.1111/j.1540-4560.1997.tb02440.x

Brewer, M. B. (1999). The psychology of prejudice: Ingroup love and outgroup hate? *Journal of Social Issues*, 55, 429–444. https://doi.org/10.1111/0022-4537.00126

Brewer, M. B. (2007). The importance of being we: Human nature and intergroup relations. *American Psychologist*, 62, 728–738. https://doi.org/10.1037/0003-066X.62.8.728

Brewer, M. B. (2016). Ethnocentrism and the optimal distinctiveness theory of social identity. In R. J. Sternberg, S. T. Fiske, & D. J. Foss (Eds.), *Scientists making a difference: One hundred eminent behavioral and brain scientists talk about their most important contributions* (pp. 360–264). New York, NY: Cambridge University Press.

Brewer, M. B., & Campbell, D. T. (1976). *Ethnocentrism and intergroup attitudes: East African evidence*. New York, NY: Sage.

Brewer, M. B., & Gaertner, S. L. (2001). Toward reduction of prejudice: Intergroup contact and social categorization. In R. Brown & S. L. Gaertner (Eds.), *Blackwell handbook of social psychology: Intergroup processes* (pp. 451–472). Malden, MA: Blackwell.

Brewer, M. B., & Miller, N. (1984). Beyond the contact hypothesis: Theoretical perspectives on desegregation. In N. Miller & M. B. Brewer (Eds.), *Groups in contact: The psychology of desegregation* (pp. 281–302). Orlando, FL: Academic Press. https://doi.org/10.1016/B978-0-12-497780-8.50019-X

Brislin, R. (1983). Cross-cultural research in psychology. *Annual Review of Psychology*, 34, 363–400. https://doi.org/10.1146/annurev.ps.34.020183.002051

Brislin, R. (1993). *Understanding culture's influence on behavior*. Fort Worth. TX: Harcourt Brace College.

Brodkin, K. (1997). Ethnocentrism within anthropology. *Anthropology News*, 38, 3. https://doi.org/10.1111/an.1997.38.3.3

Brown, D. (1999). Are there good and bad nationalisms? *Nations and Nationalism*, 5, 281–302. https://doi.org/10.1111/j.1354-5078.1999.00281.x

Brown, D. E. (1991). *Human universals*. Philadelphia, PA: Temple University Press.

Brown, D. E. (2000). Human universals and their implications. In N. Roughley (Ed.), *Being humans: Anthropological universality and particularity in transdisciplinary perspectives* (pp. 156–174). Berlin: Walter de Gruyter.

Brown, D. E. (2004). Human universals, human nature and human culture. *Daedalus*, 133, 47–54.

Brown, R. (1965). *Social psychology*. New York, NY: The Free Press.

Brown, R. (1995). *Prejudice: Its social psychology*. Oxford: Blackwell.

Brown, R. (2000). Social identity theory: past achievements, current problems and future challenges. *European Journal of Social Psychology*, 30, 745–778. https://doi.org/10.1002/1099-0992(200011/12)30:6<745::AID-EJSP24>3.0.CO;2-O

Brown, R. (2010). *Prejudice: Its social psychology* (2nd ed.). Oxford: Wiley-Blackwell.

Brown, R., & Turner, J. C. (1981). Interpersonal and intergroup behaviour. In J. C. Turner & H. Giles (Eds.), *Intergroup behaviour* (pp. 33–65). Oxford: Basil Blackwell.

Budner, S. (1962). Intolerance of ambiguity as a personality variable. *Journal of Personality*, 30, 29–50. https://doi.org/10.1111/j.1467-6494.1962.tb02303.x

Bulhan, H. A. (2015). Stages of colonialism in Africa: From occupation of land to occupation of being. *Journal of Social and Political Psychology*, 3, 239–256. https://doi.org/10.5964/jspp.v3i1.143

Burke, B. L., Martens, A., & Faucher, E. H. (2010). Two decades of terror management theory: A meta-analysis of mortality salience research. *Personality and Social Psychology Review*, 14, 155–195. https://doi.org/10.1177/1088868309352321

Campbell, D. T. (1958). Common fate, similarity, and other indices of the status of aggregates of persons as social entities. *Behavioral Science*, 3, 14–25. https://doi.org/10.1002/bs.3830030103

Campbell, D. T. (1965). Ethnocentric and other altruistic motives. In D. Levine (Ed.), *Nebraska symposium on motivation* (pp. 283–311). Lincoln, NE: University of Nebraska Press.

Campbell, D. T., & LeVine, R. A. (1961). A proposal for cooperative cross-cultural research on ethnocentrism. *Journal of Conflict Resolution*, 5, 82–108. https://doi.org/10.1177/002200276100500111

Cantril, H. (1941). *The psychology of social movements*. New York, NY: John Wiley & Sons.

Carter, C. S. (2014). Oxytocin pathways and the evolution of human behavior. *Annual Review of Psychology*, 65, 17–39. https://doi.org/10.1146/annurev-psych-010213-115110

Case, C. M. (1922). Instinctive and cultural factors in group conflicts. *American Journal of Sociology*, 28, 1–20. https://doi.org/10.1086/213423

Cashdan, E. (2001). Ethnocentrism and xenophobia: A cross-cultural study. *Current Anthropology*, 42, 760–765. https://doi.org/10.1086/323821

Cashdan, E. (2012). In-group loyalty or out-group avoidance? Isolating the links between pathogens and in-group assortative sociality. *Behavioral and Brain Sciences*, 35, 82. https://doi.org/10.1017/S0140525X11001373

Cashman, G. (2013). *What causes war? An introduction to theories of international conflict* (2nd ed.). Lanham, MD: Rowman & Littlefield.

Castano, E., & Giner-Sorolla, R. (2006). Not quite human: Infrahumanization in response to collective responsibility for intergroup killing. *Journal of Personality and Social Psychology*, 90, 804–818. https://doi.org/10.1037/0022-3514.90.5.804

Castano, E., Yzerbyt, V., Paladino, M.-P., & Sacchi, S. (2002). I belong, therefore, I exist: Ingroup identification, ingroup entitativity, and ingroup bias. *Personality and Social Psychology Bulletin*, 28, 135–143. https://doi.org/10.1177/0146167202282001

Chan, W.-T. (Ed.). (1963). *A source book in Chinese philosophy* (W.-T. Chan, Trans.). Princeton, NJ: Princeton University Press.

Chang, E. C., & Ritter, E. H. (1976). Ethnocentrism in Black college students. *Journal of Social Psychology*, 100, 89–98. https://doi.org/10.1080/00224545.1976.9711910

Cheek, N. N. (2017). Scholarly merit in a global context: The nation gap in psychological science. *Perspectives on Psychological Science*, 12, 1133–1137. https://doi.org/10.1177/1745691617708233

Chein, I. (1946). Some considerations in combating intergroup prejudice. *Journal of Educational Sociology*, 19, 412–419. https://doi.org/10.2307/2264054

Chugh, D., Bazerman, M. H., & Banaji, M. R. (2005). Bounded ethicality as a psychological barrier to recognizing conflicts of interest. In D. A. Moore, D. M. Cain, G. Loewenstein, & M. H. Bazerman (Eds.), *Conflicts of interest: Challenges and solutions in business, law, medicine, and public policy* (pp. 74–95). New York, NY: Cambridge University Press.

Cialdini, R. B., Demaine, L. J., Sagarin, B. J., Barrett, D. B., Rhoads, K., & Winter, P. L. (2006). Managing social norms for persuasive impact. *Social Influence*, 1, 3–15. https://doi.org/10.1080/15534510500181459

Cikara, M., & Van Bavel, J. J. (2014). The neuroscience of intergroup relations: An integrative review. *Perspectives on Psychological Science*, 9, 245–274. https://doi.org/10.1177/1745691614527464

Clark, L. A., & Watson, D. (1995). Constructing validity: Basic issues in objective scale development. *Psychological Assessment*, 7, 309–319. https://doi.org/10.1037/1040-3590.7.3.309

Cohrs, J. C., Moschner, B., Maes, J., & Kielmann, S. (2005). The motivational bases of right-wing authoritarianism and social dominance orientation: Relations to values and attitudes in the aftermath of September 11, 2001. *Personality and Social Psychology Bulletin*, 31, 1425–1434. https://doi.org/10.1177/0146167205275614

Coser, L. A. (1956). *The functions of social conflict*. London: Routledge.

Costa, P. T., Jr., & McCrae, R. R. (1992). Four ways five factors are basic. *Personality and Individual Differences*, 13, 653–665. https://doi.org/10.1016/0191-8869(92)90236-I

Costa-Lopes, R., Vala, J., & Judd, C. M. (2012). Similarity and dissimilarity in intergroup relations: Different dimensions, different processes. *Revue Internationale de Psychologie Sociale*, 25, 31–65.

Cottrell, C. A., & Neuberg, S. L. (2005). Different emotional reactions to different groups: A sociofunctional threat-based approach to 'prejudice'. *Journal of Personality and Social Psychology*, 88, 770–789. https://doi.org/10.1037/0022-3514.88.5.770

Cox, O. C. (1948). *Caste, class, and race: A study in social dynamics*. New York, NY: Doubleday.

Craig, M. A., Rucker, J. M., & Richeson, J. A. (in press). The pitfalls and promise of increasing racial diversity: threat, contact, and race relations in the 21st century. *Current Directions in Psychological Science*. https://doi.org/10.1177/0963721417727860

Crisp, R. J., Ensari, N., Hewstone, M., & Miller, N. (2003). A dual-route model of crossed categorisation effects. *European Review of Social Psychology*, 13, 35–73. https://doi.org/10.1080/10463280240000091

Crisp, R. J., & Turner, R. N. (2011). Cognitive adaptation to the experience of social and cultural diversity. *Psychological Bulletin*, 137, 242–266. https://doi.org/10.1037/a0021840

Crocker, J., & Schwartz, I. (1985). Prejudice and ingroup favouritism in a minimal intergroup situation: Effects of self-esteem. *Personality and Social Psychology Bulletin*, 11, 379–386. https://doi.org/10.1177/0146167285114004

Cronbach, L. J. (1957). The two disciplines of scientific psychology. *American Psychologist*, 12, 671–684. https://doi.org/10.1037/h0043943

Darwin, C. (1875). *The descent of man: And selection in relation to sex* (2nd ed.). New York, NY: D. Appleton and Company.

Dawkins, R. (1979). Twelve misunderstandings of kin selection. *Zeitschrift Für Tierpsychologie*, 51, 184–200. https://doi.org/10.1111/j.1439-0310.1979.tb00682.x

Dawkins, R. (1989). *The selfish gene*. Oxford: Oxford University Press.

Dawson, D. (1996). The origins of war: Biological and anthropological theories. *History and Theory*, 35, 1–28. https://doi.org/10.2307/2505515

De Dreu, C. K. W. (2012). Oxytocin modulates cooperation within and competition between groups: An integrative review and research agenda. *Hormones and Behavior*, 61, 419–428. https://doi.org/10.1016/j.yhbeh.2011.12.009

De Dreu, C. K. W., Greer, L. L., Kleef, G. A. V., Shalvi, S., & Handgraaf, M. J. J. (2011). Oxytocin promotes human ethnocentrism. *Proceedings of the National Academy of Sciences*, 108, 1262–1266. https://doi.org/10.1073/pnas.1015316108

De Dreu, C. K. W., & Kret, M. E. (2016). Oxytocin conditions intergroup relations through upregulated in-group empathy, cooperation, conformity, and defense. *Biological Psychiatry*, 79, 165–173. https://doi.org/10.1016/j.biopsych.2015.03.020

De Figueiredo, R. J. P., & Elkins, Z. (2003). Are patriots bigots? An inquiry into the vices of in-group pride. *American Journal of Political Science*, 47, 171–181. https://doi.org/10.1111/1540-5907.00012

De, S., Gelfand, M. J., Nau, D., & Roos, P. (2015). The inevitability of ethnocentrism revisited: Ethnocentrism diminishes as mobility increases. *Scientific Reports*, 5. https://doi.org/10.1038/srep17963

DeYoung, C. G., Hirsh, J. B., Shane, M. S., Papademetris, X., Rajeevan, N., & Gray, J. R. (2010). Testing predictions from personality neuroscience brain structure and the Big Five. *Psychological Science*, 21, 820–828. https://doi.org/10.1177/0956797610370159

Diener, E., Oishi, S., & Park, J. (2014). An incomplete list of eminent psychologists of the modern era. *Archives of Scientific Psychology*, 2, 20–31. https://doi.org/10.1037/arc0000006

Diodorus Siculus. (1814). *The historical library of Diodorus the Sicilian, in fifteen books* (G. Booth, Trans.). London: W. McDowall and J. Davis. (Original work published 1725)

Dixon, J., & Levine, M. (Eds.). (2012). *Beyond prejudice: Extending the social psychology of conflict, inequality and social change.* Cambridge: Cambridge University Press.

Djilas, A. (2005). *Najteze pitanje [The most difficult question].* Beograd: Artist.

Dollard, J. (1937). *Caste and class in a Southern town.* New Haven, CT: Yale University Press.

Dovidio, J. F., & Gaertner, S. L. (2010). Intergroup bias. In S. T. Fiske, D. T. Gilbert, & G. Lindzey (Eds.), *Handbook of social psychology* (5th ed., Vol. 2, pp. 1084–1121). Hoboken, NJ: Wiley.

Dovidio, J. F., Gaertner, S. L., & Saguy, T. (2009). Commonality and the complexity of 'we': Social attitudes and social change. *Personality and Social Psychology Review*, 13, 3–20. https://doi.org/10.1177/1088868308326751

Dovidio, J. F., Hewstone, M., Glick, P., & Esses, V. M. (2010). Prejudice, stereotyping, and discrimination: Theoretical and empirical overview. In J. F. Dovidio, M. Hewstone, P. Glick, & V. M. Esses (Eds.), *Handbook of prejudice, stereotyping, and discrimination* (pp. 3–28). London: Sage.

Dovidio, J. F., Schellhaas, F. M. H., & Pearson, A. R. (in press). The role of attitudes in intergroup relations. In D. Albarracin & B. T. Johnson (Eds.), *The handbook of attitudes.* New York, NY: Psychology Press.

Duckitt, J. (1989). Authoritarianism and group identification: A new view of an old construct. *Political Psychology*, 10, 63–84. https://doi.org/10.2307/3791588

Duckitt, J. (1992). *The social psychology of prejudice.* New York, NY: Praeger.

Duckitt, J. (2000). Culture, personality and prejudice. In S. A. Renshon & J. Duckitt (Eds.), *Political psychology: Cultural and cross cultural foundations* (pp. 89–107). Houndmills: Macmillan Press.

Duckitt, J. (2001). A dual process cognitive-motivational theory of ideology and prejudice. In M. P. Zanna (Ed.), *Advances in experimental social psychology* (Vol. 33, pp. 41–113). San Diego, CA: Academic Press.

Duckitt, J. (2010). Historical overview. In J. F. Dovidio, M. Hewstone, P. Glick, & V. M. Esess (Eds.), *The SAGE handbook of prejudice, stereotyping and discrimination* (pp. 29–44). London: Sage.

Duckitt, J. (2014). Prejudice: Its social psychology. *Journal of Multilingual and Multicultural Development*, 35, 196–198. https://doi.org/10.1080/01434632.2013.803723

Duckitt, J., & Bizumic, B. (2013). Multidimensionality of right-wing authoritarian attitudes: Authoritarianism-Conservatism-Traditionalism. *Political Psychology*, 34, 841–862. https://doi.org/10.1111/pops.12022

Duckitt, J., Bizumic, B., Krauss, S. W., & Heled, E. (2010). A tripartite approach to right-wing authoritarianism: The authoritarianism-conservatism-traditionalism model. *Political Psychology*, 31, 685–715. https://doi.org/10.1111/j.1467-9221.2010.00781.x

Duckitt, J., & Fisher, K. (2003). The impact of social threat on worldview and ideological attitudes. *Political Psychology*, 24, 199–222. https://doi.org/10.1111/0162-895X.00322

Duckitt, J., & Sibley, C. G. (2010). Personality, ideology, prejudice, and politics: A dual-process motivational model. *Journal of Personality*, 78, 1861–1894. https://doi.org/10.1111/j.1467-6494.2010.00672.x

Duckitt, J., & Sibley, C. G. (2017). The dual process motivational model of ideology and prejudice. In C. G. Sibley & F. K. Barlow, *The Cambridge handbook of the psychology of prejudice* (pp. 188–221). Cambridge: Cambridge University Press.

Duckitt, J., Wagner, C., du Plessis, I., & Birum, I. (2002). The psychological bases of ideology and prejudice: Testing a dual process model. *Journal of Personality and Social Psychology*, 83, 75–93. https://doi.org/10.1037/0022-3514.83.1.75

Dunwoody, P. T., & Funke, F. (2016). The Aggression-Submission-Conventionalism Scale: Testing a new three factor measure of authoritarianism. *Journal of Social and Political Psychology*, 4, 571–600. https://doi.org/10.5964/jspp.v4i2.168

Dutton, E., Madison, G., & Lynn, R. (2016). Demographic, economic, and genetic factors related to national differences in ethnocentric attitudes. *Personality and Individual Differences*, 101, 137–143. https://doi.org/10.1016/j.paid.2016.05.049

Eidelson, R. J. (2015). 'No cause for action': Revisiting the ethics case of Dr. John Leso. *Journal of Social and Political Psychology*, 3, 198–212. https://doi.org/10.5964/jspp.v3i1.479

Eisinga, R., Felling, A., & Peters, J. (1990). Religious belief, church involvement, and ethnocentrism in the Netherlands. *Journal for the Scientific Study of Religion*, 29, 54–75. https://doi.org/10.2307/1387030

Ekehammar, B., & Akrami, N. (2007). Personality and prejudice: From Big Five personality factors to facets. *Journal of Personality*, 75, 899–926. https://doi.org/10.1111/j.1467-6494.2007.00460.x

Ellemers, N., & Van Rijswijk, W. (1997). Identity needs versus social opportunities: The use of group-level and individual-level identity management strategies. *Social Psychology Quarterly*, 60, 52–65. https://doi.org/10.2307/2787011

Elliott, D. J. (1984). The role of music and musical experience in modern society: Toward a global philosophy of music. *International Journal of Music Education*, 4, 3–8. https://doi.org/10.1177/025576148400400101

Embree, J. F. (1950). A note on ethnocentrism in anthropology. *American Anthropologist*, 52, 430–432. https://doi.org/10.1525/aa.1950.52.3.02a00300

Engels, F., & Marx, K. (1976). *Ludwig Feuerbach and the end of classical German philosophy.* Peking: Foreign Languages Press. (Original work published 1888)

Eriksen, T. H. (2010). *Ethnicity and nationalism: Anthropological perspectives* (3rd ed.). London: Pluto Press.

Erikson, E. H. (1966). Ontogeny of ritualization in man. *Philosophical Transactions of the Royal Society of London. Series B. Biological Sciences*, 251, 337–349. https://doi.org/10.1098/rstb.1966.0019

Erikson, E. H. (1968). *Identity: Youth and crisis.* New York, NY: W. W. Norton.

Esses, V. M., Dovidio, J. F., Jackson, L. M., & Armstrong, T. L. (2001). The immigration dilemma: The role of perceived group competition, ethnic prejudice, and national identity. *Journal of Social Issues*, 57, 389–412. https://doi.org/10.1111/0022-4537.00220

Evans, E. P. (1891). Progress and perfectibility in the lower animals. *The Popular Science Monthly*, 40, 170–179.

Evans, E. P. (1894). The ethics of tribal society. *The Popular Science Monthly*, 44, 289–307.

Ezekiel, R. S. (1995). *The racist mind: Portraits of American Neo-Nazis and Klansmen.* New York, NY: Penguin.

Fabrigar, L. R., & Wegener, D. T. (2012). *Exploratory factor analysis.* Oxford: Oxford University Press.

Falk, A. (1992). Unconscious aspects of the Arab-Israeli conflict. In B. L. Boyer & R. M. Boyer (Eds.), *The psychoanalytic study of society, Vol. 17. Essays in honor of George D. and Louise A. Spindler* (pp. 213–247). Hillsdale, NJ: Analytic Press.

Farr, R., & Moscovici, S. (Eds.). (1984). *Social representations.* Cambridge: Cambridge University Press.

Farwell, L., & Wohlwend-Lloyd, R. (1998). Narcissistic processes: Optimistic expectations, favorable self-evaluations and self-enhancing attributions. *Journal of Personality*, 66, 65–83. https://doi.org/10.1111/1467-6494.00003

Faulkner, J., Schaller, M., Park, J. H., & Duncan, L. A. (2004). Evolved disease-avoidance mechanisms and contemporary xenophobic attitudes. *Group Processes & Intergroup Relations*, 7, 333 353. https://doi.org/10.1177/1368430204046142

Fazio, R. H., & Roskos-Ewoldsen, D. (2005). Acting as we feel: When and how attitudes guide behavior. In T. C. Brock & M. C. Green (Eds.), *The psychology of persuasion* (2nd ed.). New York, NY: Allyn & Bacon.

Federico, C. M. (1999). The interactive effects of social dominance orientation, group status, and perceived stability on favoritism for high-status groups. *Group Processes & Intergroup Relations*, 2, 119–143. https://doi.org/10.1177/1368430299022002

Federico, C. M., Weber, C. R., Ergun, D., & Hunt, C. (2013). Mapping the connections between politics and morality: The multiple sociopolitical orientations involved in moral intuition. *Political Psychology*, 34, 589–610. https://doi.org/10.1111/pops.12006

Feldman, S., & Stenner, K. (1997). Perceived threat and authoritarianism. *Political Psychology*, 18, 741–770. https://doi.org/10.1111/0162-895X.00077

Ferguson, A. (1768). *An essay on the history of civil society* (2nd ed.). London: A. Millar, T. Cadell, A. Kincaid, and J. Bell.

Fincher, C. L., & Thornhill, R. (2012). Parasite-stress promotes in-group assortative sociality: The cases of strong family ties and heightened religiosity. *Behavioral and Brain Sciences*, 35, 61–79. https://doi.org/10.1017/S0140525X11000021

Fishbein, M., & Ajzen, I. (1974). Attitudes towards objects as predictors of single and multiple behavioral criteria. *Psychological Review*, 81, 59–74. https://doi.org/10.1037/h0035872

Fiske, S. T., Cuddy, A. J. C., Glick, P., & Xu, J. (2002). A model of (often mixed) stereotype content: Competence and warmth respectively follow from perceived status and competition. *Journal of Personality and Social Psychology*, 82, 878–902. https://doi.org/10.1037/0022-3514.82.6.878

Fiske, S. T., & Taylor, S. E. (2017). *Social cognition: From brains to culture* (3rd ed.). Los Angeles, CA: Sage.

Foddy, M., Platow, M. J., & Yamagishi, T. (2009). Group-based trust in strangers: The role of stereotypes and expectations. *Psychological Science*, 20, 419–422. https://doi.org/10.1111/j.1467-9280.2009.02312.x

Frank, F. J., & Widaman, K. F. (1995). Factor analysis in the development and refinement of clinical assessment instruments. *Psychological Assessment*, 7, 286–299. https://doi.org/10.1037/1040-3590.7.3.286

Frank, J. D. (1967). *Sanity and survival: Psychological aspects of war and peace.* New York, NY: Random House.

Freeman, R. B., & Huang, W. (2015). Collaborating with people like me: Ethnic coauthorship within the United States. *Journal of Labor Economics*, 33, S289–S318. https://doi.org/10.1086/678973

Freud, A. (1993). *The ego and the mechanisms of defence* (C. Baines, Trans.). London: Karnac Books. (Original work published 1936)

Freud, S. (1950). Why war? In J. Starchey (Ed. & Trans.), *Collected papers* (Vol. 5, pp. 273–287). London: Hogarth Press. (Original work published 1932)

Freud, S. (1955). Group psychology and the analysis of the ego. In J. Starchey (Ed. & Trans.), *The standard edition of the complete psychological works of Sigmund Freud* (Vol. 18, pp. 65–143). London: Hogarth Press. (Original work published 1921)

Freud, S. (1961). Civilization and its discontents. In J. Starchey (Ed.), *The standard edition of the complete psychological works of Sigmund Freud* (Vol. 21, pp. 57–145). London: Hogarth Press. (Original work published 1930)

Funke, F. (2005). The dimensionality of right-wing authoritarianism: Lessons from the dilemma between theory and measurement. *Political Psychology*, 26, 195–218. https://doi.org/10.1111/j.1467-9221.2005.00415.x

Gagnon, V. P. J. (2004). *The myth of ethnic war: Serbia and Croatia in the 1990s.* Ithaca, NY: Cornell University Press.

Gailliot, M. T., Schmeichel, B. J., & Maner, J. K. (2007). Differentiating the effects of self-control and self-esteem on reactions to mortality salience. *Journal of Experimental Social Psychology*, 43, 894–901. https://doi.org/10.1016/j.jesp.2006.10.011

Gandhi, M. (1999). *The collected works of Mahatma Gandhi* (Vol. 10). New Delhi: Publications Division Government of India. Retrieved from www.gandhiserve.org/cwmg/VOL010.PDF

Gareau, F. H. (1983). The increasing ethnocentrism of American social science: An empirical study of social science encyclopedias. *International Journal of Comparative Sociology*, 24, 244–258. https://doi.org/10.1163/156854283X00170

Gat, A. (2010). Why war? Motivations for fighting in the human state of nature. In J. B. Silk & P. M. Kappeler (Eds.), *Mind the gap: Tracing the origins of human universals* (pp. 197–220). Berlin: Springer.

Gellner, E. (1994). *Encounters with nationalism.* Oxford: Blackwell.

Gibbon, E. (1788). *The history of the decline and fall of the Roman Empire* (Vol. 5). London: A. Strahan and T. Cadell.

Glenny, M. (2001). The Yugoslav catastrophe. In D. Chirot & M. E. P. Seligman (Eds.), *Ethnopolitical warfare: Causes, consequences, and possible solutions* (pp. 151–161). Washington DC: American Psychological Association.

Goodwin, R. (1996). A brief guide to cross-cultural research. In J. Haworth (Ed.), *Psychological research: Innovative methods and strategies* (pp. 78–91). London: Routledge.

Gordin, M. D. (2015). *Scientific babel: The language of science from the fall of Latin to the rise of English.* London: Profile Books.

Graham, J., Haidt, J., Koleva, S., Motyl, M., Iyer, R., Wojcik, S. P., & Ditto, P. H. (2013). Moral foundations theory: The pragmatic validity of moral pluralism. *Advances in Experimental Social Psychology*, 47, 55–130. https://doi.org/10.1016/B978-0-12-407236-7.00002-4

Graham, J., Haidt, J., & Nosek, B. A. (2009). Liberals and conservatives rely on different sets of moral foundations. *Journal of Personality and Social Psychology*, 96, 1029–1046. https://doi.org/10.1037/a0015141

Graham, J., Nosek, B. A., Haidt, J., Iyer, R., Koleva, S., & Ditto, P. H. (2011). Mapping the moral domain. *Journal of Personality and Social Psychology*, 101, 366–385. https://doi.org/10.1037/a0021847

Grant, P. B. (1993). Ethnocentrism in response to a threat to social identity. *Journal of Social Behavior and Personality*, 8, 143–154.

Graves, S., & Lee, J. (2000). Ethnic underpinnings of voting preference: Latinos and the 1996 U.S. Senate election in Texas. *Social Science Quarterly*, 81, 226–236.

Green, D. P., Abelson, R. P., & Garnett, M. (1999). The distinctive political views of hate-crime perpetrators and white supremacists. In D. A. Prentice & D. T. Miller (Eds.), *Cultural divides: Understanding and overcoming group conflict* (pp. 429–464). New York, NY: Russell Sage Foundation.

Green, D. P., & Seher, R. L. (2003). What role does prejudice play in ethnic conflict? *Annual Review of Political Science*, 6, 509–531. https://doi.org/10.1146/annurev.polisci.6.121901.085642

Greenberg, J., & Arndt, J. (2012). Terror management theory: Implications for understanding prejudice, stereotyping, intergroup conflict, and political attitudes. In P. A. M. V. Lange, A. W. Kruglanski, & E. T. Higgins (Eds.), *Handbook of theories of social psychology* (Vol. 1, pp. 398–415). London: Sage.

Greenberg, J., Solomon, S., Veeder, M., Pyszczynski, T., Rosenblatt, A., Kirkland, S., & Lyon, D. (1990). Evidence for terror management theory II: The effects of mortality salience on reactions to those who threaten or bolster the cultural worldview. *Journal of Personality and Social Psychology*, 58, 308–318. https://doi.org/10.1037/0022-3514.58.2.308

Greenwald, A. G., & Schuh, E. S. (1994). An ethnic bias in scientific citations. *European Journal of Social Psychology*, 24, 623–639. https://doi.org/10.1002/ejsp.2420240602

Greeson, L. E. (1991). Cultural ethnocentrism and imperialism in citations of American and Scandinavian psychological research. *International Journal of Psychology*, 26, 262–268. https://doi.org/10.1080/00207599108247891

Greeson, L. E. (1994). Torsten Husén: A case of ethnocentrism in U.S. educational research? *Interchange*, 25, 241–259. https://doi.org/10.1007/BF01454942

Gregor, A. J. (1969). *The ideology of fascism: The rationale of totalitarianism.* New York, NY: Free Press.

Gumplowicz, L. (1879). *Das Recht der Nationalität und Sprachen in Oesterreich-Ungarn. [The right of nationality and languages in Austria-Hungary].* Innsbruck: Wagner'schen Universitäts-Buchhandlung.

Gumplowicz, L. (1881). *Rechtsstaat und Socialismus [Legal state and socialism].* Innsbruck: Wagner'schen Universitäts-Buchhandlung.

Gumplowicz, L. (1883). *Der Rassenkampf: Sociologische Untersuchungen [The racial struggle: Sociological studies].* Innsbruck: Wagner'schen Universitäts-Buchhandlung.

Gumplowicz, L. (1884). Macierzyńtwo [Maternity]. *Prawda*, 14, 159–160.

Gumplowicz, L. (1887). *System socyologii [System of sociology].* Warsaw: Spolka Nakladowa.

Gumplowicz, L. (1892). *Die sociologische Staatsidee [The sociological idea of state].* Graz: Leuschner & Lubensky.

Gumplowicz, L. (1895). Sociale Sinnestäuschungen [Social illusions]. *New German Rundschau*, 6, 1–11.

Gumplowicz, L. (1905). *Geschichte der Staatstheorien [History of theories of state].* Innsbruck: Wagner'schen Universitäts-Buchhandlung

Gumplowicz, L. (1963). *Outlines of sociology* (I. L. Horowitz, Ed., F. W. Moore, Trans.). New York, NY: Paine-Whitman. (Original work published 1885)

Hagendoorn, L. (1995). Intergroup biases in multiple group systems: The perception of ethnic hierarchies. *European Review of Social Psychology*, 6, 199–228.

Haidt, J. (2007). Response. *Science*, 317, 597.

Haidt, J. (2012). *The righteous mind: Why good people are divided by politics and religion.* London: Penguin.

Haidt, J., & Joseph, C. (2004). Intuitive ethics: How innately prepared intuitions generate culturally variable virtues. *Daedalus*, 133, 55–66. https://doi.org/10.1162/0011526042365555

Haines, H., & Vaughan, G. M. (1979). Was 1898 a "great date" in the history of experimental social psychology? *Journal of the History of the Behavioral Sciences*, 15, 323–332. https://doi.org/10.1002/1520-6696(197910)15:4<323::AID-JHBS2300150405>3.0.CO;2-I

Hall, G. C. N., Yip, T., & Zarate, M. A. (2016). On becoming multicultural in a monocultural research world: A conceptual approach to studying ethnocultural diversity. *American Psychologist*, 71, 40–51. https://doi.org/10.1037/a0039734

Hamburg, D. A. (1986). New risks of prejudice, ethnocentrism, and violence. *Science*, 231, 533. https://doi.org/10.1126/science.231.4738.533

Hamilton, W. D. (1964). The genetic evolution of social behavior I and II. *Journal of Theoretical Psychology*, 7, 1–16.

Hammond, R. A., & Axelrod, R. (2006). The evolution of ethnocentrism. *Journal of Conflict Resolution*, 50, 926–936. https://doi.org/10.1177/0022002706293470

Harding, J., Proshansky, H., Kutner, B., & Chein, I. (1969). Prejudice and ethnic relations. In G. Lindzey & E. Aronson (Eds.), *The handbook of social psychology* (2nd ed., Vol. 5, pp. 1–76). Reading, MA: Addison Wesley.

Harre, R., & Tissaw, M. A. (2005). *Wittgenstein and psychology: A practical guide*. Aldershot: Ashgate.

Hartley, E. L. (1946). *Problems in prejudice*. New York, NY: King's Crown Press.

Haslam, N. (2006). Dehumanization: An integrative review. *Personality and Social Psychology Review*, 10, 252–264. https://doi.org/10.1207/s15327957pspr1003_4

Haslam, N. (2016). Concept creep: Psychology's expanding concepts of harm and pathology. *Psychological Inquiry*, 27, 1–17. https://doi.org/10.1080/1047840X.2016.1082418

Haslam, N., & Loughnan, S. (2014). Dehumanization and infrahumanization. *Annual Review of Psychology*, 65, 399–423. https://doi.org/10.1146/annurev-psych-010213-115045

Heaven, P. C. L. (1976). Authoritarianism and ethnocentrism: A South African sample. *Psychological Reports*, 39, 656. https://doi.org/10.2466/pr0.1976.39.2.656

Heaven, P. C. L., Rajab, D., & Ray, J. J. (1985). Patriotism, racism, and the disutility of the ethnocentrism concept. *Journal of Social Psychology*, 125, 181–185.

Hendin, H. M., & Cheek, J. M. (1997). Assessing hypersensitive narcissism: A reexamination of Murray's Narcism Scale. *Journal of Research in Personality*, 31, 588–599. https://doi.org/10.1006/jrpe.1997.2204

Henrich, J., Heine, S. J., & Norenzayan, A. (2010). The weirdest people in the world? *Behavioral and Brain Sciences*, 33, 61–83. https://doi.org/10.1017/S0140525X0999152X

Herodotus. (1947). *The history of Herodotus* (G. Rawlinson, Trans.). New York, NY: Tudor.

Herskovits, M. J. (1948). *Man and his works*. New York, NY: Knopf.

Herskovits, M. J. (1972). *Cultural relativism: Perspectives in cultural pluralism*. New York, NY: Random House.

Hill, R. J. (1981). Attitudes and behavior. In M. Rosenberg & M. H. Turner (Eds.), *Social psychology: Sociological perspectives* (pp. 347–377). New York, NY: Basic Books.

Hinkle, S., & Brown, R. (1990). Intergroup comparisons and social identity: Some links and lacunae. In D. Abrams & M. A. Hogg (Eds.), *Social identity theory: Construction and critical advances* (pp. 48–70). New York, NY: Springer.

Hirschfeld, L. A. (1996). *Race in the making: Cognition, culture, and the child's construction of human kinds*. Cambridge, MA: MIT Press.

Hitler, A. (1941). *Mein Kampf* (A. Johnson, Trans.). New York, NY: Reynal and Hitchcock. (Original work published 1925)

Ho, A. K., Sidanius, J., Kteily, N., Sheehy-Skeffington, J., Pratto, F., Henkel, K. E., … Stewart, A. L. (2015). The nature of social dominance orientation: Theorizing and measuring preferences for intergroup inequality using the new SDO7 Scale. *Journal of Personality and Social Psychology*, 109, 1003–1028. http://dx.doi.org/10.1037/pspi0000033

Ho, A. K., Sidanius, J., Pratto, F., Levin, S., Thomsen, L., Kteily, N., & Sheehy-Skeffington, J. (2012). Social dominance orientation: Revisiting the structure and function of a variable predicting social and political attitudes. *Personality and Social Psychology Bulletin*. https://doi.org/10.1177/0146167211432765

Hochschild, A. R. (2016). *Strangers in their own land: Anger and mourning on the American right*. New York, NY: New Press.

Hodson, G., Crisp, R. J., Meleady, R., & Earle, M. (in press). Intergroup contact as an agent of cognitive liberalization. *Perspectives on Psychological Science*.

Hogg, M. A., & Abrams, D. (1990). Social motivation, self-esteem, and social identity. In D. Abrams & M. A. Hogg (Eds.), *Social identity theory: Constructive and critical advances* (pp. 28–47). New York, NY: Springer.

Horowitz, I. L. (1991). *Communicating ideas: The politics of scholarly publishing* (2nd ed.). New Brunswick, NJ: Transaction Publishers.

Hovland, C. I., & Sears, R. R. (1940). Minor studies in aggression VI: Correlation of lynchings with economic indices. *Journal of Psychology*, 9, 301–310. https://doi.org/10.1080/00223980.1940.9917696

Huang, L.-L., & Liu, J. H. (2005). Personality and social structural implications of the situational priming of social dominance orientation. *Personality and Individual Differences, 38*, 267–276. https://doi.org/10.1016/j.paid.2004.04.006

Hume, D. (1767). *Essays and treatises on several subjects* (Vol. 1). London: A. Millar. (Original work published 1742)

Hyam, R. (1990). *Empire and sexuality: The British experience*. Manchester: Manchester University Press.

Ibn Khaldūn. (1958). *The Muqaddimah: An introduction to history* (F. Rosenthal, Trans.). New York, NY: Pantheon Books. (Original work published 1377)

Insko, C. A., Nacoste, R. W., & Moe, J. L. (1983). Belief congruence and racial discrimination: Review of the evidence and critical evaluation. *European Journal of Social Psychology, 13*, 153–174. https://doi.org/10.1002/ejsp.2420130206

Ishii, K. (2009). Nationalistic sentiments of Chinese consumers: The effects and determinants of animosity and consumer ethnocentrism. *Journal of International Consumer Marketing, 21*, 299–308. https://doi.org/10.1080/08961530802282232

Iyer, R., Koleva, S., Graham, J., Ditto, P., & Haidt, J. (2012). Understanding libertarian morality: The psychological dispositions of self-identified libertarians. *PLoS ONE, 7*, e42366. https://doi.org/10.1371/journal.pone.0042366

Jackman, M. R. (1994). *The velvet glove: Paternalism and conflict in gender, class, and race relations*. Berkeley, CA: University of California Press.

Jackson, J. S., Brown, K. T., Brown, T. N., & Marks, B. (2001). Contemporary immigration policy orientations among dominant-group members in Western Europe. *Journal of Social Issues, 57*, 431–456. https://doi.org/10.1111/0022-4537.00222

Jackson, L. M. (2011). *The psychology of prejudice: From attitudes to social action*. Washington DC: American Psychological Association.

Jahoda, G., & Krewer, B. (1997). History of cross-cultural and cultural psychology. In J. W. Berry, Y. H. Poortinga, & J. Pandy (Eds.), *Handbook of cross-cultural psychology, Vol. 1, 2nd ed.* (pp. 1–42). Boston, MA: Allyn and Bacon.

Japan textbooks may give rise to ethnocentrism: U.S. report. (2000, August 7). *Japan Policy & Politics*. Retrieved from www.thefreelibrary.com/Japan+textbooks+may+give+rise+to+ethnocentrism%3A+U.S.+report.-a063947154

Jetten, J., Spears, R., & Postmes, T. (2004). Intergroup distinctiveness and differentiation: A meta-analytic integration. *Journal of Personality and Social Psychology, 86*, 862–879. https://doi.org/10.1037/0022-3514.86.6.862

Jiménez-Guerrero, J. F., Gázquez-Abad, J. C., & Linares-Agüera, E. del C. (2014). Using standard CETSCALE and other adapted versions of the scale for measuring consumers' ethnocentric tendencies: An analysis of dimensionality. *BRQ Business Research Quarterly, 17*, 174–190. https://doi.org/10.1016/j.cede.2013.06.003

John, O. P., Naumann, L. P., & Soto, C. J. (2008). Paradigm shift to the integrative Big Five trait taxonomy: History, measurement, and conceptual issues. In O. P. John, R. W. Robins, & L. A. Pervin (Eds.), *Handbook of personality: Theory and research* (3rd ed., pp. 114–158). New York, NY: Guilford.

Johnson, M. K., & Marini, M. M. (1998). Bridging the racial divide in the United States: The effect of gender. *Social Psychology Quarterly, 61*, 247–258. https://doi.org/10.2307/2787111

Jones, D. (2000). Group nepotism and human kinship. *Current Anthropology, 41*, 779–809. https://doi.org/10.1086/317406

Jones, J. M., Dovidio, J. F., & Vietze, D. L. (2014). *The psychology of diversity: Beyond prejudice and racism*. Oxford: Wiley-Blackwell.

Joseph, J. (2004). *The gene illusion: Genetic research in psychiatry and psychology under the microscope*. New York, NY: Algora Publishing.

Joseph, J. (2015). *The trouble with twin studies: A reassessment of twin research in the social and behavioral sciences*. New York, NY: Routledge.

Jost, J. (2006). The end of the end of ideology. *American Psychologist*, 61, 651–670. https://doi.org/10.1037/0003-066X.61.7.651

Kakar, S. (1994). *A new Hindu identity*. UNESCO Courier, 30–31.

Kalkan, K. O. (2016, February 28). What differentiates Trump supporters from other Republicans? Ethnocentrism. *Washington Post*. Retrieved from www.washingtonpost.com/news/monkey-cage/wp/2016/02/28/what-differentiates-trump-supporters-from-other-republicans-ethnocentrism/

Kandler, C., Bleidorn, W., & Riemann, R. (2012). Left or right? Sources of political orientation: The roles of genetic factors, cultural transmission, assortative mating, and personality. *Journal of Personality and Social Psychology*, 102, 633–645. https://doi.org/10.1037/a0025560

Karasawa, M. (2002). Patriotism, nationalism, and internationalism among Japanese citizens: An etic-emic approach. *Political Psychology*, 23, 645–666. https://doi.org/10.1111/0162-895X.00302

Keith, A. (1948). *A new theory of human evolution*. London: Watts & Co.

Kellas, J. G. (1991). *The politics of nationalism and ethnicity*. London: Macmillan.

Keller, A. G. (1915). *Societal evolution: A study of the evolutionary basis of the science of society*. New York, NY: Macmillan.

Kent, D. P., & Burnight, R. G. (1951). Group centrism in complex societies. *American Journal of Sociology*, 57, 256–259. https://doi.org/10.1086/220943

Kinder, D. R. (1998). Opinion action in the realm of politics. In D. T. Gilbert, S. T. Fiske, & G. Lindzey (Eds.), *The handbook of social psychology* (4th ed., Vol. 2, pp. 778–867). New York, NY: McGraw-Hill.

Kinder, D. R., & Kam, C. D. (2009). *Us against them: Ethnocentric foundations of American opinion*. Chicago, IL: The University of Chicago Press.

Kinder, D. R., & Sears, D. O. (1981). Prejudice and politics: Symbolic racism versus racial threats to the good life. *Journal of Personality and Social Psychology*, 40, 414–431. https://doi.org/10.1037/0022-3514.40.3.414

Kinzler, K. D., Dupoux, E., & Spelke, E. S. (2007). The native language of social cognition. *Proceedings of the National Academy of Sciences*, 104, 12577–12580. https://doi.org/10.1073/pnas.0705345104

Kirschbaum, E. (2014). *Burning Beethoven: The eradication of German culture in the United States during World War I*. New York, NY: Berlinica.

Klein, J. G., & Ettenson, R. (1999). Consumer animosity and consumer ethnocentrism. *Journal of International Consumer Marketing*, 11, 5–24. https://doi.org/10.1300/J046v11n04_02

Koffka, K. (1935). *Principles of gestalt psychology*. London: Lund Humphries.

Kohn, H. (1944). *The idea of nationalism: A study in its origins and background*. Toronto: Collier Books.

Koomen, W., & Bahler, M. (1996). National stereotypes: Common representation and ingroup favouritism. *European Journal of Social Psychology*, 26, 325–331. https://doi.org/10.1002/(SICI)1099-0992(199603)26:2<325::AID-EJSP743>3.0.CO;2-E

Kosterman, R., & Feshbach, S. (1989). Toward a measure of patriotic and nationalistic attitudes. *Political Psychology*, 10, 257–274. https://doi.org/10.2307/3791647

Kroeber, A. L. (1948). *Anthropology: Race, language, culture, psychology, prehistory*. New York, NY: Harcourt, Brace.

Kropotkin, P. (1902). *Mutual aid: A factor of evolution*. London: W. Heinemann.

Kurzban, R., & Leary, M. R. (2001). Evolutionary origins of stigmatization: The functions of social exclusion. *Psychological Bulletin*, 127, 187–208. https://doi.org/10.1037/0033-2909.127.2.187

la Bruyère, J. de. (1885). *The 'Characters' of Jean de la Bruyère* (H. Van Laun, Trans.). London: Nimmo. (Original work published 1688)

Lambley, P. (1973). Authoritarianism and prejudice in South African student samples. *Journal of Social Psychology*, 91, 341–342. https://doi.org/10.1080/00224545.1973.9923057

Lane, A., Luminet, O., Nave, G., & Mikolajczak, M. (2016). Is there a publication bias in behavioural intranasal oxytocin research on humans? Opening the file drawer of one laboratory. *Journal of Neuroendocrinology*, 28, 1–15. https://doi.org/10.1111/jne.12384

Lanternari, V. (1980). Ethnocentrism and ideology. *Ethnic and Racial Studies*, 3, 52–66. https://doi.org/10.1080/01419870.1980.9993287

Las Casas, B. de. (1974). *In defense of the Indians* (S. Poole, Ed. & Trans.). DeKalb, IL: Northern Illinois University Press. (Original work published 1550)

Lasswell, H. D. (1925). Two forgotten studies in political psychology. *The American Political Science Review*, 19, 707–717. https://doi.org/10.2307/2939161

Leach, C. W., Ellemers, N., & Barreto, M. (2007). Group virtue: The importance of morality (vs. competence and sociability) in the positive evaluation of in-groups. *Journal of Personality and Social Psychology*, 93, 234–249. https://doi.org/10.1037/0022-3514.93.2.234

LeVine, R. A., & Campbell, D. T. (1972). *Ethnocentrism: Theories of conflict, ethnic attitudes, and group behavior*. New York, NY: John Wiley & Sons.

Levinson, D. J. (1949). An approach to the theory and measurement of ethnocentric ideology. *Journal of Psychology*, 27, 19–39. https://doi.org/10.1080/00223980.1949.9915992

Levi-Strauss, C. (1976). *Structural anthropology* (Vol. 2). New York, NY: Basic Books.

Lewin, K. (1948). *Resolving social conflicts: Selected papers on group dynamics*. New York, NY: Harper and Brothers.

Lewis, G. J., & Bates, T. C. (2017). The temporal stability of in-group favoritism is mostly attributable to genetic factors. *Social Psychological and Personality Science*, 8, 897–903. https://doi.org/10.1177/1948550617699250

Lewis, G. J., Kandler, C., & Riemann, R. (2014). Distinct heritable influences underpin in-group love and out-group derogation. *Social Psychological and Personality Science*, 5, 407–413. https://doi.org/10.1177/1948550613504967

Leyens, J.-P., Cortes, B., Demoulin, S., Dovidio, J. F., Fiske, S. T., Gaunt, R., … Vaes, J. (2003). Emotional prejudice, essentialism and nationalism. *European Journal of Social Psychology*, 33, 703–717. https://doi.org/10.1002/ejsp.170

Leyens, J.-P., Paladino, M. P., Rodriguez, R. T., Vaes, J., Demoulin, S., Rodriguez, A. P., & Gaunt, R. (2000). The emotional side of prejudice: The attribution of secondary emotions to ingroups and outgroups. *Personality and Social Psychology Review*, 4, 186–197. https://doi.org/10.1207/S15327957PSPR0402_06

Leyens, J.-P., Rodriguez, A. P., Rodriguez, R. T., Gaunt, R., Paladino, M. P., Vaes, J., & Demoulin, S. (2001). Psychological essentialism and the differential attribution of uniquely human emotions to ingroups and outgroups. *European Journal of Social Psychology*, 31, 395–411. https://doi.org/10.1002/ejsp.50

Liu, J. H. (1999). Social representations of history: Preliminary notes on content and consequences around the Pacific Rim. *International Journal of Intercultural Relations*, 23, 215–236. https://doi.org/10.1016/S0147-1767(98)00036-4

Liu, J. H., Lawrence, B., Ward, C., & Abraham, S. (2002). Social representations of history in Malaysia and Singapore: On the relationship between national and ethnic identity. *Asian Journal of Social Psychology*, 5, 3–20. https://doi.org/10.1111/1467-839X.00091

Liu, J. H., Wilson, M. S., McClure, J., & Higgins, T. R. (1999). Social identity and the perception of history: Cultural representations of Aotearoa/New Zealand. *European Journal of Social Psychology*, 29, 1021–1047. https://doi.org/10.1002/(SICI)1099-0992(199912)29:8<1021::AID-EJSP975>3.0.CO;2-4

Locke, J. (1825). *An essay concerning human understanding.* London: Tegg. (Original work published 1689)

Lott, B. (2009). *Multiculturalism and diversity: A social psychological perspective.* Chichester: Wiley.

Ma, X., Luo, L., Geng, Y., Zhao, W., Zhang, Q., & Kendrick, K. M. (2014). Oxytocin increases liking for a country's people and national flag but not for other cultural symbols or consumer products. *Frontiers in Behavioral Neuroscience,* 8, 266. https://doi.org/10.3389/fnbeh.2014.00266

MacDonald, K. (2001). An integrative evolutionary perspective on ethnicity. *Politics and the Life Sciences,* 20, 67–80. https://doi.org/10.1017/S0730938400005189

Mackie, D. M., Devos, T., & Smith, E. R. (2000). Intergroup emotions: Explaining offensive action tendencies in an intergroup context. *Journal of Personality and Social Psychology,* 79, 602–616. https://doi.org/10.1037/0022-3514.79.4.602

Mackie, D. M., Maitner, A. T., & Smith, E. R. (2016). Intergroup emotions theory. In T. D. Nelson (Ed.), *Handbook of prejudice, stereotyping, and discrimination* (2nd ed., pp. 149–174). New York, NY: Psychology Press.

Mackie, D. M., & Smith, E. R. (2003). Beyond prejudice: Moving from positive and negative evaluations to differentiated reactions to social groups. In D. M. Mackie & E. R. Smith (Eds.), *From prejudice to intergroup emotions: Differentiated reactions to social groups* (pp. 1–12). New York, NY: Psychology Press.

Maddens, B., Billiet, J., & Beerten, R. (2000). National identity and the attitude towards foreigners in multi-national states: The case of Belgium. *Journal of Ethnic and Migration Studies,* 26, 45–60. https://doi.org/10.1080/136918300115633

Manuck, S. B., & McCaffery, J. M. (2014). Gene-environment interaction. *Annual Review of Psychology,* 65, 41–70. https://doi.org/10.1146/annurev-psych-010213-115100

Marinkovic, V., Stanisic, N., & Kostic, M. (2011). Consumer ethnocentrism of Serbian citizens. *Sociologija,* 53, 43–58. https://doi.org/10.2298/SOC1101043M

Marsella, A. J. (1998). Toward a 'global-community psychology': Meeting the needs of a changing world. *American Psychologist,* 53, 1282–1291. https://doi.org/10.1037/0003-066X.53.12.1282

Marsella, A. J., & Pedersen, P. (2004). Internationalizing the counseling psychology curriculum: Toward new values, competencies, and directions. *Counselling Psychology Quarterly,* 17, 413–423.

Martin, L. L., & van den Bos, K. (2014). Beyond terror: Towards a paradigm shift in the study of threat and culture. *European Review of Social Psychology,* 25, 32–70. https://doi.org/10.1080/10463283.2014.923144

Martindale, D. (1976). American sociology before World War II. *Annual Review of Sociology,* 2, 121–143. https://doi.org/10.2307/2946089

Marx, K., & Engels, F. (1970). *The German ideology.* London: Lawrence & Wishart. (Original work published 1846)

Mavor, K. I., Louis, W. R., & Sibley, C. G. (2010). A bias-corrected exploratory and confirmatory factor analysis of right-wing authoritarianism: Support for a three-factor structure. *Personality and Individual Differences,* 48, 28–33. https://doi.org/10.1016/j.paid.2009.08.006

Mayr, E. (1982). *The growth of biological thought: Diversity, evolution and inheritance.* Cambridge, MA: Belknap Press.

McCauley, C. (2001). The psychology of group identification and the power of ethnic nationalism. In D. Chirot & M. E. P. Seligman (Eds.), *Ethnopolitical warfare: Causes, consequences, and possible solutions* (pp. 343–362). Washington DC: American Psychological Association.

McCauley, C. (2008, September). *The political power of ethnicity: A psychological perspective.* Paper presented at the Conference on Rethinking Ethnicity and Ethnic Strife: Multidisciplinary Perspectives, Budapest, Hungary.

McCrae, R. R. (2010). The place of the FFM in personality psychology. *Psychological Inquiry*, 21, 57–64. https://doi.org/10.1080/10478401003648773

McCrae, R. R., & Costa, P. T., Jr. (2008). A five-factor theory of personality. In O. P. John, R. W. Robins, & L. A. Pervin (Eds.), *Handbook of personality: Theory and research* (3rd ed., pp. 159–181). New York, NY: Guilford.

McEvoy, C. J. (2002). A consideration of human xenophobia and ethnocentrism from a sociobiological perspective. *Human Rights Review*, 3, 39–49. https://doi.org/10.1007/s12142-002-1018-x

McFarland, S., Ageyev, V. S., & Abalakina-Paap, M. A. (1992). Authoritarianism in the former Soviet Union. *Journal of Personality and Social Psychology*, 63, 1004–1010. https://doi.org/10.1037/0022-3514.63.6.1004

McFarland, S., Webb, M., & Brown, D. (2012). All humanity is my ingroup: A measure and studies of identification with all humanity. *Journal of Personality and Social Psychology*, 103, 830–853. https://doi.org/10.1037/a0028724

McGary, H. (1998). Paternalism and slavery. In T. L. Lott (Ed.), *Subjugation and bondage: Critical essays on slavery and social philosophy* (pp. 187–208). Lanham, MD: Rowman & Littlefield.

McGee, W. J. (1898). The Seri Indians. *Annual Report of the Bureau of American Ethnology (1895–1896)*, 17, Part 1, 1–344.

McGee, W. J. (1899a). The beginning of mathematics. *American Anthropologist*, 1, 646–674. https://doi.org/10.1525/aa.1899.1.4.02a00040

McGee, W. J. (1899b). The trend of human progress. *American Anthropologist*, 1, 401–447. https://doi.org/10.1525/aa.1899.1.3.02a00010

McGee, W. J. (1900). Primitive numbers. *Annual Report of the Bureau of American Ethnology (1897–1898)*, 19, 825–851.

McWhae, L. E., Paradies, Y., & Pedersen, A. (2015). Bystander antiprejudice on behalf of Muslim Australians: The role of ethnocentrism and conformity. *Australian Community Psychologist*, 27, 6–20.

Mead, M. (1928). *Coming of age in Samoa: A psychological study of primitive youth for Western civilisation*. New York, NY: W. Morrow.

Medin, D. L. (1989). Concepts and conceptual structure. *American Psychologist*, 44, 1469–1481. https://doi.org/10.1037/0003-066X.44.12.1469

Mehler, J., Jusczyk, P., Lambertz, G., Halsted, N., Bertoncini, J., & Amiel-Tison, C. (1988). A precursor of language acquisition in young infants. *Cognition*, 29, 143–178. https://doi.org/10.1016/0010-0277(88)90035-2

Melanson, P. H. (1972). The political science profession, political knowledge and public policy. *Politics & Society*, 2, 489–500. https://doi.org/10.1177/003232927200200407

Meloen, Van der Linden, & De Witte, H. (1996). A test of the approaches of Adorno et al., Lederer and Altemeyer of authoritarianism in Belgian Flanders: A research note. *Political Psychology*, 17, 643–656. https://doi.org/10.2307/3792131

Merton, R. K. (1957). *Social theory and social structure*. Glencoe, IL: Free Press.

Merton, R. K. (1973). *The sociology of science: Theoretical and empirical investigations* (N. W. Storer, Ed.). Chicago, IL: The University of Chicago Press.

Migdal, M. J., Hewstone, M., & Mullen, B. (1998). The effects of crossed categorization on intergroup evaluations: A meta-analysis. *British Journal of Social Psychology*, 37, 303–324. https://doi.org/10.1111/j.2044-8309.1998.tb01174.x

Mihalyi, L. J. (1984). Ethnocentrism vs. nationalism: Origin and fundamental aspects of a major problem for the future. *Humboldt Journal of Social Relations*, 12, 95–113.

Miller, J. E., O'Neal, R., & McDonnell, H. M. (1970). *Literature of the Eastern world*. Atlanta, GA: Scott, Foresman, and Company.

Mills, C. W. (1956). *The power elite.* New York, NY: Oxford University Press.

Miscevic, N. (2010). Nationalism. In E. N. Zalta (Ed.), *The Stanford encyclopedia of philosophy* (Summer 2010). Retrieved from http://plato.stanford.edu/archives/sum2010/entries/nationalism/

Moghaddam, F. M. (1987). Psychology in the three worlds: As reflected by the crisis in social psychology and the move toward indigenous third-world psychology. *American Psychologist, 42*, 912–920. https://doi.org/10.1037/0003-066X.42.10.912

Moghaddam, F. M. (1990). Modulative and generative orientations in psychology: Implications for psychology in the three worlds. *Journal of Social Issues, 46*, 21–41.

Moghaddam, F. M. (1996). Theories of intergroup relations. In F. N. Magill (Ed.), *International Encyclopaedia of Psychology* (Vol. 1, pp. 927–931). London: Fitzroy Dearborn.

Montaigne, M. (2003). *The complete essays* (M. A. Screech, Ed. & Trans.). London: Penguin. (Original work published 1580)

Moon, C., Cooper, R. P., & Fifer, W. P. (1993). Two-day-olds prefer their native language. *Infant Behavior and Development, 16*, 495–500. https://doi.org/10.1016/0163-6383(93)80007-U

Mosca, G. (1939). *The ruling class* (Hannah D. Kahn, Trans.). New York, NY: McGraw Hill.

Moscovici, S. (1972). Society and theory in social psychology. In J. Isreal & H. Tajfel (Eds.), *The context of social psychology. A critical assessment* (pp. 17–68). London: Academic Press.

Moscovici, S. (1973). Foreword. In C. Herzlich (Ed.), *Health and illness: A social psychological analysis.* London: Academic Press.

Moses, R. (1982). The group self and the Arab-Israeli conflict. *International Review of Psycho-Analysis, 9*, 55–65.

Mueller, J. (2000). The banality of 'ethnic war'. *International Security, 25*, 42–70. https://doi.org/10.1162/016228800560381

Mummendey, A., Klink, A., & Brown, R. (2001). Nationalism and patriotism: National identification and out-group rejection. *British Journal of Social Psychology, 40*, 159–172. https://doi.org/10.1348/014466601164740

Mummendey, A., & Wenzel, M. (1999). Social discrimination and tolerance in intergroup relations: Reactions to intergroup difference. *Personality and Social Psychology Review, 3*, 158–174. https://doi.org/10.1207/s15327957pspr0302_4

Murdock, G. P. (1949). *Social structure.* New York, NY: Macmillan.

Murphy, G., Murphy, L. B., & Newcomb, T. M. (1937). *Experimental social psychology: An interpretation of research upon the socialization of the individual.* New York, NY: Harper and Brothers.

Myers, D. G. (1993). *Social psychology* (4th ed.). New York, NY: McGraw-Hill.

Naidoo, A. V. (1996). Challenging the hegemony of Eurocentric psychology. *Journal of Community and Health Sciences, 2*, 9–16.

Navarrete, C. D., & Fessler, D. M. T. (2006). Disease avoidance and ethnocentrism: The effects of disease vulnerability and disgust sensitivity on intergroup attitudes. *Evolution and Human Behavior, 27*, 270–282. https://doi.org/10.1016/j.evolhumbehav.2005.12.001

Navarrete, C. D., Fessler, D. M. T., & Eng, S. J. (2007). Elevated ethnocentrism in the first trimester of pregnancy. *Evolution and Human Behavior, 28*, 60–65. https://doi.org/10.1016/j.evolhumbehav.2006.06.002

Nelson, L. J., Moore, D. L., Olivetti, J., & Scott, T. (1997). General and personal mortality salience and nationalistic bias. *Personality and Social Psychology Bulletin, 23*, 884–892. https://doi.org/10.1177/0146167297238008

Nicolas, S., Collins, T., Gounden, Y., & Roediger, H. L. (2011). The influence of suggestibility on memory. *Consciousness and Cognition, 20*, 399–400. https://doi.org/10.1016/j.concog.2010.10.019

Nisbett, R. E. (1990). The anti-creativity letters: Advice from a senior tempter to a junior tempter. *American Psychologist*, 45, 1078–1082. https://doi.org/10.1037/0003-066X.45.9.1078

Nisbett, R. E., Peng, K., Choi, I., & Norenzayan, A. (2001). Culture and systems of thought: Holistic versus analytic cognition. *Psychological Review*, 108, 291–310. https://doi.org/10.1037/0033-295X.108.2.291

Noor, F. A. (2003). Blood, sweat and Jihad: The radicalization of the political discourse of the Pan-Malaysian Islamic Party (PAS) from 1982 onwards. *Contemporary Southeast Asia*, 25, 200–232. https://doi.org/10.1355/CS25-2B

Oishi, S., Kesebir, S., & Snyder, B. H. (2009). Sociology: A lost connection in social psychology. *Personality and Social Psychology Review*, 13, 334–353. https://doi.org/10.1177/1088868309347835

Open Science Collaboration. (2015). Estimating the reproducibility of psychological science. *Science*, 349, aac4716. https://doi.org/10.1126/science.aac4716

Opotow, S. (1990). Moral exclusion and injustice: An introduction. *Journal of Social Issues*, 46, 1–20. https://doi.org/10.1111/j.1540-4560.1990.tb00268.x

Opotow, S., Gerson, J., & Woodside, S. (2005). From moral exclusion to moral inclusion: Theory for teaching peace. *Theory Into Practice*, 44, 303–318. https://doi.org/10.1207/s15430421tip4404_4

Opotow, S., & Weiss, L. (2000). New ways of thinking about environmentalism: Denial and the process of moral exclusion in environmental conflict. *Journal of Social Issues*, 56, 475–490. https://doi.org/10.1111/0022-4537.00179

Orey, B. D., & Park, H. (2012). Nature, nurture, and ethnocentrism in the Minnesota twin study. *Twin Research and Human Genetics*, 15, 71–73. https://doi.org/10.1375/twin.15.1.71

Outten, H. R., Schmitt, M. T., Miller, D. A., & Garcia, A. L. (2012). Feeling threatened about the future: Whites' emotional reactions to anticipated ethnic demographic changes. *Personality and Social Psychology Bulletin*, 38, 14–25. https://doi.org/10.1177/0146167211418531

Ozkirimli, U. (2000). *Theories of nationalism: A critical introduction*. Houndmills: Macmillan Press.

Parenti, M. (1967). Ethnic politics and the persistence of ethnic identification. *The American Political Science Review*, 61, 717–726. https://doi.org/10.2307/1976090

Pareto, V. (1935). *The mind and society*. London: Jonathan Cape.

Park, R. E. (1914). Racial assimilation in secondary groups with particular reference to the Negro. *American Journal of Sociology*, 19, 606–623.

Parker, C. S. (2010). Symbolic versus blind patriotism distinction without difference? *Political Research Quarterly*, 63, 97–114. https://doi.org/10.1177/1065912908327228

Penke, L., Denissen, J. J. A., & Miller, G. F. (2007). The evolutionary genetics of personality. *European Journal of Personality*, 21, 549–587. https://doi.org/10.1002/per.629

Peres, Y., & Schrift, R. (1978). Intermarriage and interethnic relations: A comparative study. *Ethnic and Racial Studies*, 1, 428–451. https://doi.org/10.1080/01419870.1978.9993243

Perez, A. R., Rodriguez, N. D., Rodriguez, V. B., Leyens, J. P., & Vaes, J. (2011). Infra-humanization of outgroups throughout the world: The role of similarity, intergroup friendship, knowledge of the outgroup, and status. *Anales de Psicología / Annals of Psychology*, 27, 679–687.

Perlmutter, H. V. (1954). Some characteristics of the xenophilic personality. *Journal of Psychology*, 38, 291–300. https://doi.org/10.1080/00223980.1954.9712938

Perlmutter, H. V. (1956). Correlates of two types of xenophilic orientation. *Journal of Abnormal and Social Psychology*, 52, 130–135. https://doi.org/10.1037/h0045166

Pesic, V. (1993). The cruel face of nationalism. *Journal of Democracy*, 4, 100–103. https://doi.org/10.1353/jod.1993.0053

Petrovic, D. (1994). Ethnic cleansing – An attempt at methodology. *European Journal of International Law*, 5, 342–359. https://doi.org/10.1093/oxfordjournals.ejil.a035875

Pettigrew, T. F. (1991). Normative theory in intergroup relations: Explaining both harmony and conflict. *Psychology & Developing Societies*, 3, 3–16. https://doi.org/10.1177/097133369100300102

Pettigrew, T. F., Jackson, J. S., Brika, J. B., Lemaine, G., Meertens, R. W., Wagner, U., & Zick, A. (1997). Outgroup prejudice in Western Europe. *European Review of Social Psychology*, 8, 241–273. https://doi.org/10.1080/14792779843000009

Pettigrew, T. F., & Tropp, L. R. (2006). A meta-analytic test of intergroup contact theory. *Journal of Personality and Social Psychology*, 90, 751–783. https://doi.org/10.1037/0022-3514.90.5.751

Phillips, L., Penn, M. L., & Gaines, S. O., Jr. (1993). A hermeneutic rejoinder to ourselves and our critics. *Journal of Black Psychology*, 19, 350–357. https://doi.org/10.1177/00957984930193012

Pinker, S. (2011). *The better angels of our nature*. London: Allen Lane.

Poppe, E., & Linssen, H. (1999). In-group favouritism and the reflection of realistic dimensions of difference between national states in Central and Eastern European nationality stereotypes. *British Journal of Social Psychology*, 38, 85–102. https://doi.org/10.1348/014466699164059

Popper, K. (2002). *The logic of scientific discovery*. London: Routledge. (Original work published 1935).

Pratto, F. (1999). The puzzle of continuing group inequality: Placing together psychological, social, and cultural forces in social dominance theory. *Advances in Experimental Social Psychology*, 31, 191–263. https://doi.org/10.1016/S0065-2601(08)60274-9

Pratto, F., Sidanius, J., & Levin, S. (2006). Social dominance theory and the dynamics of intergroup relations: Taking stock and looking forward. *European Review of Social Psychology*, 17, 271–320. https://doi.org/10.1080/10463280601055772

Pratto, F., Zezelj, I., Maloku, E., Turjacanin, V., & Brankovic, M. (Eds.). (2017). *Shaping social identities after violent conflict: Youth in the Western Balkans*. Cham: Palgrave Macmillan.

Preece, J. J. (1998). Ethnic cleansing as an instrument of nation-state creation: Changing state practices and evolving legal norms. *Human Rights Quarterly*, 20, 817–842. https://doi.org/10.1353/hrq.1998.0039

Proshansky, H. M. (1966). The development of intergroup attitudes. In L. W. Hoffman & M. L. Hoffman (Eds.), *Review of child development research* (pp. 311–371). New York, NY: Russell Sage Foundation.

Pyszczynski, T., Greenberg, J., & Solomon, S. (1999). A dual-process model of defense against conscious and unconscious death-related thoughts: An extension of terror management theory. *Psychological Review*, 106, 835–845. https://doi.org/10.1037/0033-295X.106.4.835

Pyszczynski, T., Solomon, S., & Greenberg, J. (2015). Thirty years of terror management theory: From genesis to revelation. *Advances in Experimental Social Psychology*, 52, 1–70. https://doi.org/10.1016/bs.aesp.2015.03.001

Rabinowitz, J. L. (1999). Go with the flow or fight the power? The interactive effects of social dominance orientation and perceived injustice on support for the status quo. *Political Psychology*, 20, 1–24. https://doi.org/10.1111/0162-895X.00135

Raden, D. (2003). Ingroup bias, classic ethnocentrism, and non-ethnocentrism among American whites. *Political Psychology*, 24, 803–828. https://doi.org/10.1046/j.1467-9221.2003.00355.x

Raskin, R., & Terry, H. (1988). A principal-components analysis of the Narcissistic Personality Inventory and further evidence of its construct validity. *Journal of Personality and Social Psychology*, 54, 890–902. https://doi.org/10.1037/0022-3514.54.5.890

Rattansi, A. (2007). *Racism: A very short introduction.* New York, NY: Oxford University Press.

Ray, J. J., & Doratis, D. (1972). Religiocentrism and ethnocentrism: Catholic and Protestant in Australian schools. *Sociological Analysis*, 32, 170–179. https://doi.org/10.2307/3710000

Redfield, J. (1985). Herodotus the Tourist. *Classical Philology*, 80, 97–118. https://doi.org/10.1086/366908

Reicher, S., & Hopkins, N. (2001). *Self and nation.* London: Sage.

Reichl, A. J. (1997). Ingroup favouritism and outgroup favouritism in low status minimal groups: Differential responses to status-related and status-unrelated measures. *European Journal of Social Psychology*, 27, 617–633. https://doi.org/10.1002/(SICI)1099-0992(199711/12)27:6<617::AID-EJSP829>3.0.CO;2-T

Reise, S. P., Waller, N. G., & Comrey, A. L. (2000). Factor analysis and scale revision. *Psychological Assessment*, 12, 287–297. https://doi.org/10.1037/1040-3590.12.3.287

Rey, A. M., & Gibson, P. R. (1998). Beyond high school: Heterosexuals' self-reported anti-gay/lesbian behaviors and attitudes. *Journal of Gay & Lesbian Social Services*, 7, 65. https://doi.org/10.1300/J041v07n04_05

Riefler, P., & Diamantopoulos, A. (2009). Consumer cosmopolitanism: Review and replication of the CYMYC scale. *Journal of Business Research*, 62, 407–419. https://doi.org/10.1016/j.jbusres.2008.01.041

Riefler, P., Diamantopoulos, A., & Siguaw, J. A. (2012). Cosmopolitan consumers as a target group for segmentation. *Journal of International Business Studies*, 43, 285–305. https://doi.org/10.1057/jibs.2011.51

Riek, B. M., Mania, E. W., & Gaertner, S. L. (2006). Intergroup threat and outgroup attitudes: A meta-analytic review. *Personality and Social Psychology Review*, 10, 336–353. https://doi.org/10.1207/s15327957pspr1004_4

Roccas, S., Klar, Y., & Liviatan, I. (2006). The paradox of group-based guilt: Modes of national identification, conflict vehemence, and reactions to the in-group's moral violations. *Journal of Personality and Social Psychology*, 91, 698–711. https://doi.org/10.1037/0022-3514.91.4.698

Rokeach, M. (1960). *The open and closed mind: Investigations into the nature of belief systems and personality systems.* New York, NY: Basic Books.

Rokeach, M., & Mezei, L. (1966). Race and shared belief as factors in social choice. *Science*, 151, 167–172. https://doi.org/10.1126/science.151.3707.167

Rorty, R. (1986). On ethnocentrism: A reply to Clifford Geertz. *Michigan Quarterly Review*, 25, 525–534.

Rorty, R. (1989). *Contingency, irony, and solidarity.* Cambridge: Cambridge University Press.

Rose, P. I. (1966). *They and we: Racial and ethnic relations in the United States.* New York, NY: Random House.

Rosenberg, M. (1965). *Society and the adolescent self-image.* Princeton, NJ: Princeton University Press.

Rosenberg, M. (1979). *Conceiving the self.* New York, NY: Basic Books.

Rosenblatt, P. C. (1964). Origins and effects of group ethnocentrism and nationalism. *Journal of Conflict Resolution*, 8, 131–146. https://doi.org/10.1177/002200276400800204

Ross, M. H. (1983). Political decision making and conflict: Additional cross-cultural codes and scales. *Ethnology*, 22, 169–192. https://doi.org/10.2307/3773578

Ross, M. H. (1991). The role of evolution in ethnocentric conflict and its management. *Journal of Social Issues*, 47, 167–185. https://doi.org/10.1111/j.1540-4560.1991.tb01829.x

Rubin, M., & Hewstone, M. (1998). Social identity theory's self-esteem hypothesis: A review and some suggestions for clarification. *Personality and Social Psychology Review*, 2, 40–62. https://doi.org/10.1207/s15327957pspr0201_3

Rushton, J. P. (1989). Genetic similarity, human altruism, and group selection. *Behavioral and Brain Sciences*, 12, 503–518. https://doi.org/10.1017/S0140525X00057320

Rushton, J. P. (2005). Ethnic nationalism, evolutionary psychology and genetic simi-larity theory. *Nations and Nationalism*, 11, 489–507. https://doi.org/10.1111/j.1469-8129.2005.00216.x

Sachdev, I., & Bourhis, R. Y. (1987). Status differentials and intergroup behaviour. *European Journal of Social Psychology*, 17, 277–293. https://doi.org/10.1002/ejsp.2420170304

Sachdev, I., & Bourhis, R. Y. (1991). Power and status differentials in minority and majority group relations. *European Journal of Social Psychology*, 21, 1–24. https://doi.org/10.1002/ejsp.2420210102

Sagiv, L., & Schwartz, S. H. (1995). Value priorities and readiness for out-group social con-tact. *Journal of Personality and Social Psychology*, 69, 437–448. https://doi.org/10.1037/0022-3514.69.3.437

Sales, S. M. (1973). Threat as a factor in authoritarianism. *Journal of Personality and Social Psychology*, 28, 44–57. https://doi.org/10.1037/h0035588

Salter, F. K. (2007). *On genetic interests: Family, ethnicity, and humanity in an age of mass migration.* New Brunswick, NJ: Transaction.

Schatz, R. T., & Staub, E. (1997). Manifestations of blind and constructive patriotism: Personality correlates and individual-group relations. In E. Staub & D. Bar-Tal (Eds.), *Patriotism: In the lives of individual and nations* (pp. 229–245). Chicago, IL: Nelson-Hall.

Schatz, R. T., Staub, E., & Lavine, H. (1999). On the varieties of national attachment: Blind versus constructive patriotism. *Political Psychology*, 20, 151–174. https://doi.org/10.1111/0162-895X.00140

Scheepers, P., Felling, A., & Peters, J. (1989). Ethnocentrism in the Netherlands: A typo-logical analysis. *Ethnic and Racial Studies*, 12, 289–308. https://doi.org/10.1080/01419870.1989.9993636

Scheepers, P., Felling, A., & Peters, J. (1990). Social conditions, authoritarianism and ethno-centrism: A theoretical model of the early Frankfurt School updated and tested. *European Sociological Review*, 6, 15–29. https://doi.org/10.1093/oxfordjournals.esr.a036543

Schermerhorn, R. A. (1970). *Comparative ethnic relations: A framework for theory and research.* New York, NY: Random House.

Schmid, K., Ramiah, A. A., & Hewstone, M. (2014). Neighborhood ethnic diversity and trust: The role of intergroup contact and perceived threat. *Psychological Science*, 25, 665–674. https://doi.org/10.1177/0956797613508956

Schmitt, M. T., Branscombe, N. R., & Kappen, D. M. (2003). Attitudes towards group-based inequality: Social dominance or social identity? *British Journal of Social Psychology*, 42, 161. https://doi.org/10.1348/014466603322127166

Schwartz, S. H. (1992). Universals in the content and structure of values: Theoretical advances and empirical tests in 20 countries. *Advances in Experimental Social Psychology*, 25, 1–65. https://doi.org/10.1016/S0065-2601(08)60281-6

Schwartz, S. H. (1994). Are there universal aspects in the structure and contents of human values? *Journal of Social Issues*, 50, 19–45. https://doi.org/10.1111/j.1540-4560.1994.tb01196.x

Schwartz, S. H. (1999). A theory of cultural values and some implications for work. *Applied Psychology: An International Review*, 48, 23–47. https://doi.org/10.1111/j.1464-0597.1999.tb00047.x

Schwartz, S. H. (2012). An overview of the Schwartz theory of basic values. *Online Readings in Psychology and Culture*, 2. https://doi.org/10.9707/2307-0919.1116

Schwartz, S. H., Cieciuch, J., Vecchione, M., Davidov, E., Fischer, R., Beierlein, C., … Konty, M. (2012). Refining the theory of basic individual values. *Journal of Personality and Social Psychology*, 103, 663–688. https://doi.org/10.1037/a0029393

Scott, J. (2007). Ludwig Gumplowicz. In J. Scott (Ed.), *Fifty key sociologists: The formative theorists* (pp. 58–60). London: Routledge.

Seeyle, H. N., & Brewer, M. B. (1970). Ethnocentrism and acculturation of North Americans in Guatemala. *Journal of Social Psychology*, 80, 147–155. https://doi.org/10.1080/00224545.1970.9712535

Sekulic, D. (2004). Civic and ethnic identity: The case of Croatia. *Ethnic and Racial Studies*, 27, 455. https://doi.org/10.1080/01491987042000189240

Shaffer, B., & Duckitt, J. (2013). The dimensional structure of people's fears, threats, and concerns and their relationship with right-wing authoritarianism and social dominance orientation. *International Journal of Psychology*, 48, 6–17. https://doi.org/10.1080/00207594.2012.696651

Sharma, S., Shimp, T., & Shin, J. (1995). Consumer ethnocentrism: A test of antecedents and moderators. *Journal of the Academy of Marketing Science*, 23, 26–37. https://doi.org/10.1007/BF02894609

Sherif, M. (1966). *In common predicament: Social psychology of intergroup conflict and cooperation.* Boston, MA: Haughton Mifflin.

Sherif, M. (1973). *The psychology of social norms.* New York, NY: Octagon Books. (Original work published 1936)

Sherif, M., Harvey, O. J., White, B. J., Hood, W. R., & Sherif, C. W. (1961). *Intergroup conflict and cooperation: The Robbers Cave Experiment.* Norman: University of Oklahoma Book Exchange.

Sherif, M., & Sherif, C. W. (1969). *Social psychology.* New York, NY: Harper & Row.

Shimp, T. A., & Sharma, S. (1987). Consumer ethnocentrism: Construction and validation of the CETSCALE. *Journal of Marketing Research*, 24, 280–289. https://doi.org/10.2307/3151638

Siamagka, N.-T., & Balabanis, G. (2015). Revisiting consumer ethnocentrism: Review, reconceptualization, and empirical testing. *Journal of International Marketing*, 23, 66–86. https://doi.org/10.1509/jim.14.0085

Sibley, C. G., & Duckitt, J. (2008). Personality and prejudice: A meta-analysis and theoretical review. *Personality and Social Psychology Review*, 12, 248–279. https://doi.org/10.1177/1088868308319226

Sidanius, J., Cotterill, S., Sheehy-Skeffington, J., Kteily, N., & Carvacho, H. (2017). Social dominance theory: Explorations in the psychology of oppression. In C. G. Sibley & F. K. Barlow, *The Cambridge handbook of the psychology of prejudice* (pp. 149–187). Cambridge: Cambridge University Press.

Sidanius, J., & Liu, J. (1992). Racism, support for the Persian Gulf War, and the police beating of Rodney King: A social dominance perspective. *Journal of Social Psychology*, 132, 685–699. https://doi.org/10.1080/00224545.1992.9712099

Sidanius, J., & Pratto, F. (1999). *Social dominance: An intergroup theory of social hierarchy and oppression.* New York, NY: Cambridge University Press.

Sidanius, J., Pratto, F., & Rabinowitz, J. L. (1994). Gender, ethnic status, and ideological asymmetry: A social dominance interpretation. *Journal of Cross-Cultural Psychology*, 25, 194–216. https://doi.org/10.1177/0022022194252003

Silverman, B. I. (1974). Consequences, racial discrimination, and the principle of belief congruence. *Journal of Personality and Social Psychology*, 29, 497–508. https://doi.org/10.1037/h0036211

Simpson, J. A., & Weiner, E. S. C. (Eds.). (1989). *The Oxford English Dictionary* (2nd ed., Vol. 5). Oxford: Clarendon Press.

Singer, P. (2000). *Darwinian left: Politics, evolution and cooperation.* Hartford, CT: Yale University Press.

Smith, A. D. (2001). *Nationalism: Theory, ideology, history*. Cambridge: Polity.

Smith, A. D. (2010). *Nationalism: Theory, ideology, history* (2nd ed.). Cambridge: Polity.

Smith, C. (2013). Adam Ferguson and ethnocentrism in the science of man. *History of the Human Sciences*, 26, 52–67. https://doi.org/10.1177/0952695112467027

Smith, E. R., & Mackie, D. M. (2016). Group-level emotions. *Current Opinion in Psychology*, 11, 15–19. https://doi.org/10.1016/j.copsyc.2016.04.005

Smith, M. B. (1992). Nationalism, ethnocentrism, and the new world order. *Journal of Humanistic Psychology*, 32, 76–91. https://doi.org/10.1177/0022167892324005

Smith, P. B., & Bond, M. H. (1998). *Social psychology across cultures* (2nd ed.). London: Prentice Hall Europe.

Sniderman, D. M., & Piazza, T. (1993). *The scar of race*. Cambridge, MA: The Belknap Press of Harvard University Press.

Solomon, S., Greenberg, J., & Pyszczynski, T. (1991). A terror management theory of social behavior: The psychological functions of self-esteem and cultural worldviews. *Advances in Experimental Social Psychology*, 24, 93–159. https://doi.org/10.1016/S0065-2601(08)60328-7

South, S. C., Oltmanns, T. F., & Turkheimer, E. (2002). Personality and the derogation of others: Descriptions based on self- and peer report. *Journal of Research in Personality*, 37, 16–33. https://doi.org/10.1016/S0092-6566(02)00526-3

Spencer, H. (1874). *The study of sociology*. London: H. S. King.

Spencer, H. (1892a). *The principles of ethics* (Vol. 1). London: Williams and Norgate.

Spencer, H. (1892b). Three letters to Kaneko Kentaro. Retrieved from http://praxeology.net/HS-LKK.htm

Staerklé, C., Sidanius, J., Green, E. G. T., & Molina, L. E. (2010). Ethnic minority-majority asymmetry in national attitudes around the world: A multilevel analysis. *Political Psychology*, 31, 491–519. https://doi.org/10.1111/j.1467-9221.2010.00766.x

Stangor, C., & Thompson, E. P. (2002). Needs for cognitive economy and self-enhancement as unique predictors of intergroup attitudes. *European Journal of Social Psychology*, 32, 563–575. https://doi.org/10.1002/ejsp.114

Staub, E. (1997). Blind versus constructive patriotism: Moving from embeddedness in the group to critical loyalty and action. In D. Bar-Tal & E. Staub (Eds.), *Patriotism: In the lives of individuals and nations* (pp. 213–228). Chicago, IL: Nelson-Hall.

Steinmetz, G. (2013). Major contributions to sociological theory and research on empire, 1830s–present. In G. Steinmetz (Ed.), *Sociology and empire: The imperial entanglements of a discipline* (Vol. 22, pp. 1–50). Durham, NC: Duke University Press.

Stephan, W. G., & Stephan, C. W. (1984). The role of ignorance in intergroup relations. In N. Miller & M. B. Brewer (Eds.), *Groups in contact: The psychology of desegregation* (pp. 229–255). Orlando: Academic Press.

Stephan, W. G., & Stephan, C. W. (2000). An integrated threat theory of prejudice. In S. Oskamp (Ed.), *Reducing prejudice and discrimination* (pp. 23–46). Hillsdale, NJ: Lawrence Erlbaum.

Stephan, W. G., Ybarra, O., & Morrison, K. R. (2009). Intergroup threat theory. In T. D. Nelson (Ed.), *Handbook of prejudice, stereotyping, and discrimination* (pp. 43–60). New York, NY: Psychology Press.

Stone, W. F., Lederer, G., & Christie, R. (1993). The status of authoritarianism. In W. F. Stone, G. Lederer, & R. Christie (Eds.), *Strength and weakness: The authoritarian personality today* (pp. 229–245). New York, NY: Springer.

Suhay, E., Kalmoe, N., & McDermott, C. (2007). *Why twin studies are problematic for the study of political ideology: Rethinking 'Are Political Orientations Genetically Transmitted?'* Paper presented at the Annual Meeting of the International Society of Political Psychology, Portland, OR.

Sumner, W. G. (1906). *Folkways: A study of the sociological importance of usages, manners, customs, mores, and morals*. Boston, MA: Ginn and Company.

Sumner, W. G. (1911). *War and other essays*. New Haven, CT: Yale University Press.

Sumner, W. G. (1913). *Earth-hunger and other essays*. New Haven, CT: Yale University Press.

Sumner, W. G., Keller, A. G., & Davie, M. R. (1928). *The science of society*. New Haven, CT: Yale University Press.

Swann, W. B. J., Gomez, A., Buhrmester, M. D., Lopez-Rodriguez, L., Jimenez, J., & Vazquez, A. (2014). Contemplating the ultimate sacrifice: Identity fusion channels pro-group affect, cognition, and moral decision making. *Journal of Personality and Social Psychology*, 106, 713–727. https://doi.org/10.1037/a0035809

Swann, W. B. J., Gómez, Á., Dovidio, J. F., Hart, S., & Jetten, J. (2010). Dying and killing for one's group. *Psychological Science*, 21, 1176–1183. https://doi.org/10.1177/0956797610376656

Swann, W. B. J., Gómez, A., Seyle, D. C., Morales, J. F., & Huici, C. (2009). Identity fusion: The interplay of personal and social identities in extreme group behavior. *Journal of Personality and Social Psychology*, 96, 995–1011. https://doi.org/10.1037/a0013668

Swann, W. B. J., Jetten, J., Gomez, A., Whitehouse, H., & Bastian, B. (2012). When group membership gets personal: A theory of identity fusion. *Psychological Review*, 119, 441–456. https://doi.org/10.1037/a0028589

Tacitus. (2003). *The annals & The histories* (M. Hadas, Ed., A. J. Church & W. Brodribb, Trans.) (New edition). New York, NY: Modern Library.

Tajfel, H. (1981). *Human groups and social categories: Studies in social psychology*. Cambridge: Cambridge University Press.

Tajfel, H. (1982). Social psychology of intergroup relations. *Annual Review of Psychology*, 33, 1–39. https://doi.org/10.1146/annurev.ps.33.020182.000245

Tajfel, H. (1983). Prejudice. In R. Harre & R. Lamb (Eds.), *The dictionary of personality and social psychology* (pp. 268–271). Cambridge, MA: The MIT Press.

Tajfel, H., Billig, M., Bundy, R. P., & Flament, C. (1971). Social categorization and intergroup behaviour. *European Journal of Social Psychology*, 1, 149–178. https://doi.org/10.1002/ejsp.2420010202

Tajfel, H., Jahoda, G., Nemeth, C., Campbell, J. D., & Johnson, N. (1970). The development of children's preference for their own country. *International Journal of Psychology*, 5, 245–253. https://doi.org/10.1002/j.1464-066X.1970.tb00002.x

Tajfel, H., Jahoda, G., Nemeth, C., Rim, Y., & Johnson, N. B. (1972). The devaluation by children of their own national and ethnic group: Two case studies. *British Journal of Social and Clinical Psychology*, 11, 235–243. https://doi.org/10.1111/j.2044-8260.1972.tb00808.x

Tajfel, H., & Turner, J. C. (1986). The social identity theory of intergroup behavior. In S. Worchel & W. G. Austin (Eds.), *Psychology of intergroup relations* (2nd ed., pp. 7–24). Chicago, IL: Nelson Hall.

Taleb, N. N. (2010). *The black swan: The impact of the highly improbable* (Revised). London: Penguin Books.

Taruskin, R. (2009). *On Russian music*. Berkeley, CA: University of California Press.

Taylor, D. M., & Jaggi, V. (1974). Ethnocentrism and causal attribution in a South Indian context. *Journal of Cross-Cultural Psychology*, 5, 162–171. https://doi.org/10.1177/002202217400500202

Taylor, S. E., Peplau, L. A., & Sears, D. O. (1997). *Social psychology* (9th ed.). Upper Saddle River, NJ: Prentice Hall.

Templin, J. A. (1999). The ideology of a chosen people: Afrikaner nationalism and the Ossewa Trek, 1938. *Nations and Nationalism*, 5, 397–418. https://doi.org/10.1111/j.1354-5078.1999.00397.x

Teo, T., & Febbraro, A. R. (2003). Ethnocentrism as a form of intuition in psychology. *Theory & Psychology*, 13, 673–694. https://doi.org/10.1177/09593543030135009

Todorov, T. (2010). *The fear of barbarians: Beyond the clash of civilizations* (A. Brown, Trans.). Cambridge: Polity. (Original work published 2008)

Triandis, H. C. (1989). The self and social behaviour in differing cultural contexts. *Psychological Review*, 96, 506–520. https://doi.org/10.1037/0033-295X.96.3.506

Triandis, H. C. (2000). Culture and conflict. *International Journal of Psychology*, 35, 145–152. https://doi.org/10.1080/002075900399448

Triplett, N. (1898). The dynamogenic factors in pacemaking and competition. *The American Journal of Psychology*, 9, 507–533. https://doi.org/10.2307/1412188

Turner, J. C. (1978). Social comparison, similarity and ingroup favouritism. In H. Tajfel (Ed.), *Differentiation between social groups: Studies in the social psychology of intergroup relations* (pp. 235–250). London: Academic Press.

Turner, J. C. (1981). The experimental social psychology of intergroup behaviour. In J. C. Turner & H. Giles (Eds.), *Intergroup behaviour*. Oxford: Basil Blackwell.

Turner, J. C. (1982). Towards a cognitive redefinition of the social group. In H. Tajfel (pp. 15–40). Cambridge: Cambridge University Press.

Turner, J. C. (1991). *Social influence*. Pacific Grove, CA: Brooks-Cole.

Turner, J. C. (1999). Some current issues in research on social identity and self-categorization theories. In R. S. N. Ellemers & B. Doosje (Eds.), *Social identity context, commitment, content* (pp. 6–34). Oxford: Blackwell.

Turner, J. C., Hogg, M. A., Oakes, P. J., Reicher, S. D., & Wetherell, M. S. (1987). *Rediscovering the social group: A self-categorization theory*. Oxford: Basil Blackwell.

Turner, J. C., & Reynolds, K. J. (2003). Why social dominance theory has been falsified. *British Journal of Social Psychology*, 42, 199–206. https://doi.org/10.1348/014466603322127184

Turner, J. C., & Reynolds, K. J. (2010). The story of social identity. In T. Postmes & N. R. Branscombe (Eds.), *Rediscovering social identity: Key readings* (pp. 13–32). New York, NY: Psychology Press.

Turner, J. C., Reynolds, K. J., Haslam, S. A., & Veenstra, K. E. (2006). Reconceptualizing personality: Producing individuality by defining the personal self. In T. Postmes & J. Jetten (Eds.), *Individuality and the group* (pp. 11–36). London: Sage.

Tuschman, A. (2013). *Our political nature: The evolutionary origins of what divides us*. Amherst, NY: Prometheus Books.

Vaes, J., Bain, P. G., & Leyens, J.-P. (2014). Understanding humanness and dehumanization: Emerging themes and directions. In P. G. Bain, J. Vaes, & J.-P. Leyens (Eds.), *Humanness and dehumanization* (pp. 323–336). New York, NY: Psychology Press.

Vaes, J., Paladino, M. P., Castelli, L., Leyens, J.-P., & Giovanazzi, A. (2003). On the behavioral consequences of infrahumanization: The implicit role of uniquely human emotions in intergroup relations. *Journal of Personality and Social Psychology*, 85, 1016–1034. https://doi.org/10.1037/0022-3514.85.6.1016

van den Berghe, P. L. (1967). *Race and racism: A comparative perspective*. New York, NY: John Wiley & Sons.

van den Berghe, P. L. (1978). Race and ethnicity: A sociobiological perspective. *Ethnic and Racial Studies*, 1, 401–411. https://doi.org/0.1080/01419870.1978.9993241

van den Berghe, P. L. (1981). *The ethnic phenomenon*. Westport, CN: Praeger.

van den Berghe, P. L. (1990). Why most sociologists don't (and won't) think evolutionarily. *Sociological Forum*, 5, 173–185. https://doi.org/10.1007/BF01112591

van den Berghe, P. L. (1995). Does race matter? *Nations and Nationalism*, 1, 357–368. https://doi.org/10.1111/j.1354-5078.1995.00357.x

van den Berghe, P. L. (1999). Racism, ethnocentrism and xenophobia: In our genes or in our memes? In K. Thienpont & R. Cliquet (Eds.), *In-group/out-group behaviour in modern societies: An evolutionary perspective* (pp. 21–33). Brussels: NIDI CBGS.

van den Berghe, P. L. (2012). Colour vs. race: A distinction or a difference? *Ethnic and Racial Studies*, 35, 1174–1176. https://doi.org/10.1080/01419870.2011.643816

van der Geest, S. (2005). Introduction: Ethnocentrism and medical anthropology. In S. van der Geest & R. Reis (Eds.), *Ethnocentrism: Reflections on medical anthropology* (2nd ed., pp. 1–23). Amsterdam: Het Spinhuis.

van der Veer, P. (1999). Hindus: A superior race. *Nations and Nationalism*, 5, 419–430. https://doi.org/10.1111/j.1354-5078.1999.00419.x

van Dijk, T. A. (1993). *Elite discourse and racism*. Newbury Park, CA: Sage.

Van Ijzendoorn, M. H. (1989). Moral judgment, authoritarianism, and ethnocentrism. *Journal of Social Psychology*, 129, 37–45.

Vico, G. (1948). *New science of Giambattista Vico* (T. G. Bergin & M. H. Fisch, Trans.) (3rd ed.). Ithaca, NY: Cornell University Press. (Original work published 1744)

Vincent, G. E. (1911). The rivalry of social groups. *American Journal of Sociology*, 16, 469–484. https://doi.org/10.1086/211909

Volkan, V. D. (1997). *Bloodlines: From ethnic pride to ethnic terrorism*. New York, NY: Ferrar, Straus, and Giroux.

Wachtel, P. L. (1980). Investigation and its discontents: Some constraints on progress in psychological research. *American Psychologist*, 35, 399–408. https://doi.org/10.1037/0003-066X.35.5.399

Wakefield, J. C. (2007). Why psychology needs conceptual analysts: Wachtel's 'discontents' revisited. *Applied and Preventive Psychology*, 12, 39–43. https://doi.org/10.1016/j.appsy.2007.07.014

Waldzus, S., & Mummendey, A. (2004). Inclusion in a superordinate category, in-group prototypicality, and attitudes towards out-groups. *Journal of Experimental Social Psychology*, 40, 466–477. https://doi.org/10.1016/j.jesp.2003.09.003

Waldzus, S., Mummendey, A., Wenzel, M., & Weber, U. (2003). Towards tolerance: Representations of superordinate categories and perceived ingroup prototypicality. *Journal of Experimental Social Psychology*, 39, 31–47. https://doi.org/10.1016/S0022-1031(02)00507-3

Wallace, H. A. (1973). *The price of vision: The diary of Henry A. Wallace, 1942–1946* (J. M. Blum, Ed.). Boston, MA: Houghton Mifflin.

Wang, Q. (2017). Putting culture in the middle in judging scholarly merit. *Perspectives on Psychological Science*, 12, 1166–1170. https://doi.org/10.1177/1745691617724240

Warr, P. B., Faust, J., & Harrison, G. J. (1967). A British Ethnocentrism Scale. *British Journal of Social and Clinical Psychology*, 6, 267–277. https://doi.org/10.1111/j.2044-8260.1967.tb00529.x

Warwick, D. P. (1980). The politics and ethics of cross-cultural research. In H. C. Triandis & W. W. Lambert (Eds.), *Handbook of cross-cultural psychology* (Vol. 1, pp. 329–372). Boston, MA: Allyn and Bacon.

Watson, J. B. (1925). *Behaviorism*. London: Kegan Paul, Trench, Trubner.

Watts, M. W. (1996). Political xenophobia in the transition from socialism: Threat, racism and ideology among East German youth. *Political Psychology*, 17, 97–126. https://doi.org/10.2307/3791945

Webster, G. D., Jonason, P. K., & Schember, T. O. (2009). Hot topics and popular papers in evolutionary psychology: Analyses of title words and citation counts in *Evolution and Human Behavior*, 1979–2008. *Evolutionary Psychology*, 7, 147470490900700300. https://doi.org/10.1177/147470490900700301

Wegener, D. T., & Fabrigar, L. R. (2000). Analysis and design for nonexperimental data: Addressing causal and noncausal hypotheses. In H. T. Reis & C. M. Judd (Eds.), *Handbook of research methods in social and personality psychology* (pp. 412–450). New York, NY: Cambridge University Press.

Wenzel, M., Mummendey, A., & Waldzus, S. (2007). Superordinate identities and intergroup conflict: The ingroup projection model. *European Review of Social Psychology*, 18, 331–372. https://doi.org/10.1080/10463280701728302

White, R. T. (1990). Internationalism versus parochialism in educational research. *The Review of Higher Education*, 14, 47–62. https://doi.org/10.1353/rhe.1990.0003

Whiting, J. (2006). The Nicomachean account of philia. In R. Kraut (Ed.), *The Blackwell guide to Aristotle's Nicomachean Ethics* (pp. 276–304). Malden, MA: Blackwell.

Wicker, A. W. (1969). Attitudes versus actions: The relationship of verbal and overt behavioral responses to attitude objects. *Journal of Social Issues*, 25, 41–78. https://doi.org/10.1111/j.1540-4560.1969.tb00619.x

Williams, R. M., Jr. (1994). The sociology of ethnic conflicts: Comparative international perspectives. *Annual Review of Sociology*, 20, 49–79. https://doi.org/10.1146/annurev.so.20.080194.000405

Wilson, E. O. (1975). *Sociobiology: The new synthesis.* Cambridge, MA: Harvard University Press.

Wilson, E. O. (1978). *On human nature.* Cambridge, MA: Harvard University Press.

Wilson, E. O. (2012). *The social conquest of Earth.* New York, NY: Liveright.

Wilson, E. O. (2014). *The meaning of human existence.* New York, NY: Liveright.

Wilson, M. S., & Liu, J. H. (2003). Social dominance orientation and gender: The moderating role of gender identity. *British Journal of Social Psychology*, 42, 187–198.

Wittgenstein, L. (1953). *Philosophical investigations.* Oxford: Blackwell.

Worchel, S. (1999). *Written in blood: Ethnic identity and the struggle for human harmony.* New York, NY: Worth Publishers.

Worchel, S., & Coutant, D. (1997). The tangled web of loyalty: Nationalism, patriotism, and ethnocentrism. In D. Bar-Tal & E. Staub (Eds.), *Patriotism: In the lives of individuals and nations* (pp. 190–210). Chicago, IL: Nelson Hall.

Yarkoni, T. (2010). The abbreviation of personality, or how to measure 200 personality scales with 200 items. *Journal of Research in Personality*, 44, 180–198. https://doi.org/10.1016/j.jrp.2010.01.002

Yen, C.-L., & Cheng, C.-P. (2010). Terror management among Taiwanese: Worldview defence or resigning to fate? *Asian Journal of Social Psychology*, 13, 185–194. https://doi.org/10.1111/j.1467-839X.2010.01328.x

Yen, C.-L., & Cheng, C.-P. (2013). Researcher effects on mortality salience research: A meta-analytic moderator analysis. *Death Studies*, 37, 636–652. https://doi.org/10.1080/07481187.2012.682290

Young, K. (1930). *Social psychology: An analysis of social behavior.* New York, NY: F. S. Crofts.

Zagefka, H. (2009). The concept of ethnicity in social psychological research: Definitional issues. *International Journal of Intercultural Relations*, 33, 228–241. https://doi.org/10.1016/j.ijintrel.2008.08.001

Zagefka, H., & Brown, R. (2002). The relationship between acculturation strategies, relative fit and intergroup relations: immigrant-majority relations in Germany. *European Journal of Social Psychology*, 32, 171–188. https://doi.org/10.1002/ejsp.73

Zarate, M. A., Hall, G. N., & Plaut, V. C. (2017). Researchers of color, fame, and impact. *Perspectives on Psychological Science*, 12, 1176–1178. https://doi.org/10.1177/1745691617710511

Zeugner-Roth, K. P., Žabkar, V., & Diamantopoulos, A. (2015). Consumer ethnocentrism, national identity, and consumer cosmopolitanism as drivers of consumer behavior: A social identity theory perspective. *Journal of International Marketing*, 23, 25–54. https://doi.org/10.1509/jim.14.0038

Zimmermann, J. G. (1797). *Essay on national pride* (S. H. Wilcocke, Trans.). London: C. Dily. (Original work published 1758)

APPENDIX A

DEFINITIONS OF ETHNOCENTRISM AND THEMATIC ANALYSIS

The following definitions served as the basis for the thematic analysis of ethnocentrism as reported in Bizumic and Duckitt (2012). It should be noted that many other definitions of ethnocentrism can certainly be included within these themes.

A. Ethnic group self-centredness

"Regarding one's own race or ethnic group as of supreme importance" (Simpson & Weiner, 1989, p. 424)

"belief that the ingroup is the center of everything" (S. E. Taylor, Peplau, & Sears, 1997, p. 179)

"ethnocentric judgments ... are based on feelings that one's own group is the center of what is reasonable and proper in life" (Brislin, 1993, p. 38)

"Ethnocentrism focuses on a 'we group' feeling where the ingroup is the center and all outgroups are judged in relation to it" (Balabanis et al., 2001, p. 159)

"Ethnocentrism is the technical name for this view of things in which one's own group is the center of everything, and all others are scaled and rated with reference to it. Folkways correspond to it to cover both the inner and the outer relation." (Sumner, 1906, p. 13)

Specific facets of ethnic group self-centredness

1. Preference (major theme: a tendency to prefer and like one's ingroup over outgroups)

"a relative preference for one's ingroup over most outgroups" (Berry & Kalin, 1995, p. 303)

"the phenomenon that members of a particular group favor members of their group to members of out-groups" (D. M. Taylor & Jaggi, 1974, p. 162)

"the point of view that one's own way of life is to be preferred to all others" (Herskovits, 1948, p. 68)

"a preference of one's own ethnicity over outgroups" (Peres & Schrift, 1978, p. 429)

"Cooperative relations with ingroups members" / "Absence of cooperation with outgroup members" (LeVine & Campbell, 1972, p. 12)

2. Superiority (major theme: a belief that one's ingroup is better than or superior to others)

"a sense of superiority to any out-group" (Sumner, 1911, p. 11)

"Each group ... boasts itself superior, exalts its own divinities" (Sumner, 1906, p. 13)

"prejudicial attitudes between in-groups and out-groups by which our attitudes, customs and behaviour are unquestionably and uncritically treated as superior to their social arrangements" (Abercrombie, Hill, & Turner, 1994, p. 151)

"this sentiment of superiority is called ethnocentrism. Every tribe or nation believes itself, at least in some matters, superior to all others – if not in military or economic strength, possibly in scholarship, art, or morals" (Young, 1930, p. 20)

"A belief in the superiority of one's own ethnic and cultural group" (Myers, 1993, p. 397)

"group-egotism, which, among other things, causes so many peoples to denominate themselves 'Men,' as distinguished from the rest of the world, who do not measure up to that exalted title" (Keller, 1915, p. 58) "the tendency to exalt the in-group" (Murdock, 1949, pp. 83–84)

"an attitude of uncritically assuming the superiority of the in-group culture" (Moghaddam, 1996, p. 927)

"the attitude that regards one's own group or culture as superior" (Bohannan, 1993, p. 80)

"[belief that the ingroup] is superior to all outgroups" (S. E. Taylor et al., 1997, p. 179)

"Each group nourishes its own … vanity" (Sumner, 1906, p. 13)

"the term implies that others can be judged according to one, central set of standards. An implication of the judgements is that one group is clearly better, even superior, than the other since its members practice proper and correct behaviors" (Brislin, 1993, p. 38)

"the inclination to judge others in terms of standards and values of one's own group" (American Psychological Association, 2001, p. 92)

"self-regard or hyperevaluation of the ingroup" (Brewer & Campbell, 1976, p. 74)

"the overevaluation of one's own group in comparison with other groups, especially those perceived as rivals" (J. D. Frank, 1967, p. 104)

"See selves as virtuous and superior" (LeVine & Campbell, 1972, p. 12)

"See own standards of value as universal, intrinsically true. See own customs as original, centrally human" (LeVine & Campbell, 1972, p. 12)

"See selves as strong" / "See outgroups as weak" (LeVine & Campbell, 1972, p. 12)

"[thinking] of their in-group as the standard of what is good and proper, and of other groups as good only to the extent that they are similar to the in-group" (Triandis, 2000, p. 151)

"Each group thinks its own folkways the only right ones, and if it observes that other groups have other folkways, these excite its scorn" (Sumner, 1906, p. 13)

3. Purity (major theme: a desire to maintain the purity of one's ingroup and a rejection of mixing with outgroups)

"concerned to keep the blood pure" (Sumner et al., 1928, p. 1897)

"a lack of acceptance of cultural diversity, a general intolerance for outgroups" (Berry & Kalin, 1995, p. 303)

"Social distance" (LeVine & Campbell, 1972, p. 12)

4. Exploitativeness (major theme: a belief that one's ingroup interests take precedence over outgroup interests)

"readiness to defend the interests of the in-group against the out-group" (Sumner, 1911, p. 11)

"a hierarchical, authoritarian view of group interaction in which ingroups are rightly dominant, outgroups subordinate" (Adorno et al., 1950, p. 150)

"Sanctions against ingroup theft" / "Sanctions for outgroup theft, or absence of sanctions against" (LeVine & Campbell, 1972, p. 12)

"Sanctions against ingroup murder" / "Sanctions for outgroup murder or absence of sanctions against outgroup murder" (LeVine & Campbell, 1972, p. 12)

5. Group cohesion (major theme: a belief that one's ingroup should be integrated, cohesive, cooperative, and unified)

"The sentiment of cohesion, internal comradeship" (Sumner, 1911, p. 11)

"ingroup integration" (Brewer & Campbell, 1976, p. 74)

"Sanctions against ingroup theft" (LeVine & Campbell, 1972, p. 12)

"Sanctions against ingroup murder" (LeVine & Campbell, 1972, p. 12)

"Cooperative relations with ingroup members" (LeVine & Campbell, 1972, p. 12)

6. Devotion (major theme: a strong and ardent dedication to one's ingroup)

"The sentiment of ... devotion" (Sumner, 1911, p. 11)

"exaggerated tendency to identify with one's own ethnic group" (American Psychological Association, 2001, p. 92)

"submissive attitudes regarding ingroup" (Adorno et al., 1950, p. 150)

"Obedience to ingroup authorities" (LeVine & Campbell, 1972, p. 12)

"Willingness to remain an ingroup member" (LeVine & Campbell, 1972, p. 12)

"Willingness to fight and die for ingroup" (LeVine & Campbell, 1972, p. 12)

B. Outgroup negativity

(Major theme: a general dislike and devaluation of outgroups)

"Each group ... looks with contempt on outsiders" (Sumner, 1906, p. 13)

"a corresponding disdain for all other groups" (Myers, 1993, p. 397)

"the tendency to ... depreciate the other groups" (Murdock, 1949, pp. 83–84)

"contemptuous of other groups and cultures" (Bohannan, 1993, p. 80)

"the devaluation of other-group characteristics" (Phillips et al., 1993, p. 429)

"hostile relations between ingroup and outgroups" (Brewer & Campbell, 1976, p. 74)

"derogatory stereotyping of outgroup characteristics" (Brewer & Campbell, 1976, p. 74)

"it involves stereotyped negative imagery and hostile attitudes regarding outgroups" (Adorno et al., 1950, p. 150)

"See outgroup as contemptible, immoral, and inferior" (LeVine & Campbell, 1972, p. 12)

"Outgroup hate" (LeVine & Campbell, 1972, p. 12)

"Absence of conversion to outgroup membership" (LeVine & Campbell, 1972, p. 12)

"Absence of willingness to fight and die for outgroups" (LeVine & Campbell, 1972, p. 12)

"Absence of obedience to outgroup authorities" (LeVine & Campbell, 1972, p. 12)

"Absence of cooperation with outgroup members" (LeVine & Campbell, 1972, p. 12)

"Virtue in killing outgroup members in warfare" (LeVine & Campbell, 1972, p. 12)

"Use of outgroups as bad examples in the training of children" (LeVine & Campbell, 1972, p. 12)

"Blaming of outgroup for ingroup troubles" (LeVine & Campbell, 1972, p. 12)

"Distrust and fear of the outgroup" (LeVine & Campbell, 1972, p. 12)

C. Mere ingroup positivity

(Major theme: a general positive attitude towards the ingroup)

"the valuation of own-group characteristics" (Phillips et al., 1993, p. 429)

"Each group nourishes its own pride" (Sumner, 1906, p. 13)

"ingroup members' positive evaluation of the group as a whole" (Turner et al., 1987, p. 57)

"stereotyped positive imagery … regarding ingroup" (Adorno et al., 1950, p. 150)

APPENDIX B

THE ETHNOCENTRISM SCALE 1: THE 36-ITEM VERSION

The original 58-item version of the scale has been tested in cross-cultural studies in student populations as reported in Bizumic et al. (2009). The 36-item version has been created based on a confirmatory factor analysis of the combined sample from Study Two in Bizumic et al. (2009). The 36-item version has been extensively tested on YourMorals.Org and in several Australian samples, and had good psychometric properties. Note that the items that should be reverse-scored are marked with R. The items are reproduced here with permission from the publisher of the journal article.

Devotion

1. The values, way of life and beliefs of my culture or ethnic group must be preserved whatever the sacrifices.
2. I have a total loyalty to our people and our way of life.
3. No matter what happens, I will ALWAYS support my cultural or ethnic group and never let it down.
4. I just DON'T have the kind of strong and passionate attachment to my people and our culture that would make me make serious sacrifices for their interests. (R)
5. I cannot imagine myself ever developing an intense, passionate total devotion and commitment to my ethnic or cultural group. (R)
6. I think it is foolish to be completely and unconditionally devoted to one's cultural or ethnic group. (R)

Group cohesion

1. We should focus all our energy on trying to develop a greater sense of unity, community and solidarity in our cultural group.
2. It is absolutely vital that all true members of my ethnic or cultural group forget their differences and strive for greater unity and cohesion.
3. We, as a cultural group, should be more integrated and cohesive, even if it reduces our individual freedoms.
4. We don't need more unity and cohesion in our cultural group; we should rather encourage people to be more ready to think for themselves and express themselves and their individuality in whatever way they wish. (R)
5. Personal freedoms and allowing people from our cultural group to do exactly what they want to do are more important than achieving unity and cohesion. (R)
6. Instead of greater unity and more cohesion, our people need more change, innovation, and freedom for individuals to express themselves however they want to. (R)

Preference

1. In most cases, I like people from my culture more than I like others.
2. I feel much more relaxed and comfortable in the company of people from my cultural or ethnic group than I feel in the company of others.
3. In general, I prefer doing things with people from my own culture than with people from different cultures.
4. I do NOT prefer members of my own cultural or ethnic group to others. (R)
5. I don't think I have any particular preference for my own cultural or ethnic group over others. (R)
6. I would probably be quite content living in a cultural or ethnic group that is very different to mine. (R)

Superiority

1. The world would be a much better place if all other cultures and ethnic groups modelled themselves on my culture.
2. On the whole, people from my culture tend to be better people than people from other cultures.
3. In general, other cultures do not have the inner strength and resilience of our culture.
4. Our cultural or ethnic group is NOT more deserving and valuable than others. (R)
5. I don't believe that my cultural or ethnic group is any better than any other. (R)
6. It is simply NOT true that our culture and our customs are any better than other cultures and other customs. (R)

Purity

1. It is better for people from different ethnic and cultural groups not to marry.
2. Our culture would be much better off if we could keep people from different cultures out.
3. I prefer not to be around people from very different cultures.
4. I'd really enjoy working and being with people from completely different cultures and ethnic groups. (R)
5. I'd like to live in a neighbourhood where there are many people from all sorts of quite different cultural and ethnic groups to mine. (R)
6. I like the idea of a society in which people from completely different cultures, ethnic groups, and backgrounds mix together freely. (R)

Exploitativeness

1. We should always put our interests first and not be oversensitive about the interests of other cultures or ethnic groups.
2. In dealing with other ethnic and cultural groups our first priority should be that we make sure that we are the ones who end up gaining and not the ones who end up losing.
3. We need to do what's best for our own people, and stop worrying so much about what the effect might be on other peoples.
4. We should always show consideration for the welfare of people from other cultural or ethnic groups even if, by doing this, we may lose some advantage over them. (R)
5. In dealing with other cultures we should always be honest with them and respect their rights and feelings. (R)
6. I would be extremely unhappy if our actions had negative effects on other cultures, no matter how much advantage we might be gaining. (R)

APPENDIX C

THE ETHNOCENTRISM SCALE 2: THE 36-ITEM AND 12-ITEM VERSIONS

This revised version is based on the 36-item version in Appendix B. This version has been developed in order to primarily target ethnicity as opposed to ethnicity and culture. In addition, the version improves on the readability of items in the original measure, and is recommended to be used in the general population, as each subscale has a readability in the 60s–70s on the Flesch Kincaid Reading Ease scale. The items from the 12-item version are marked with an asterisk (*). The 12 items were selected following Yarkoni's (2010) method to abbreviate longer psychological measures. The readability of the final 12-item scale is also appropriate for use in the general population, with a Flesch Kincaid Reading Ease of 67.8. Both versions have been tested in community samples and showed excellent psychometric properties. The items that should be reverse-scored are marked with R.

Devotion

1. No matter what happens, I will ALWAYS support my ethnic group and never let it down.*
2. I just DON'T have the kind of strong attachment to my ethnic group that would make me make serious sacrifices for its interests.* (R)
3. The values, way of life and beliefs of my ethnic group must be preserved whatever the sacrifices.
4. I have a total loyalty to people from my ethnic group.
5. I cannot imagine myself ever developing a total devotion and commitment to my ethnic group. (R)
6. I think it is foolish to be unconditionally devoted to one's ethnic group. (R)

Group cohesion

1. It is absolutely vital that all members of our ethnic group think and behave as one.★
2. We, as an ethnic group, must unite, even if all our personal freedoms are lost.★
3. Instead of promoting unity in our ethnic group, we should let people do whatever they wish. (R)
4. It is more important that members of our ethnic group think for themselves than that they all think the same. (R)
5. It is of utmost importance that all members of our ethnic group ALWAYS cooperate with each other.
6. I oppose those saying that everyone in our ethnic group should be forced to behave the same. (R)

Preference

1. In general, I prefer doing things with people from my own ethnic group than with people from other ethnic groups.★
2. I don't think I have any particular preference for my own ethnic group over others.★ (R)
3. In most cases, I like people from my ethnic group more than I like others.
4. I would probably be quite content living in an ethnic group that is very different to mine. (R)
5. I do NOT prefer members of my own ethnic group to others. (R)
6. I feel much more relaxed and comfortable in the company of people from my ethnic group than I feel in the company of others.

Superiority

1. I don't believe that my ethnic group is any better than any other.★ (R)
2. The world would be a much better place if all other ethnic groups modelled themselves on my ethnic group.★
3. In general, other ethnic groups do not have the inner strength and resilience of ours.
4. Our ethnic group is NOT more deserving and valuable than others. (R)
5. It is simply NOT true that our ethnic group and our customs are any better than other ethnic groups and other customs. (R)
6. On the whole, people from my ethnic group tend to be better people than people from other ethnic groups.

Purity

1. I like the idea of a society in which people from completely different ethnic groups mix together freely.* (R)
2. I prefer not to be around people from very different ethnic groups.*
3. It is better for people from different ethnic groups not to marry.
4. Our ethnic group would be much better off if we could keep people from different ethnic groups out.
5. I'd really enjoy working and being with people from completely different ethnic groups. (R)
6. I'd like to live in a neighbourhood where there are many people from all sorts of quite different ethnic groups to mine. (R)

Exploitativeness

1. We need to do what's best for our own ethnic group, and stop worrying so much about what the effect might be on others.*
2. We should always be considerate for the welfare of people from other ethnic groups even if, by doing this, we may lose some advantage over them.* (R)
3. In dealing with other ethnic groups we should always be honest with them and respect their rights and feelings. (R)
4. We should always put our ethnic group's interests first and not be very sensitive about the interests of other ethnic groups.
5. In dealing with other ethnic groups our first priority should be that we make sure that we are the ones who end up gaining and not the ones who end up losing.
6. I would be extremely unhappy if our actions had negative effects on other ethnic groups, no matter how much advantage we might be gaining. (R)

INDEX

Note: Page numbers in **bold** refer to a table and in *italics* refer to a figure.